GENTLEMEN, WE WILL STAND AND FIGHT

Le Cateau, 1914

Wisdom is better than weapons of war: but one sinner destroyed much good.

ECCLESIASTES IX, 18

GENTLEMEN, WE WILL STAND AND FIGHT

Le Cateau, 1914

ANTONY BIRD

THE CROWOOD PRESS

First published in 2008 by
The Crowood Press Ltd
Ramsbury, Marlborough
Wiltshire SN8 2HR

www.crowood.com

British Library Cataloguing-in-Publication Data
A catalogue record for this book is available from the British Library.

ISBN 978 1 84797 062 6

A note on measurements

Throughout this book, measurements have been given in imperial with the metric equivalent in parenthesis. In the case of distances quoted in yards, however, due to the impreciseness of most of the many figures given and the closeness of yards and metres (1yd = 0.91m), the metric conversion has been omitted in the interests of the ease of reading. Figures given as part of a weapon designation, such as 18-pounder, have also been left unconverted.

Typeset by SR Nova Pvt Ltd., Bangalore, India.
Printed and bound in Great Britain by The Cromwell Press, Trowbridge

Contents

List of Maps

Introduction

On 25 August 1914 Field Marshal Sir John French, commander of the British Expeditionary Force, had many reasons to be a worried man. At his new headquarters in St Quentin, northern France, 18 miles (30km) south of Le Cateau, he was of course aware that troops in both of his corps* had been fighting and retreating for two days since their first battle against Gen von Kluck's 1st Army at Mons on 23 August; indeed, he had been with Gen Smith-Dorrien at the latter's forward HQ at Sars-la-Bruyère at dawn that morning and had issued orders to retreat later that same night. The British Second Corps under Smith-Dorrien, the corps that had borne the brunt of the German attack, had without doubt suffered a defeat, but a defeat that rapidly became suffused with glory and myth. Within two weeks the legend of the Angel of Mons was current, an angel clad in white with flaming sword who barred the way to the German horde.** But there nothing mythical about British marksmanship at the battle, which had cut down the Germans who had 'come over in mass formation', their spiked helmets clearly visible to the British defending the canal, emerging like Birnam Wood from the dense forest to the north of the canal.*** The second wave of attacking troops had used the dead bodies of their comrades as cover.

* The British had never before gone to war with a two-corps structure; it was set up to conform to French Army organization.
** Before the month was out the myth of countless Russian divisions passing through Scotland on their way to the Western Front, with the snow still on their boots (in August?) was also to take a hold on the popular imagination.
*** Except that like all legends, British markmanship may have become slightly exaggerated over the years. Lt Roupell, whom we will meet again, wrote later of how he got his platoon of East Surreys on the canal to lower their aim, when he saw their bullets hitting the upper branches of the wood out of which the enemy was advancing. He got their attention by striking them with the flat of his sword.

'Papa' Joffre, French C-in-C.

Sir John French, BEF C-in-C, with French officers.

4th Royal Fusiliers in the Grande Place, Mons, 22 August 1914.

Sir John French was also of course uncomfortably aware that there were alarming gaps in the Allied lines, not only between his two corps, First Corps under Gen Haig and Second Corps under Gen Smith-Dorrien, but also between First Corps and the French 5th Army to their east and south, which was pulling back from Charleroi. Both the British corps were under orders to meet up at Le Cateau. The 5th Army was commanded by Gen Lanrezac, with whom French was on frosty terms to say the least. He did know, however, by the 25th that Lanrezac, by French standards of the time an almost timorous general, was about to counterattack, under pressure from Joffre, the French commander-in-chief, in what was to become known to the British as the Battle of Guise (29 August).*

Communications between his own subordinate commanders and between himself and the French commands were haphazard and often reliant on the motor car or horse. To the west of Second Corps there was a screen of French cavalry, under Gen Sordet, together with a division of French territorials under Gen D'Amade, based in Cambrai. Both these divisions were to prove themselves invaluable in the BEF's hour of need, but of course they were not

*Bizarrely, French, who could not speak French, shared the first three letters of his name with the last three in Joffre's name, both of which have six letters. Some thought of this as an omen of some kind.

under British command. Gen Sordet was receiving reinforcements on the 25th, which were crossing from east to west across the BEF's area of operations, causing much dislocation in their wake.

As always in war there was a mass of inconsistent intelligence reports from his own cavalry and Royal Flying Corps, as well as from the French commands, which had to be sifted and interpreted, and Sir John was hardly sophisticated in the use of intelligence. In fact it would be fair to say that he lacked the intellectual rigour needed to find what would now be called the critical path between competing data.* But the fog of war was beginning to lift. And what it was revealing was the stark fact that the BEF was in grave danger.

The war was only three weeks old and Sir John had arrived in France on the 9th. The British Army, and Sir John, a cavalryman, had come to the Franco-Belgian border fully prepared to take the offensive; no army, after all, chooses to start a campaign with a retreat. Its deployment, compared with its performance at the outset of the Boer War, was a model of efficiency. There was an optimistic assumption in both military and non-military circles that the speedy advance of the BEF to its position on the left of the Allied line would tip the balance against the German assault, although of course the Royal Navy was the ultimate guarantor of victory. Sir John, with his 110,000-strong force, was tasked by Herbert Asquith's government, in Lord Kitchener's Instructions, to restore Belgian neutrality by co-operating with the Allied armies. In pursuit of this aim, right up until the eve of Mons, 23 August, Sir John was intending to move north of the Mons–Conde canal, urged on by Joffre, who made reassuring noises about Lanrezac's position and intentions, as well as enemy strength. These French reports Sir John was not in a position to disregard, even had he wished to, and in any case the BEF was obliged to conform to the movements of its much larger ally. On the left of the Allied line, facing the strong right wing of the Schlieffen-inspired German attack, the BEF made up only about 15 per cent of the Allied force.

Sir John's outstanding achievement at this time was his decision that the BEF must retreat. By this decision alone, which on the evening of Mons was not as inevitable as it now appears,** and leaving aside whatever else might be said about his personal and military failings, Sir John passed the Iron Duke's supreme test of generalship: to know when to retreat.*** A fighting retreat

---

*Lt-Col George Barrow, the intelligence officer of the cavalry, brought information of German whereabouts to GHQ by the simple expedient of telephoning Belgian post offices. Two of his subordinates were police detectives with bicycles.

**Admiral Jellicoe's adoption of the convoy system in 1917 was another crucial decision that appears with hindsight to have been more inevitable than it was at the time. Indeed, the very decision to send the BEF to France was not a foregone conclusion.

***Field Marshal Haig was to fail the Wellington test of generalship by not shutting down the third Battle of Ypres in October 1917, before the mud made it almost impossible to move the guns forwards, an offensive that some historians consider he should never have undertaken in the first place.

is, after all, recognized as an operation of war. The Retreat from Mons is the British equivalent of Joffre's abandonment of the cherished Plan XVII. This plan, with the latest revision of which the French went to war, was based on an all-out assault to recapture Alsace/Lorraine, the territories lost in 1871, an offensive that they believed would simultaneously weaken the German right wing. In the event it achieved neither objective and the German right wing remained strong. Of course to a large extent Sir John had the retreat decision made for him by the pressure of events (although his sub-chief of staff, Sir Henry Wilson, was not exactly helpful, to put it mildly, even drafting orders for a Second Corps attack on the 24th) and in any case it may not have gone against the grain of his personality: his biographer, Richard Holmes, suggests that Sir John was driven by love, a genuine love for the old professional army and his horror at the thought of its destruction.

And further to his credit, French's eventual decision to retreat south to Compiègne rather than south-west towards Amiens and his channel ports effectively hoodwinked von Kluck, who expected him to do the latter. After Le Cateau von Kluck himself shifted part of his army, II Cavalry Corps, to the south-west (Bapaume) in search of the BEF, to the consternation of von Bulow, the commander of 2nd Army to his left, who was in fact his superior.

Although Sir John could take some comfort from the fact that he was retreating into friendly territory while the Germans were extending their lines of supply, the position of the BEF north of Le Cateau for the three days of 23–5 August was now exactly one that Lord Kitchener had cautioned him against in his Instructions. The relevant passage (fourth paragraph) reads as follows:

> . . . while every effort must be made to coincide most sympathetically with the plans and wishes of our Ally, the gravest consideration will devolve upon you as to participation in forward movements where large bodies of French troops are not engaged and where your Force may be unduly exposed to attack. Should a contingency of this sort be contemplated, I look to you to inform me fully and give me time to communicate to you any decision His Majesty's Government may come to in the matter. In this connection I wish you distinctly to understand that your command is an entirely independent one and you will in no case come in any sense under the orders of any Allied general.

In other words Sir John had to look to his front, watch his flanks and keep in touch with his rear, accept automatically no commands from his main ally, who vastly outnumbered him, but co-operate fully with him, and guard Britain's only field army, all the time while opposed to Europe's most powerful armed forces. French was to discover to his chagrin (at his meeting with Kitchener on 1 September) that his status as commander of an independent force was subject to supervision and control by the Cabinet.

11

Sir John was also of course aware that his force was on the left of a mass of five French armies that had been fighting, together with the Belgian Army, since 20 August and that everywhere the German armies were on foreign soil. After all, Gen Sir Henry Wilson, his francophile sub-chief of staff, was the architect of the mobilization plans and was in close touch with French GQG, assisted by Col Huguet, the French liaison officer at the BEF. Indeed, Wilson bore a unique responsibility for the decision to deploy the BEF in France on the left of the line at the outbreak of hostilities, although of course he cannot be held responsible for all its doleful consequences. It could be said that without Wilson the BEF would not be here at all – and that without Count von Schlieffen neither would von Kluck. But although Sir John professed to be a serious student of military strategy, the name von Schlieffen meant little to him. What he did know by 25 August – and which he had not known on 22 August – was how formidable the German army confronting him was. It consisted of four corps, or 320,000 men, although von Kluck was diverting troops to Antwerp, where six Belgian divisions had gone into shelter. Von Kluck seemed determined to press attacks with an alarming lack of caution; he was a more audacious commander than von Bulow of the 2nd Army to his left. There were approximately 18,000 German soldiers for every mile of von Kluck's front,* and even this density would have made von Schlieffen uneasy, for whom the right wing was all. Sir John's force had the misfortune to be at the *Schwerpunkt* of the enveloping attack and von Kluck was a dedicated follower and executor of the Schlieffen plan. In the plan's 1905 formulation von Kluck had ten days to get from Mons to Amiens.

The fact that the Germans were using their reserve divisions in their front lines was not known to Sir John at the moment; nor did he know that the German troops were sleeping by the roadsides in their efforts to press on. What he did know was that his two corps were now spread out in and around the small market town of Le Cateau Cambresis (1914 population of about 10,000), the site of his previous headquarters, along a front of more than 25 miles (40km), having lost contact with each other by their separate passing of the ancient Forest of Mormal. They had last been in close touch at Bavai, north of the forest. The two corps could only communicate with each other through GHQ and even that was haphazard, to say the least. French held a low opinion of Smith-Dorrien's military abilities, which was not improving his peace of mind. The physical condition of the troops was already a concern, especially the reservists, who had come straight from civilian life. Many of them simply could not keep up on the march. One young subaltern, K.F.B. Tower of the 2nd Royal Fusiliers (1st Division), had one such man

---

*A somewhat incomprehensible statistic, giving von Kluck three men for every foot of front.

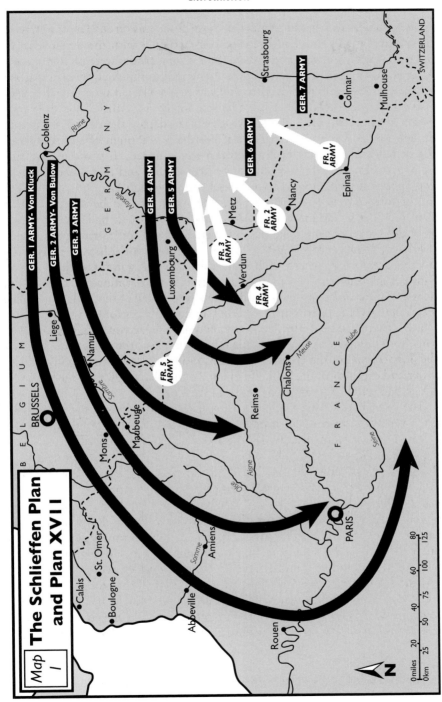

Map 1. **The Schlieffen Plan and Plan XVII**

in his platoon, 'a most extraordinarily ugly little man'. The man begged not to be sent back to base, saying he had won a prize in a dance marathon in Hackney; Tower relented. The man continued to fall out, but fought at Mons and '. . . gave a very fine account of himself. On the second day of the Retreat he collapsed at the side of the road and died in my arms.' (Quoted in Gardner, *see* Bibliography.)

It was no longer possible, even if it ever had been, to form a common front with Gen Lanrezac's 5th Army. French was not to know until 26 August of Marshal Joffre's decision to form a new army, the 6th, on the French left wing. He could only know vaguely that French casualties, due largely to their frontal attacks, were mounting alarmingly and would total 300,000 by the end of what was to become known as the Battles of the Frontiers. French casualties already amounted to more than the total number of troops in the BEF, their soldiers being 'shot down like rabbits', dressed in their red trousers. Unknown of course to Sir John, von Kluck's intelligence about the BEF was if anything even more patchy than French's intelligence about 1st Army. Even after Le Cateau von Kluck was still under the impression that he taken on nine divisions, five more than he had actually engaged.

On the 25th the fortress of Namur fell to the Germans, with 5,000 Belgian troops taken prisoner. Liège had surrendered on the 17th. These were bitter blows and shocked the world, both neutral and combatant, although military academies had long agreed that no fortress was immune to modern siege guns.

1914 recruitment poster.

Of some comfort to the Allies, and Sir John could only be vaguely aware of it, the rapid Russian advance into East Prussia had already upset the whole Schlieffen Plan timetable, and had brought about the simultaneous war on two fronts that it had been designed to forestall. But Sir John could not know that by the end of the month the Russian 2nd Army would be destroyed and that its commander, Samsonov, would go off into the forest and shoot himself.

On the BEF front the fortress of Mauberge, with its garrison of 40,000 troops, was left to its own devices, French admitting that for a fleeting moment it offered the promise of a safe haven for the BEF. Von Bulow left a sizeable force, in fact the whole of his IX Corps, to bottle up its troops, to the annoyance of von Kluck; three divisions were out of the line until 7 September, when Mauberge surrendered. Further south, the defences on the perimeter of Paris were being prepared; the Government fled to Bordeaux on 2 September, leaving its defence to its military governor, Gen Gallieni, who announced, 'I have been empowered to defend Paris against the invader. This task I shall carry out to the end.' The situation as it confronted Sir John on 25 August would have taxed the resolve of a commander of Wellington's stamp.

Memories of the war with Prussia in 1870–71 were very real, the war that Napolean III had so ineptly declared. Anna Matisse, the mother of Henri, who had witnessed the Prussians pass through Le Cateau and St Quentin in 1871, had already buried her valuables in her cellar at Bohain by the time the Germans reached Mons. (She was to survive the occupation, with its endless requisitions and looting, but refusing to leave even when the Germans offered free passage to the old and infirm in 1918.) Andre Maurois, the author, went off to the war on the 28th and later wrote:

> My father looked me over with the severity of an old soldier. 'You must polish
> up your buttons.' He was sad at my leaving but full of hope for France and
> happy to see a son of his taking part in the war of revenge of which he had
> dreamed ever since 1871.

But if Sir John had been in direct touch with his battalion officers he would have learnt much that would have given him encouragement. Everywhere the British troops had fought with a skill and gallantry that amounted on occasion to self-sacrifice. On the 24th, for example, in a desperate 5th Division rearguard action at Elouges, south-west of Mons, involving the 1st Cheshires, the 1st Norfolks, 119th Battery Royal Field Artillery and the 9th Lancers, with some 4th Dragoon Guards, von Kluck's attempts at envelopment were successfully frustrated, albeit at great cost to the Cheshires: only 200 of them answered the roll call that night, and eleven of their officers languished in Torgau prison for the duration. If the BEF had suffered nearly 5,000 casualties by the evening of the 25th, the German 1st Army must have suffered at least three times as many.

The quick-firing skill of the professional volunteer soldier, with his new short .303 Lee-Enfield bolt-action rifle and its ten-round magazine (re-filled in clips of five rounds) was devastating to massed German infantry. It was probably the best rifle issued to all the combatant forces on the Western Front in the war; the French Lebel rifle, because of poor design, would often fail to reload from the magazine. What was also proving a vital asset in the small BEF was its fieldcraft: time and again, both at Mons itself and in subsequent encounters, its ability to disengage from a numerically superior enemy saved units from annihilation. It was a skill that was going to be needed at Le Cateau. The Cheshires had fought on because orders to retire did not get through; this was to happen again to many units at Le Cateau.

French's beloved cavalry had performed brilliantly in dozens of engagements, almost to the point of self-destruction, with lance, sabre and firearm, as well as in its scouting role; the 9th Lancers at Elouges were stopped by a single wire fence and 'galloped about like rabbits'. Although he would not like to admit it, it was invaluable fighting dismounted; unlike French cavalry, it carried the same rifle as the infantry and experience in the Boer War had taught it the value of cavalry shooting.* One historian of the period (Stephen

The 11th Hussars choosing softer ground for the horses.

*The French cavalry carbine was derided by the British as useless; their tactics were based on the Napoleonic belief in the shock of the armoured charge.

Badsey) has recently claimed that the British cavalry corps was 'massively superior' to the equivalent German arm. He was presumably not referring to the 9th Lancers at Elouges; their charge was magnificent, but it was not an act of war. But in their dual role as intelligence-gatherers and as protectors of the moving army, the cavalry division had already in the opening moves of the war more than proved its worth.

But Sir John himself was in no sense in control of events. If what followed on 26 August was a battle that the British, in the person of Sir Horace Smith-Dorrien and his division commanders, elected to fight, it was von Kluck who held the initiative. It was fought as always by the officers and men with what they had to hand. It was a soldier's battle fought almost one hundred years after the last great British battle on continental soil, Waterloo, and on the anniversary of the battle of Crécy (1346).

Not only was it fought no more than a day's ride away from the field of Waterloo, it was fought with weapons and tactics that would not have been unfamiliar to the Duke of Wellington: the horse-drawn field guns, often in range of the enemy infantry, the screen of cavalry (French cavalry still wore breastplates and plumed helmets, and the French infantry had a distinctly Napoleonic appearance with their red and blue), the massed infantry, the buglers calling the fire orders; none would have been out of place on 18 June 1815, which was a Sunday as was the day of the Battle of Mons. In 1914 most British infantry officers still carried their swords into battle and Highland officers their claymores, sharpened by the armourers. German and French officers also wore swords, the swords carried by German officers at Mons and Le Cateau marking them out as primary targets for the British infantry. In the heat of battle swords proved to be something of a hindrance; in the battle to come on the 26th, Lt Ian Stewart, an 18-year-old platoon commander in 2nd Argyll and Sutherland Highlanders, was leading a charge when he fell, claymore in hand, like his Jacobite ancestors at Culloden. His sergeant leant over him saying, 'poor wee kid', only to receive the caustic reply that he had tripped over the sword. A similar accident befell Lt Montgomery, with happy results, as we shall see. German regiments carried their colours into battle unfurled. Uhlans carried bugles as part of their issue as well as their lances. The headgear of Jäger infantry strongly resembled the shako of Wellington's day, and confused British infantry at first with their un-Germanic appearance. Just as the thin red line in the Crimea had not been uniformly red, the thin line at Le Cateau was not uniformly khaki; there was many a splash of tartan amongst the men and officers of the BEF.

Both Le Cateau and Waterloo were fought after three days of intense battle and retreat. Both were preceded by thunderstorms. One difference was that at Le Cateau the field of battle had been harvested while at Waterloo the corn stood uncut. Waterloo was smaller, and hence more crowded with troops and shrouded in black gunpowder smoke. Le Cateau was wholly innocent of barbed wire, which had yet to make its baleful appearance on the Western Front, although the 2nd Royal Scots, 8th Brigade, stripped some barbed wire from the gardens of Audencourt and used in front of their trenches; the first recorded use of wire in this now-familiar role.

Even though the effective range of weapons had increased by a factor of ten to as much as 1,200yd for rifles and 9,000yd for field guns (whose gunners could now bring optical range-finders into play and whose projectiles were far more sophisticated than the roundshot of Wellington's day), many actions at Le Cateau were fought at ranges where the two sides were in close proximity. This reflects the unchanging fact of infantry warfare: if the commander can bring superior force close up to the enemy, he can either kill him or force his surrender, although the emergence of the clip-holding magazine rifle, the range-finder and the well-sited machine gun had unquestionably favoured the defence. At Le Cateau as at Waterloo gunners needed to see their targets; there was no question of pre-registering the guns.

The number of British troops involved at Le Cateau, say 60,000, was more than Wellington had had at his disposal but less than his total command. Both battles were hastily improvised defensive affairs. In both cases the flank between the British and the sea gave commanders cause for concern. It may be fanciful but it is forgivable to regard the British infantry at Mons and Le Cateau with their .303 Lee-Enfields as the direct descendants of the Anglo-Welsh archers of Crécy and Agincourt, and of the squares at Waterloo armed with muskets. After all, one of the legends of Mons was the archers appearing in the sky to shepherd the men of 1914. Certainly one eyewitness at Le Cateau was reminded of Waterloo by the wrecked gun batteries of the right flank, and of course many of the battalions at Le Cateau had Waterloo battle honours in their regimental history. Waterloo was a more bloody battle (8,558 British losses against 7,812 at Le Cateau) if only because Wellington was not prepared to give up any ground. But Waterloo was of course crushingly decisive. Seven years of almost continuous warfare for the British had brought them to the decisive moment since their expeditionary force under Sir John Moore had been driven comprehensively out of Spain in 1808.

If Le Cateau bore similarities to nineteenth-century battles, such was the pace of technological change in the Great War that within four years battles on the Western Front were to take on a twentieth-century aspect, with hundreds of tanks and thousands of aircraft co-operating in all-arms assaults on the Kaiser's armies. Instead of the hundreds of guns deployed at Le Cateau, guns were brought up in their thousands, so that on the opening day of the Battle of the Somme (1 July 1916) there was one gun for every twenty yards of the frontage attacked. At Cambrai in November 1917, little more than 5 miles (8km) from where the BEF now stood, 324 tanks were massed for the initial assault. Nearly six million men were to enter the ranks of the British Army before the end of hostilities. The scout planes of the Royal Flying Corps and the requisitioned motor transport of the BEF in August 1914 were but harbingers of the nature of warfare to come. The bugler, an already anachronistic figure, was to be replaced by the officer's whistle which, with the synchronized watch, was to become another of the mournful symbols of the war. The sword soon became purely ceremonial. Even the vaunted marksmanship of the infantry, so nourished before the war, was becoming by 1917 a thing of distant memory.

The battlefield of Le Cateau on 26 August 1914 was wholly bereft of motor transport, as indeed battlefields were to remain for at least two years. Guns, ammunition wagons and all other forms of transport were horse-drawn. At the end of the day, on the Roman road, as Lt Gen Smith-Dorrien was being driven in his car, part of the long line of beaten but not defeated 5th Division troops, he heard gunfire in the west. He didn't send a staff officer to see for whom the guns were firing; he got on his horse, which was being led alongside, and went to see for himself. It was Gen Sordet's 75mm field guns, whose distinctive crack Sir Horace already recognized. The Frenchman had not let him down. But it was a horse that Sir Horace used to get about the field, just as it had been for Wellington or Marlborough. Its name, alas, has not been recorded.

Professional soldiers, like Capt Dunn of the Royal Welch Fusiliers, were to regret the inevitable passing, during the war years at least, of the close-knit, clannish, organic, professional Edwardian army, based as it was on regional recruiting among the working class, with officers who came almost exclusively from a social class whose right to hand down orders, by virtue of their position in the social structure, was not questioned and whose guiding principle was one of *noblesse oblige*. A great many of those paternalistic officers lay dead in the Flanders mud by Christmas 1914. The part-time Territorials who went to the front after the time covered in this book enjoyed a style of discipline that was based more on an easy understanding or even comradeship between officers and men, although it never got as matey as the Australian model. As Gary Sheffield has written, these two different strands of officer–men relations became intermingled in the BEF. In August 1914, however, it was the old-style regular officers who led the men, some of them crusty martinets maybe, obsessed with trivialities maybe, profoundly anti-intellectual probably, but all of them taking their duties towards their men very seriously indeed. The late Victorian officer's credo of leading by example was still very much alive.

19

For the men perhaps even more than the officers the battalions that went to war in 1914 defined the boundaries of their known world, although the colonel loomed large in all aspects of an officer's life; the colonel's permission was required for a young officer to marry, for example, and he certainly governed the etiquette adopted in the mess. There had been a rush to marry, or at least get engaged, among many officers in the last few days before setting off to France; Lt Rory Macleod, a gunner who we will meet later, had asked his Irish sweetheart to marry him just days before the troopship sailed. For many officers the battalion was their world; officers would typically marry late in life and many were 'wedded to the regiment'. The older officers still referred to their battalions by their numbers in the line of battle as their predecessors had at Waterloo; the 2nd Battalion the Suffolk Regiment was thus the 2nd/12th. In fact it was only in 1881 that the old battalion numbers were officially swept away and the BEF as it was in 1914 was born, with its regiments of linked battalions, one always serving overseas, based on local recruiting and its extended family of reservists.

When Capt C.A.L. Brownlow, a gunner later awarded the DSO, wrote that 'I have no remembrance to equal in any way that of the old regiments of the BEF marching to the Battle of Mons', he was speaking for the great majority of the 1914 regulars. Or as R.V. Dolbey RAMC, a captain in the KOSB, put it, writing after the war about the Retreat, 'None but a regular army could have done it, and after the war we shall worship the gods of spit and polish and barrack-square again.'

In many respects the BEF of 1914 had the characteristics of an old family firm, with all the fierce loyalties, paternalism and built-in discipline that one would expect in such an organization, which were inevitably lost as the war went on and the BEF took on more and more the features of a large corporation. Such was the magnitude of change and death in the old family firm that it is somewhat inconsistent and even incongruous that the BEF that went to war in August 1914 with five divisions was still called by the same name as the army of a million men that crossed the Hindenburg Line in 1918. On 26 August 1914 the old family firm that was called the BEF was still intact, but it was the high noon of the Edwardian army, based upon Edwardian social divisions and the primary product of the first Industrial Revolution, steel, produced by coal and iron. It was on the cusp of the second Industrial Revolution, which added the internal combustion engine, based on petroleum, as a further power source. The fact that the army largely reverted to its pre-war type after the war says a lot about the permanence and conservatism of British institutions; but that is another story.

On 26 August 1914 for Lt Gen Sir Horace Smith-Dorrien there was to be no Blücher; and before Le Cateau there was certainly no ball. All Sandhurst officer cadets were (and are) required to know their military history and many would have been aware of the site of the battle of Malplaquet (1709) just south of Mons. It had been a very bloody battle by eighteenth-century standards, fought against the despotism of Louis XIV. And nobody could of course know that twenty-six years later Guderian's *Panzers* would roll through this same undulating country on their way to the Channel, as had the Prussian legions in 1870 on their way to Paris, to which they laid siege. Le Cateau lay in the cockpit of European wars, but the precedents and auguries were mixed.

On 26 August 1914 Sir John French – in response to a lengthy note from Sir Horace Smith-Dorrien informing him that he intended to make a stand at Le Cateau – sent back by wire an immediate reply to Bertry, just south-west of Le Cateau, where Sir Horace had set up his battle HQ. This reply arrived at Bertry at 5.00am on the 26th. It read:

> If you can hold your ground the situation appears likely to improve. 4th Division must co-operate. French troops are taking the offensive on right of 1st Corps. Although you are given a free hand as to method, this telegram is not intended to convey the impression that I am not anxious for you to carry out the retirement and you must make every effort to do so.

This communication, which to the non-military eye might appear equivocal with its double negative, Smith-Dorrien took to be approval of his earlier decision to 'stand and fight'. Its condition, that Second Corps' primary orders were to continue the Retreat, did not run counter to his own instincts, although he knew that that manoeuvre might have to be conducted late in the day. The reference to the French 5th Army was irrelevant to Smith-Dorrien; he would rather have had something reassuring concerning help from First Corps on his right and French troops on his left, but it was not unreasonable to assume that at least First Corps could perform a blocking or masking role on his right flank. He was given no intelligence on the enemy, but he had his own shrewd idea of what he was up against. In any case, he could now do nothing else but fight. The battle that ensued has been called by John Terraine 'one of the most remarkable British feats of arms of the whole war'.

But the stage was also set for tragedy, farce and glory. Tragedy because more than half the British field army faced destruction from von Kluck, who had more than three times its men and guns, if he only knew it. Farce, or tragicomedy, because forever after Sir John French was obsessed with continuing his feud with his *bête noir*, Sir Horace Smith-Dorrien. Personal animosities loomed large in the psychological makeup of Sir John French. And for Sir John the feud found its focus on the events of 26 August. He was damned if he was going to go out of his way to help Sir Horace, whose orders were to get Second Corps away to the south. French was to quit St Quentin even as the exhausted troops were streaming back from Le Cateau, without informing Sir Horace of his new location. Even French's biographer, Richard Holmes, admits that 'from 26 August onwards he lavished the full force of his hatred upon Smith-Dorrien'. John Terraine was more charitable: he merely said that French had a grievance, possibly resulting from a guilty conscience.

The bitterness of old soldiers may be sterile and farcical in retirement, but in August 1914 it was materially to affect the help French was willing to give Smith-Dorrien's Corps. In retirement, in fact while still in uniform, Sir John, because of his animus against Sir Horace, was to denigrate the achievement of Second Corps at Le Cateau and the heroism and sacrifice of its veterans. That is the final pathos. If Mons is to be forever remembered for the Angel, Le Cateau is remembered for the malevolent Sir John French.

And yet even though the Germans were left in possession of the field at the end of the day, the battle fought to the west and south of Le Cateau on 26 August 1914 can be considered, in the words of the historian of the Royal Artillery, 'one of the most important delaying actions recorded in history'. And there was the glory. But to one young officer was vouchsafed a vision not of the glory of war, but of the sorrow and the pity yet to come. Lt Maurice Baring was with the men as they marched singing into Mauberge on their way up to Mons. He wrote at the end of October:

> The thought of these men swinging on into horror undreamt of – the whole German Army – came to me like the stab of a sword and I had to go and hide in a shop for the people not to see the tears running down my cheeks.*

*Maurice Baring, 1874–1945, of the banking family, educated at Eton and Trinity College, Cambridge, man of letters, Anglo-Catholic. He served on the staff of the RFC during the war and published a memoir of his war in 1920. He was a convinced practical joker.

1

To Bertry: 23–5 August

The Smith-Dorrien–French Feud

Horace Smith-Dorrien was born into a large, upper-middle-class military family in Hertfordshire in 1858. The family was not rich; at his death in 1930 Horace's estate was valued at £6,519 3s. In many respects his career followed the conventional pattern of a late Victorian officer: after Harrow School he was commissioned into the 95th Foot (later the Sherwood Foresters) and attended the Royal Military College, Sandhurst. By 1879 he was fighting Zulus at Isandhlwana, and in 1898 he was fighting the Mahdi's army at Omdurman. In between there were long spells playing polo in India, where it is said that he could remember the names of all the officers in his division as well as of their polo ponies. At Staff College, Camberley, in 1887 he was said not to know where to find the library but he still managed to pass his final examinations. He married late, as was usual for regimental officers at the time, in September 1902 at St Peter's, Eaton Square, London, to Olive Crofton, also from a well-connected military family. By this time he might have considered that his period of active soldiering was coming to an end. He had, after all, just returned from three bruising years fighting the Boers, for a time as a brigade commander under Lord Roberts. In 1912 he was promoted full general and given the prestigious appointment of Southern Command. There he was when war broke out on 4 August 1914 and there he remained when the BEF sailed for France. As a lieutenant general there were in effect only two jobs open to him with the BEF and both those were taken. He was fifty-six years old with three boys under ten and devoted to his wife. But he was unlikely to stay on the home front for long.

But that is not quite the whole story of his pre-1914 career. Even as a young subaltern he had displayed considerable organizational skill, which had come to the attention of his superiors, and it was this skill that saved his life. When Col Durnford's redcoats were being cut down by the Zulus at Isandhlwana, Smith-Dorrien was with the transport wagons distributing ammunition. He was dressed in blue patrols: for some reason this made him a less attractive target for the Zulus (all those who got away were wearing blue) and he managed to make off on horseback and then on foot after some useful work with his revolver.* Fifty-six European soldiers escaped and 626 were killed, all with assegais. Smith-Dorrien undoubtedly helped some soldiers to safety. There was talk of a VC but it came to nothing.

Lt-Gen Sir Horace Smith-Dorrien, Second Corps commander.

At Aldershot Sir Horace succeeded Sir John French to the command and he – together with Haig as his successor, according to historians of the period – made possible the very high standards of the professional BEF that went to war in 1914.

Lt-Gen Sir Douglas Haig, First Corps commander.

*He later wrote to his parents, 'It seems a miracle that I am alive to tell you about it.'

As with all feuds, the origins of that between French and Smith-Dorrien are obscure. Perhaps French didn't even need a reason to develop a phobia; in any case the mere fact that Smith-Dorrien, an infantryman, had had the temerity to put forward views on the tactical role of cavalry that were opposed to Sir John's was reason enough. But he did more than just put forward views: he insisted that cavalry officers learn infantry tactics. Smith-Dorrien had, of course, done nothing more than join the reforming wing, led by Lord Roberts, in the debate over the role of cavalry, against the *arme blanche* led by French. There was also the matter of military police patrols in Aldershot: Smith-Dorrien stood them down to save troops from harassment, which made Sir John more than usually red-faced.

The feud was common knowledge in the Army. Although not a martinet, Smith-Dorrien himself was not exactly placid; his temper has been variously ascribed to bad teeth and to the fact that he was born eleventh of fifteen children.* Always smartly turned out himself, he does not have the reputation, which Allenby of the cavalry has, of being a stickler for correct dress at all times – indeed, Allenby was known among the troops as 'chin-strap' for his obsession with this item of equipment. Smith-Dorrien was careful with money and faithful to his wife, both virtues not shared by French. Although he was not an intellectual soldier like Wilson or Lanrezac, his writing – like his actions – display a clarity and robustness that should be the envy of many an academic, although his diary, written at the behest of the King, is unfortunately free of indiscretions. The feud was already well entrenched by August 1914. We should note here that Haig and Smith-Dorrien were also on opposing sides in the cavalry debate. The British Army, like the French, was riven with schisms concealed as doctrinal debates, and promotion was often largely a matter of hitching one's career-wagon to the most promising star.

During the winter of 1914–15, like many senior officers, Smith-Dorrien would become concerned about the growing number of cases of deserters found behind the lines and the effect these might have on the morale of front-line troops; he was invariably in favour of the death penalty in such cases. It is perhaps for this attitude, his upper middle-class background and his polo-playing that Stephen Badsey has called him a 'fairly typical' general of his generation. But it is a surprising and unhelpful description.

The feud went public with the publication of an interview (conducted by telephone) with Smith-Dorrien in the *Weekly Despatch* of February 1917, and became a central feature of French's book *1914* (published 1919) to which Smith-Dorrien quite justifiably replied in a privately published statement. The feud centred around the events of the first week of hostilities and, in particular, the decision to offer battle at dawn on 26 August. The battle fought that day was to cast a long shadow.

*Douglas Haig was born the youngest of eleven children, of whom nine survived.

The Battle of Mons

On 17 August 1914 Sir James Grierson, commander-designate of Second Corps, died of a heart attack in a train on the way to the front – he was extremely corpulent and his dining habits were lavish even by the standards of Edwardian cuisine. It was a loss universally felt, not least because Sir James was an acknowledged expert on the German Army and order of battle; he had been a guest of the Kaiser at the annual German Army manoeuvres. Kitchener sent for Sir Horace despite French having asked for Sir Herbert Plumer; this was not entirely surprising, Sir Horace being a protégé of Kitchener's. On the 18th, Sir Horace shook hands with the King, with whom he was on familiar terms, bade farewell to his family and by the 20th he was in France. His fellow lieutenant general was Sir Douglas Haig, commanding First Corps. He took with him his personal staff officers: Major Hope Johnstone AMS, Capt W.A.T. Bowly ADC and Col W. Rycroft AQMG. At this stage, by his own admission, he knew next to nothing of the situation at the front. He confessed no feelings of personal self-doubt at the prospect of being in command of nearly 40,000 men under a commander-in-chief in whom he had less than full confidence, although he did not share Haig's robust certainty of a direct connection with the Lord God of Hosts. It was now his manifest duty and destiny to fight the invading German armies of the German Empire, which by its 'evil machinations' was seeking to achieve hegemony over Europe by military power.

By the 21st he was at Corps HQ at Bavai to meet his chief of staff, Brig-Gen Forestier-Walker, followed by a meeting with the chief at Le Cateau. Here he got the general impression that Second Corps was to move up to the line of the Mons–Condé canal with a view to pushing on beyond it in a right wheel. By the 22nd his staff had set up HQ at a modest manor house at Sars-la-Bruyère, 6 miles (10km) south-west of Mons. It had no telephone but the Royal Engineers later fixed up a telegraph connection with GHQ. That afternoon he motored round the outposts and was not happy with what he found: a thinly-held front of 21 miles (33km) with poor fields of fire and the indefensible town of Mons in a salient. The canal was almost as much a hindrance to the British as a barrier to the enemy. He reconnoitred a fall-back position: in his heart he knew that there was no prospect of any offensive action by Second Corps. But he slept the sleep of the innocent that night; it was the last good night's sleep that he, or indeed anyone in the BEF, was going to get for a long time.

At 0600 the next day French turned up at Sars and a conference of the divisional generals of Second Corps (Gen Hamilton of 3rd Division, Gen Fergusson of 5th Division and Gen Allenby of the Cavalry Division) met to hear the latest intelligence reports and to receive orders: the BEF was faced by no more than two German corps; Sir Horace was to move forward, stay put, or fall back if necessary. Sir Horace's second line seemed to meet with the Chief's approval, as far as he could tell. And with that Sir John went back to Le Cateau, via Valenciennes to inspect the recently arrived 19th Brigade. He was thought to have been 'on splendid form'. Smith-Dorrien 'chafed': by that time the Battle of Mons had already started in earnest. At the end of the day, the first European battle for the British for ninety-nine years, the German buglers sounded 'cease fire' and two British divisions had stopped six German. First Corps under Gen Haig had not been engaged, but had stood sentinel on the right flank, facing east and north.

Command and Control

It was not the custom in the early twentieth century for army commanders to share the same physical dangers that their men suffered, although corps, division and brigade commanders certainly did on occasions: fifty-seven officers in the Great War of the rank of brigadier-general and above were killed by enemy fire. A shell burst in front of Sir Horace's car at Mons early on the 23rd and he was within range of German shell-fire on the 26th. All of the division commanders came under shell-fire on that day as they rode out to the front lines, and lieutenant colonels were nearly as likely to be killed as their men, as were the brigadiers. Von Arnim, the equivalent of a brigadier in the British Army, was killed at Le Cateau on the 26th. Gen Franchet d'Esperey, a corps commander, led a brigade into battle at Guise on 29 August. Haig, while commanding First Corps, famously rode up the Menin road during the height of First Ypres. Von Kluck himself, exceptionally, had a brush with French cavalry just before the Marne battle and was badly wounded by a shell in 1915. All could have been killed.

Wellington, in the thick of the action at Waterloo, very nearly suffered the same fate as Sir John Moore at Corunna. By the time Lord Raglan was commanding in the Crimea, however, or Grant and Lee in the American Civil War, commanders at army level were acting in the role of managing directors rather than line managers; Lord Raglan was as likely to be killed by Russian action at Balaclava in 1854 as Sir John French was to be killed by German action at Mons, even allowing for the fact that Raglan was ordering individual units into action. The problem for army commanders, now that they were more distant from the battle itself and no longer concerned with tactics, was that communication technology had not kept pace with the growth in the level of organizational complexity: armies were now counted in hundreds of thousands, yet all movements had to go through the appropriate chain of command, by one method of communication or other.

In northern France in 1914 there was a partial and unreliable telephone system. Even a town as big as Bertry, say 5,000 people, might have only a single telephone. There were the army signallers (Royal Engineers) who could only do so much with their cables. There was as yet no effective mobile wireless system; the telegraph needed a transmitting station and a receiving station. The BEF had no despatch riders. What it did have was the RAC Corps of Volunteer Motor Drivers, among whom were the Duke of Westminster (known as 'Bendor') and Lord Dalmeny. Six of these aristocratic gentlemen, including the duke, were attached to GHQ at Le Cateau, driving staff officers to liaison meetings at corps and division HQs. They were of course driving their own cars, all of which had passed a technical inspection by the RAC.

The unavoidable truth was that even a distance of around just 20 miles (30km) from BEF HQ to its constituent corps was too far for effective communication, especially when the roads were clogged with military and civilian traffic; most roads were in any case in those days hardly designed for motor traffic. No one has imputed cowardice to Sir John, but both at Le Cateau and at St Quentin he was a little eager to move south, more so at St Quentin. Both moves were to inconvenience Smith-Dorrien, a man who was easily irritated by his C-in-C. Army commanders such as French made do with what communications they had with the knowledge that the telephone wires were not secure from enemy interference. This knowledge, combined with the fragmented and partial signals net, meant that in practice movement orders were issued in general terms, the details to be worked out by commanders on the ground (known as the 'umpire' system). Spy mania was at its height, but a staff officer in a Rolls-Royce driven by Hugh Grosvenor, 2nd Duke of Westminster, was about as secure as you could get as a means of communication. The main danger to drivers behind the lines, particularly in the French area of operations, was 'lunatic' Territorials or even civilians, armed with shotguns, who set up road-blocks in their hunt for 'spies'. At times, interpreters were kept from meetings for fear of security leaks. Here is Lt Gen Sir William Robertson QMG on the means of communication on the Western Front:

> Telegraph and telephone by wire and cable, wireless telegraphy, telegraphy through the ground (power buzzer), visual signalling with electric lamps, helio and flags, carrier pigeons, messenger dogs, message-carrying rockets, firework signals, despatch riders, mounted orderlies, cyclists and finally runners, were all employed in turn, according to circumstances.

In August 1914, although Sir John could not know it, the German signals net was even more primitive than the British, in spite of their world lead in electronics, and was to prove a constant source of exasperation to commanders in the field from von Kluck down to the lieutenant colonels. Both the British and German cavalry were equipped with bulky radio sets, which could be used to intercept enemy signals.

Sir William might have added the RFC to his list. During the battle, on the 26th, GHQ sent up a number of aeroplanes for both reconnaissance and liaison. One airman was sent to locate Gen Haig; another made a forced landing near Smith-Dorrien's HQ at Bertry. A third made a successful landing near Bertry and was able to make a report to Sir Horace. The airman took off again for St Quentin, a dangerous move at the best of times since British soldiers tended to fire at all aeroplanes. GHQ made no use of any information obtained and it did not affect the course of the battle, although the *Official History* says it was 'valuable'.* There was of course no air-to-ground radio communication, although German aircraft had already developed a technique of dropping markers to indicate targets, mainly gun batteries; the German air force, with over 400 aeroplanes, entered the war better prepared than the British. The BEF had no anti-aircraft guns. Lt Hodgson, who we will meet later, has recorded that late in 1914 his 18-pounder battery tried shooting at hostile aircraft with his guns at high elevation, firing shrapnel, with no success. Soldiers would loose off their rifles at aeroplanes they saw to be German, all of which they called 'Taubes' after a common German type of 1914; one was shot down in the 4th Division area on 25 August.

Illustration by Ludwig Hohlwein of a German Albatros scout plane, designed by Ernst Heinkel. This type of aircraft was used at Le Cateau to spot targets for the artillery.

*Brig Sir James Edmonds' *Official History of the Great War* is, according to Paddy Griffith, 'positively the best book ever written, or ever likely to be written, about the Great War on the Western Front – and by quite a large margin'.

The Retreat Begins

On 23 August at BEF HQ at Le Cateau there were two crucial events that tell us a great deal about French's style of generalship and the problems of communication: Gen Forestier-Walker's comings and goings from Second Corps HQ and Capt Spears' visit from Gen Lanrezac's HQ. At 7.15pm on the 23rd, the evening of Mons, Smith-Dorrien sent by wire from Sars the following message to GHQ at Le Cateau, 30 miles (50km) south:

> 3rd Division report at 6.47pm the Germans are in front of his main position and are not attacking at present, they are however working round 3rd Division on left flank. If it should appear that there is a danger of my centre being pierced I can see no course but to order a general retirement on Bavai position [10 miles south]. Have I your permission to adopt this course if it appears necessary?

It was this threat to Gen Hamilton's Division that had Smith-Dorrien driving to Haig's HQ with Brig Forestier-Walker to request urgent help, help which was forthcoming in the shape of Gen Haking's three battalions.

At 9.00pm a message came back from Le Cateau which summoned the Second Corps chief of staff (Forestier-Walker) to appear in person at Army HQ; he arrived at 11.00pm and went into immediate conference with Sir Archibald Murray, the chief of staff, exchanging merely a few words with the C-in-C about the regrettable loss of Grierson. Forestier-Walker got back to Sars at 3.30am on the 24th with the orders that the whole BEF was to retire, commencing at 5.00am, the details to be worked out by Second and First Corps staff. This general retreat order, according to Smith-Dorrien's later statement, came as a total surprise to him: 'A wish to retire never entered my head.' This is surely some exaggeration; the corps commander was at pains to avoid the charge of pessimism, and so claimed that the offensive spirit was strong throughout the BEF and that it was Sir John who abandoned hopes of an offensive before he did. In any event, Smith-Dorrien, right up to the moment Forestier-Walker got back from Le Cateau, was expecting to resume action at dawn on his second line, in spite of the fact that he was in a better picture regarding German strength than GHQ was and in spite of his expressed wish to retire on Bavai. The warning orders to the divisions were sent out on Forestier-Walker's return, Haig's staff under the direction of his chief of staff, Brig-Gen Johnny Gough,* having already prepared the details of retreat orders. Haig's retreat order reached him by telegram at 2.00am, one and a half hours ahead of Forestier-Walker's return to Sars. Gough had been at Le Cateau with Forestier-Walker (the two men did not get on) but had chosen to stay there, sending the orders by wire. Forestier-Walker felt obliged

---

*Killed by a sniper in February 1915 while visiting his old regiment, the 2nd Rifle Brigade, near Neuve Chapelle; his brother was Brig-Gen Hubert Gough of the cavalry.

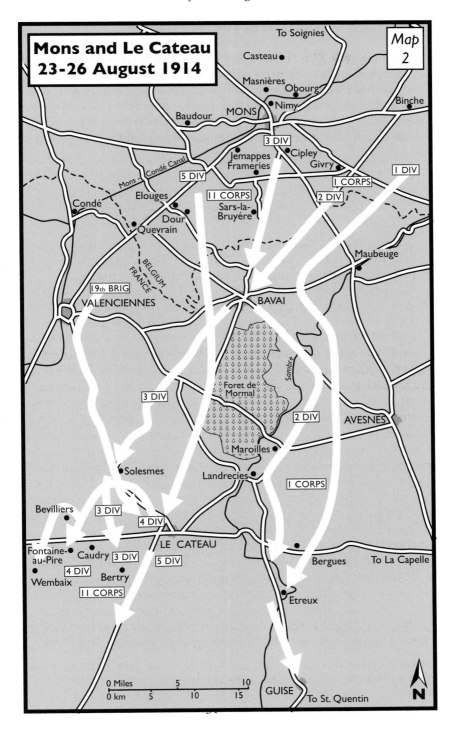

**Mons and Le Cateau
23-26 August 1914**

Map
2

To Soignies

Casteau

Masnières
Obourg
Binche
Baudour
MONS
Nimy

3 DIV
Cipley
Jemappes
Frameries
Givry
I DIV
5 DIV
I CORPS
Mons – Condè Canal
Elouges
II CORPS
2 DIV
Condé
Sars-la-
Bruyére
Dour
Quevrain
Maubeuge
BELGIUM
FRANCE
19th BRIG
VALENCIENNES
BAVAI

Sambre

Foret de
Mormal
2 DIV
AVESNES

3 DIV

Maroilles

Solesmes
Landrecies
I CORPS
Bevilliers
3 DIV
4 DIV
Fontaine-
au-Pire
Caudry
3 DIV
5 DIV
LE CATEAU
Bergues
To La Capelle
4 DIV
Bertry
Wembaix
II CORPS
Etreux

0 Miles   5   10
0 km   5   10   15
GUISE
To St. Quentin
N

to make the return journey by road, carrying the orders, for reasons not entirely clear, in spite of Smith-Dorrien's original message requesting retreat to Bavai having been sent by telegraph. Haig received the additional order that he should cover the retirement of Second Corps, which clearly made no sense. He ignored it, beyond issuing orders to form a rearguard at Le Bonnet.

It was a time when an elapse of even four hours was critical in organizing an orderly retreat, which was roughly the amount of time taken by Forestier-Walker in his staff car on the road, going both ways. Smith-Dorrien blamed French for the dilatory manner in which the vital retreat order reached him, rather than his chief of staff. At the very least, both road and wire could have been used. In the event, the fact that the BEF got away from the Mons position that night in an orderly retreat owed nothing to the staff at GHQ – the army simply muddled through. But this preventable delay in getting the retreat orders out to battalion level in Second Corps was responsible in large part for the unplanned battle at Elouges the next day, where the BEF suffered more casualties than at Mons. In fact one of the first things that Smith-Dorrien did after Forestier-Walker got back from his round trip was to send off a personal note to Sir John, as follows:

> .... the situation we are embarking on is one of the most difficult which can occur, namely breaking off a fight at its hottest and adopting retirement tactics, without offering great advantages to an enemy.

Sir Horace clearly already had one eye on the history books. Sir John acknowledged the note and confirmed that he would visit both corps commanders the same day (24th). Both these notes were sent by telegraph wire. It was at the 24th meeting that French told Smith-Dorrien, when asked to clarify the details of the retreat order, 'you can do as you like'. This dismissive remark, which speaks volumes, is recorded without comment in Sir Horace's memoir but not at all in Sir John's. The meeting on the 24th (French met both corps commanders separately) was the last for Sir Horace until the small hours of the 27th. Sir John was keen to keep his face-to-face meetings with Sir Horace to the minimum; they were not good for his temper, always simmering at the best of times.

The two corps were concentrated briefly at Bavai. Smith-Dorrien shifted his HQ to Hon, just south of the Belgian border. His losses from all causes over the two days of fighting now amounted to 3,784 officers and men: serious but gratifyingly smaller than those he felt sure had been inflicted on the enemy. First Corps losses were no more than 150. What was worrying was that the relentless progress south of von Kluck's 1st Army was not being appreciatively slowed. The Battle of Mons had effectively slowed von Kluck down by no more than twenty-four hours. He had had a shock but his losses did not amount to more than 5 per cent of his army (although of course the percentage losses were much higher in the fighting formations). He was desperate to resume contact with the main body of the BEF.

On the morning of the 23rd, while Second Corps BEF – in particular the 4th Middlesex and the 4th Royal Fusiliers – was fighting for its life in the Mons salient, Gen Lanrezac was at his advance position at Philippeville. (Acting) Captain Edward Spears was with him, the Anglo-French liaison officer who had already tried and failed to bring the two chiefs into some sort of mutual understanding. The French general spent the morning pacing up and down the Grand Place, watching the miserable refugees passing through the town. There was a telephone link with Le Cateau at the Mairie, Lanrezac's HQ, and messages passed to and fro, the last at 6.00pm to the effect that the British would hold at the Mons position even though they knew the BEF were threatened with three enemy corps and that at least one French corps appeared to be falling back. This conversation (with Col Macdonogh, chief intelligence officer) was before Smith-Dorrien's request to retire on Bavai. Using the line in the post office across the Place, Spears assured Col Macdonogh that the French were not in full flight: the airman reporting the retreating French soldiers must have mistaken a refugee column for troops. This merely confirmed what GHQ wished the situation to be; at this stage GHQ still seemed to be in a state of ignorance about how severe the fight had been at Mons, with Gen Wilson living in a fantasy world of his own.

But when Spears emerged from the post office the whole French staff with the general had decamped. He followed them down the road to Chimay where he learned that Lanrezac had ordered the whole 5th Army to retire. This was momentous news: Joffre might know it; French couldn't know it. This time, instead of trusting to the telephone, Spears got in his little Sunbeam car and drove the two hours to Le Cateau, arriving about 11.00pm. The news he brought resulted in the retreat order to the BEF; his visit in person had just preceded that of Forestier-Walker and although he was treated in the rather brusque manner appropriate to his lowly military rank, he managed to get his message across. According to Spears' biographer, Max Egremont, a subaltern had saved the BEF. This is a pardonable exaggeration: French in his memoir gave more credit to his growing realization of German strength, but there is no doubt that Spears' news of 5th Army's new southerly movement made the scales drop from his eyes. Forestier-Walker confirmed later that it was the French 5th Army move that had convinced the C-in-C of the exposed position in which the BEF now stood. Of course, French also had Smith-Dorrien's request to retire on Bavai, but we know that he was always sceptical about requests from that particular quarter. Up to now French had been effectively duped by Joffre, regarding both German strength and French movements; he had been living in a Panglossian world. The timely news that Spears brought to Le Cateau had a greater influence on the retreat decision than the combined wisdom of the ten professional GHQ staff officers, supposedly the best Britain had to offer. In any event, the pressure of events on Sir John was now overwhelming, and there was nowhere for the BEF to go but south.

The Retreat to Le Cateau

But for now the BEF was saving itself, 5th Division retreating to the west of 3rd Division (they were later to switch), First Corps coming in from the north-east. For most fit young men a walk of 25 miles (40km) or so should not present an intolerable burden, but the BEF faced many difficulties in their march: the heat (the late summer of 1914 was one of glorious weather), the cobbled roads, the unsuitable battledress (the infantry would have been better off in tropical kit), the burden the infantry always carry (say 56lb/25kg); the bitter disappointment, the thirst, the lack of sleep, rifles carried often with bayonets fixed, the constant alerts. For the British, the Retreat from Mons is still fixed in the national consciousness and rightly ranks as a battle honour for all battalions who took part.

If the German troops were uplifted by thoughts of marching in triumph down the Paris boulevards, and that the Kaiser and the Fatherland were entities worth dying for, then British morale was sustained by the certain knowledge that they were not a beaten army and by a perhaps less-articulated belief in King and Country. The joyous welcome from the French lifted their spirits, as did the wine proffered by the roadside, although zealous officers would knock over buckets of wine for fear of the consequences – French officers would try to prevent their thirsty men from drinking too much water, lest it did them damage.

The BEF 'came into Bavai singing', according to one eyewitness, some of the older men singing 'The Girl I left Behind Me', which became altered to:

> Oh, we don't give a fuck
> For old von Kluck
> An' all his fucking Army!'

The columns of troops singing irreverent songs as they marched has become one of the accepted images of the war. There was in fact not a great deal of singing, irreverent or otherwise, on the roads either side of Bavai by troops, who had more pressing matters to contend with. The *Official History* records that the BEF 'stumbled along like robots' as they came into Bavai, 'and this was only the start of the Retreat'. Marching songs do not in any case come naturally to English soldiers, who are more inclined to break into song in the estaminet after some *vin blanc*, a relaxation that was to be denied them for some time. Later songs were to achieve a haunting, sardonic beauty wonderfully attuned to the mood in the trenches:

If you want to find the old battalion,
I know where they are, I know where they are,
I know where they are –
They're hanging on the old barbed wire,
They're hanging on the old barbed wire,
I've seen 'em, I've seen 'em,
Hanging on the old barbed wire.

It is hard to imagine German soldiers singing the equivalent of this ditty:

Send for the boys of the Girls' Brigade
To set old England free:
Send for my mother, my sister or my brother
But for God's sake don't send me.

An exhausted German soldier, August 1914.

Private Frank Richards (he remained a private throughout the war) can take up the narrative here. He was a reservist, as were about half the BEF at this date, called back to the 2nd Royal Welch Fusiliers, a regular battalion, at the outbreak of war and therefore older than the average age of the other men. On 4 August the 2nd Royal Welch – who clung to the old English spelling of 'Welch' – had a strength of twenty officers and 580 other ranks, which was brought up to twenty-nine officers and 1,066 other ranks by the recalling of reservists and general mobilization. The reserves called back to their regiments at the outbreak of war were thus vital to the deployment of the BEF; half of the 148 regular infantry battalions (excluding the foot guards) were serving abroad, mostly in India (fifty-one battalions), and home-based battalions had to send drafts abroad to keep them up to strength. The navy brought all the regular battalions back home without loss, but this took many weeks to accomplish.

The 2nd Royal Welch (23rd of Foot) were part of the independent 19th Brigade, formed from battalions of the lines of communication and rushed up to Valenciennes by train late on the 22nd. They therefore did not form part of the line at Mons but became part of the fighting retreat along the western flank under the command of the cavalry. The other battalions in the Brigade were the 1st Middlesex, the 2nd Argyll and Sutherland Highlanders and the 1st Cameronians (Scottish Rifles); their fortunes were to vary greatly in the battle to come. Richards later wrote:

> It was at Vicq that we first realized that there was a war in progress. We advanced out of the village across open country. High shrapnel was exploding in the air some miles in front of us, and an officer and twelve of us were sent out about half a mile in front of the company and took up an outpost position at some crossroads. About midnight orders came for us to rejoin our company, which was now lined up on a railway. Rations for the next day were issued out. The bread ration was a 2lb loaf between four men. It was the last bread ration we were to get for many a day, for our service had now begun in earnest. We marched all that night and the greater part of the next day, and dug trenches on the evening of the 24 August, outside a village, the name of which I never heard, or else I have forgotten it. Old men and women from the village gave a hand in the digging. While visiting outposts that evening Major Walwyn was shot through the foot with a spent bullet – the battalion's first casualty in the war.
>
> We were only in those trenches a few hours before we were on the march again; we didn't know where to, or why. We were issued out with an extra fifty rounds of ammunition, making in all 200 rounds to carry. We marched all night again and all next day, halting a few times to fire at German scouting aeroplanes but not hitting one. At one halt of about twenty minutes we realized that the Germans were still not far away, some field-artillery shells bursting a few yards from my platoon, but nobody was damaged. We reservists

fetched straight out of civil life were suffering the worst on this non-stop march, which would have been exhausting enough if we had not been carrying 50lb weight or so of stuff on our backs. And yet these two days and nights were only the start of our troubles.

Capt J.C. Dunn, the medical officer of the Royal Welch, who shared much of the privations of the men, later recorded this little incident from the Retreat:

> We managed to keep the men fairly well together, though it was a bit of a job to prevent some of them falling out to lie down and sleep. I saw a man leave the ranks and wander towards the gate of a farm we were passing. Taking hold of his arm I asked him where he was going; he looked at me with a fixed stare, and mumbled that he was going to have a sleep. I pushed him back into the ranks, and the movement of the other men kept him going ... his senses were numbed by want of sleep for so long.

Another incident on the Retreat, on the 24th, was recorded by Lt George Roupell of the 1st East Surreys (14th Brigade):

> The company was resting by the side of the road during a halt; all the men very tired and half of them asleep as soon as they sat down. Then the order came to fall in; someone, probably half asleep, pressed his trigger and let off a round of ammunition which hit both Hines [his batman] and Hopper [a sergeant]. We had no transport and consequently no means of carrying them away. They were bandaged up and put into a farm at the side of the road. Later on the farm people got them away in a cart and they were not captured.
>
> Found supplies at the side of the road. As we were in the rear of the column the supply company could not deliver our rations to us direct but dumped them by the roadside. A small party was sent on ahead to divide up the rations and the column was rationed without halting. As each man went by he was given two biscuits, a tin of bully beef, and every second man, a pot of jam.
>
> Picked up signal wagon; threw valises [officers' kit] away and used it to carry men. Took over trenches dug by cavalry at Eth and spent the night in them.

The BEF had brought to France from its peacetime training a great respect for private property, an attitude reinforced by harsh military rules against looting. But to pass by farms with perfectly serviceable carts, and to leave them for the use of the Germans instead of requisitioning them for British use, seemed to officers like Major Peebles of the 2nd Suffolks the height of folly. To the thirsty troops the order forbidding men from helping themselves to fruit growing in orchards by the road seemed unnecessarily harsh. The

Lt George Roupell of the East Surreys, pictured later in his career as a brigadier.

order (in the KRRC) that handkerchiefs, white, were not allowed was at least understandable, if hardly indicative of trust in the men's steadfastness. To begin with, infantry and cavalry avoided damaging unharvested crops and the troops stuck to the roads, while refugees in their desperate hurry to get away from Mons would go across fields. There are tales, probably apocryphal, of soldiers hesitating to knock loop-holes in farm buildings to use as firing points. Later, after Bavai, men would burn sheaves of corn to dry out their clothing and some resorted to more desperate measures. Gunner J.W. Palmer (First Corps) remembered:

> We were then told we must live off the land, we must get everything we can from empty houses otherwise the Germans would have it. Well, I remember seeing the Munsters, they got about five cows in front of them and they tried to drive them along and I think they were going to kill them at night ... but I don't think that the Munsters had beef for supper.

Gunner Palmer had strong feelings for his horses:

> As the days went on, the horse's belly got more up into the middle of its back, and the cry was frequently down the line, 'Saddler – a plate and a punch!' This meant that the saddler had to come along and punch some more holes in the horse's leather girth to keep the saddle on.

The BEF would shoot horses that became too lame, whereas the Germans would merely turn them out into the fields.

The Germans helped themselves to what they wanted by right of conquest and were bound only by those rules of civilized behaviour that they chose to follow, although they were of course subject to their own military discipline. British use of Belgian and French property (including rolling stock and railway engines taken over for military use) all had to be accounted for and eventually paid for.

The BEF had been enjoined by Kitchener in his message to the original five divisions to resist temptations 'both in wine and women'* and to 'look upon looting as a disgraceful act', but it is hard to see how this could be applied to the occasional apple. It seems that military law could not distinguish between an apple and a silver spoon. After a day or two, however, apples were considered outside the scope of looting. Charlie Watts, an NCO with the 1st Hampshires (4th Div) remembered, 'I'd say our main diet during the retreat was German blood and French apples.'

On 2 September Lt Johnston (3rd Worcesters, 7th Brigade, 3rd Div), who we will meet later, a cricket-playing Old Whykehamist of unimpeachable rectitude, found a case of liqueurs in his billet and had no qualms about adding it to his supplies, there being 'no use leaving the stuff behind for the Germans'. A day later he broke into some abandoned shops in Meaux and helped himself to equipment for his signals section: that was clearly requisitioning, for which he left a note for the owners to claim against the army; the boundary between looting ('liberating' in the next war) and requisitioning became a fine one.

Frank Richards had found the *jeunes filles* of Amiens not without their charms: 'Billy and I spent a very agreeable evening and the two young ladies who we picked up with proved to be true daughters of France.' Kitchener's message, which had the legal status of an Order of the Day, with its injunction to resist 'intimacy' with women, became a laughing stock at Lanrezac's HQ; but Kitchener was always a bit prissy, unlike Gen Montgomery in the next war, and hardly experienced himself in that department.

At this time the East Surreys had become split up so that Roupell's half (A and C Companies) arrived at what was to become the battlefield south-west of Le Cateau while the other two companies arrived at the town itself. They were to take up positions to the east of the town, after making a fighting retreat through the streets. Roupell managed to get three hours sleep on the 25/26th:

> On treck all day. Sent out at night to find Brigade HQ on a bicycle. Very tired; a wet and dark night and Major Tew had no idea where I could find the Brigade HQ. Rode about for several hours, nearly had my bicycle taken by the Queen's Bays and eventually got back to our billet about 1.00am [on the 26th] without having found Brigade HQ. Went to sleep in straw and was almost left behind when the company moved off at 4.00am.

*In the next war the *Instructions for British Servicemen in France 1944* were less bossy: 'If you should happen to imagine that the first pretty French girl who smiles at you intends to dance the can-can or take you to bed, you will risk stirring up a lot of trouble for yourself – and for our relations with the French.'

Capt Jack of the 1st Cameronians (Scottish Rifles), also with 19th Brigade, has given us a mounted staff officer's perspective from the same road as Richards on the 24th:

> The hazy dawn of a fine summer morning ends an entirely sleepless night, and finds the brigade near Elouges commencing to entrench a defensive position. The country in front is open, with low whale-backed ridges providing an excellent field of fire. ...
>
> We have been placed under command of the Cavalry Division, and I am sent to Andregnies for orders. Riding along I meet General Allenby whose tall handsome figure sits a beautiful dark charger. One of his staff tells me that the 19th Brigade is to assist the cavalry in securing the left flank of the BEF.
>
> All this time we hear a very severe action raging a few miles north-east and east in the nests of slag-heaps, furnaces and industrial villages lying between us and Mons; the front is clearly marked by the smoke of bursting shells.
>
> About 7.30am and the 2nd Cavalry Brigade with Horse Artillery batteries trot past us to take up covering positions near the Mons–Valenciennes road. My word! They look superb, business-like and resolute.
>
> The brigade is now on its way, but ready to deploy for action ... The sun is baking hot, and the roads are crammed with fleeing inhabitants, their cattle, and wagons piled high with belongings. They keep asking us where to go and should have been evacuated before now for their sakes as well as ours as they greatly hamper the column. Besides, there may be German spies among them. A pitiful sight!
>
> Sir Horace Smith-Dorrien, the lean, wiry Second Corps commander, a fine soldier, overtakes me on his way back from the front in a car. He inquires how the men are getting along. I reply that they are in grand heart but overloaded in this heat, especially the reservists who are not yet fit for hard marching and that the incessant blocks on the roads due to refugees are a great bother. He nods and is driven on ...
>
> Our destination is changed from Presieu to Jenlain, so thither I ride in the afternoon to arrange quarters, and to collect farm picks and spades for entrenching at night as the men's small tools are useless for serious digging. The villagers are, however, very chary about lending their gear.
>
> The brigade arrives toward 6.00pm, having covered fully 18 miles since leaving the canal this morning, and with only one proper meal from the field kitchens during a halt. The men are tired, foot-sore from the cobbled roads, and irritated at a retreat for which they can see no necessity. They consider themselves quite a match for the 'bosches'.

Refugees

Isabelle Rimbaud, the sister of the poet Arthur Rimbaud, lived with her husband Pierre near Roche, on the Belgian border. They decided, unlike the Matisse family, to get away and they chose Rheims, where they had a friend who would take them in. Isabelle was faced with the agonising choices of what to leave behind for the Germans and what to take with them. They had to hire a car – no easy matter when so many people had the same idea. They had to get the deputy mayor to sign the necessary pass, in the manner of French bureaucracy. She packed a valise with her most precious possessions, hid some plate and papers in the double bottom of a chest and left everything else in her cupboards, with the keys in the locks. She made the beds and left napkins on the dining room table, 'for French soldiers will certainly precede the Germans, and the first, our defenders and brothers, have a claim on everything we can provide.' They did not get away until the 29th, just ahead of the advancing Germans. They joined the throng of gloomy emigrants, many of whom had for some reason put on their best Sunday clothes. Isabelle Rimbaud thought that this was an attempt to make a good impression on the invaders; it could equally have been because they didn't want to leave their best clothes behind and wearing them was the only way of taking them with them.

Middle class refugees. The congestion of refugees, often more pitiful than these, was a hindrance to the BEF.

'Police on foot, horseback or cycle guide all these poor scared creatures like so much cattle and make them keep moving southwards; for if by any chance the procession were to stop, the confusion would become hopeless.' They became mingled up with the survivors from a Breton regiment, who had lost all their officers. When they reached Rheims, the 'Prussians' were already in the city and the cathedral was being shelled. 'Then begins for me and Pierre the most horrible torture.' It was an experience that was being replicated all over north-eastern France.

Battle at Landrecies

On the night of the 25/26th there occurred the incident at Landrecies, to the south of the Forest of Mormal, barely 10 miles (16km) across the Sambre canal east of Le Cateau in the First Corps area, which stands out not merely for the heroism and ferocity shown, but for what it shows us about the febrile nature of the BEF leadership at this time. It was a hastily planned attack in battalion strength carried out at night by German infantry driven up in motor lorries and dressed in French uniforms. It was put together with that skill and speed of improvisation for which the German Army is renowned. Night attacks were not usual at this time – though later, during the long years of static trench warfare, night raids were to become a regular and much-hated form of aggressive tactics. They brought a field gun with them, equipped with star-shell, as well as conventional ammunition. The defenders were two companies of the 3rd Coldstream Guards (4th Guards Brigade), although the whole brigade was in the town. The brigade had gone into billets in the afternoon, which does not say much for the urgency with which the corps was treating the Retreat. An attack of similar strength was mounted from the forest on nearby Maroilles, which was repulsed by the Berkshires and the 1st KRRC (60th Rifles).

At 8.30pm on the 25th one company of The Coldstream under Capt the Hon. A. Monck was picketing the north-west entrance to the town when they heard (it was now dark) the sound of infantry approaching. There had been warnings of a German attack, but Monck held his fire when he heard the singing of French marching songs (the Germans had a captured French officer with them). The unknown troops were upon them when an electric torch revealed French uniforms (seemingly considered an acceptable *ruse de guerre*). At the moment when the torch revealed troops in field grey further back in the column, the machine-gunner (Monck had one of the two battalion machine guns) was bayoneted and a pell-mell fight ensued. There was much shouting and shooting, firing of revolvers, wild stabbing with bayonets, all of which alerted Capt Longueville who rushed up to join the fray with his company, which had been in reserve. Col Fielding and Maj Matheson arrived, shouted out their presence and took command. The Germans, although still outnumbering The Coldstream two to one, were driven back out of the town whence they had come.

At this point a light field gun began firing shrapnel and star-shell at close range, which made things 'very unpleasant' for the defenders, according to a contemporary account. A barn caught fire that was extinguished by a Private Wyatt, later awarded the VC for this action. Col Fielding got a British field gun up and with its third shot knocked out the German gun. Fighting continued for a while until 1.30am when the Germans made off in motor lorries, taking their wounded with them. Losses on the British side were about 170, the majority wounded, who were left in the hospital at Landrecies when the brigade retired the next day. What is interesting about this action is what ensued.

Haig was in Landrecies at the time. He was extremely alarmed, thought that they were being attacked by a brigade, was heard to say 'we must sell our lives dearly', ordered the destruction of secret papers and went off in a car with a staff officer (Brig Charteris) to his HQ to demand assistance from Second Corps in a message to GHQ. Charteris did in fact save some papers by stuffing them in his pocket. To be fair to Haig, this reaction was uncharacteristic of him; an explanation that has been advanced is that he was suffering from diarrhoea resulting from treatment for constipation (he himself remarking on it in his diary). This was Haig's first close-quarter exposure to the gunfire of a modern European army and on this occasion his diary is remarkably honest about his near-panic over the attack of such a small force, although he naturally credits himself with galvanizing the 'sleepy and half-hearted' Guards commanders, particularly Brig Scott-Kerr. But French's reaction to an attack by a total of 1,000 men with one field gun on a force under Haig's command of 36,000 men was even more hysterical. At 5.00am on the 26th he sent Col Huguet, his liaison officer, off to Lanrezac's HQ with the message that,

> First Corps has been violently attacked in its billets between Le Cateau and Landrecies and is falling back – if it can – on Guise to the south; if not southeast in the direction of La Capelle. Tomorrow the BEF will continue its retreat towards Peronne[!]. Can 5th Army come to FM French's aid by sheltering First Corps until it can rejoin the main body of the British forces?

We should note here French's use of the words 'main body' (i.e. Second Corps plus 4th Division). We must remember that the two corps were not separate armies; they needed each other and yet they could not talk to each other. They were one force and yet divided, with separate commands. What French clearly meant was that he wished the two corps to be conjoined for mutual assistance and for Lanrezac to draw closer to Haig. This had indeed been his intention ever since the night of the 23rd. GHQ's Operation Order No. 8, issued on the 25th but drawn up earlier, ordered Haig to retreat in the direction of Busigny, that is, south-west towards Second Corps, and stated that the overall objective of the Retreat was to cover the advanced base of Amiens. And yet Haig marched due south, as we shall see, towards Etreux, under GHQ's orders, in the morning of the 26th, after another short night of interrupted sleep; and Lanrezac did not alter his line of march. Haig was now exhibiting signs of almost indecent haste to get away; he ordered the Retreat to start at 2.00am on the 26th. We will return later to the details of these new orders.

Since French was thinking of Second Corps as the 'main body' (which in a sense it was, including as it did the Cavalry Division) it helps further to explain his inaction the next day: in his mind it was a stand-alone force. The new two-corps structure in fact had made it possible for Smith-Dorrien to fight a four-division battle on his own. Unfortunately for Smith-Dorrien and the men of Second Corps, everywhere in Europe the products of the industrial revolution, combined with conscription, had made it possible for the first time in history to keep armies of hundreds of thousands of soldiers in the field indefinitely. These armies – two or three times larger than the original BEF – were now fighting, however imperfectly, as armies under a single lieutenant-general, at some distance from their bases. Second Corps was going to have to punch above its weight.

Smith-Dorrien with justification refused to send troops to his right, i.e. towards Landrecies, which increased still further French's irritation with him, although Lanrezac did in fact offer assistance. The whole Landrecies episode cannot simply be put down to temporary confusion arising from a night action. In his memoirs French characteristically exaggerated the fight, by writing about 800 or 900 dead and repeating the story of an attack in brigade strength, a narrative he needed to maintain to justify his reaction. One does wonder, however, that if Smith-Dorrien had appealed to him in like fashion on the 25th whether his reaction would have been similar. Would he have appealed to Haig, whom he held in high regard, to go to Smith-Dorrien's aid? In the much greater crisis the next day he did not. In fact on the 26th Smith-Dorrien made no appeal to GHQ for assistance from First Corps; he presumably regarded such an appeal as superfluous. On the 23rd when he had wanted urgent help from Haig he went in person to get it.

French's diary for the 25th has a revealing sentence: 'No sooner had anxiety on Haig's account ceased than trouble re-occurred with S-D.' Smith-Dorrien was the source of constant trouble as far as GHQ was concerned and they had no faith in his ability to get himself out of it. Late on the 25th French, as this diary extract makes clear, already seemed to have more than an inkling that Smith-Dorrien was not going to carry out the retreat orders to the letter. This was not exactly mind-reading. After all, GHQ had already by this time organized the trench-digging along the line of the Cambrai–Le Cateau road, or at the very least was aware of it as a precautionary measure, and Smith-Dorrien had surveyed the ground. French himself was no stranger to what was to become the battlefield. But as far as French was concerned, wherever Smith-Dorrien went, trouble was not far behind. Smith-Dorrien was the first to request falling back to Bavai; this was not what French had wanted to hear. He had wanted to rest his troops at Bavai; this was not what French had wanted to hear. He had pestered French for guidance on the Retreat. He had not been helpful over the Landrecies affair. And now it looked like he was squaring up for a fight.

It may be worth mentioning in this context, if only in passing, the fact that a loan made by Haig to French of £2,000 in 1899 was still outstanding, and that both French and Haig were cavalrymen, members of a fraternity, although that fact didn't prevent Haig from having a very low opinion of French's abilities; his August diary includes the entry 'I know that French is quite unfit for this great command.' French and Haig were certainly found unfit for command on this day (25th), which John Terraine has called the most 'alarming' day of the Retreat.*

Smith-Dorrien Decides to Stand at Le Cateau

French's intervention on behalf of First Corps in the early morning of the 26th shows how inappropriate it was for an army commander to get involved at the level of tactical command from his HQ a dozen miles away. At Mons he had played no part whatever at the tactical level, his 'orders' on the morning of the battle being vague to the point of useless, even delegating the arrangements for a possible retreat to his chief of staff, Murray. If he had then underplayed his hand, he had now on the 26th overplayed it in the Landrecies incident, with unfortunate consequences.

Smith-Dorrien reached Le Cateau at 3.30pm on the 25th, somewhat ahead of his forces, to find the C-in-C already on his way to St Quentin, which was 'unfortunate'. Gen Murray, by now distraught, was still there but with no news of the whereabouts of First Corps; he was expecting its leading troops to arrive in the town well before nightfall. He was to have a physical collapse later that night; as Haig had remarked in his diary, Murray was 'an old woman'. GHQ had now effectively misplaced almost half its army as far as Smith-Dorrien was concerned – they were in fact about 8 miles (13km) away to the east. This is curious because Gen Johnny Gough, Haig's Chief of Staff, was in Le Cateau at the time receiving yet more orders for the line of retreat, which was still in the direction of Le Cateau/Busigny, from where the two corps would be in close touch. Wilson was already expressing concern in his diary at the gap now opened up between the two corps and said it was 'mad'

---

*The 4th (Guards) Brigade, with the 4th Brigade, fought a larger, more costly rearguard battle in woodland at Villers Cotterets on 1 September, which is now less remembered than the affair at Landrecies.

that Haig was not going any further than Landrecies that night. Haig himself, in a frank and revealing entry in his diary for the 25th, wrote:

> During the afternoon an officer came out from GHQ to ask when the corps would be able to reach the neighbourhood of Le Cateau, and to take its place in a defensive line which had been partially prepared by civil labour.

Smith-Dorrien also stated in his memoir that the field of battle where he would surely meet the enemy next day was chosen by the staff of GHQ; GHQ staff had organized the digging of trenches by local people, mostly teenagers and those over military age; there are no reports that tell of a spontaneous outpouring of volunteer labour to defend this corner of France, but neither was there any of the defeatism witnessed in St Quentin two days later. Gen Snow (4th Div) wrote that the French peasantry were 'impressed' into digging. Others were under the impression that French Territorial officers had been in charge; in any case the efforts, however well meant, were extremely amateur.

The position to the south and west of the town Smith-Dorrien found quite a good one to defend; and there was enough daylight left to look over the ground with Forestier-Walker and allot the ground for his divisions to occupy. It was a position not unfamiliar to him from exercises on Salisbury Plain or the Surrey heaths. It was a position greatly superior to that at Bavai, where there had been brief talk of taking up a defensive stance. He was worried about the right flank and defending the town of Le Cateau itself; but he had First Corps somewhere out there. His staff set up an HQ at Bertry, in the *Mairie* (town hall), south and west of Le Cateau and west of the Roman road leading south-west towards St Quentin. The nearest telephone/telegraph link was at Bertry railway station, half a mile away. At 6.00pm a note was received from Gen Wilson, sub-chief of staff at GHQ, warning Sir Horace that orders would shortly be issued for continuing the Retreat. That order did in fact arrive at Bertry at 9.00pm, and Sir Horace duly ordered Second Corps to continue the retirement the next day at 7.00am (the time of this order was not recorded).

Sir Horace actually countermanded this order and made his decision to make a stand at a conference of his divisional commanders and staff some time after 2.00am on the 26th. He quotes himself as saying 'Very well gentlemen we will fight and I will ask General Snow to act under me as well.' The notification to GHQ was prepared. General Snow's division, the 4th, had arrived at Le Cateau and nearby stations on the 24th and had marched off to the north-west (around Solesmes) under orders from the C-in-C. In the late afternoon of the 25th his rearguard (12th Brigade) was holding off the leading German troops. The division was without its baggage train, but its timely arrival must have been instrumental in Smith-Dorrien's decision to fight. Gen Snow later wrote that it was pure luck that it arrived at the same

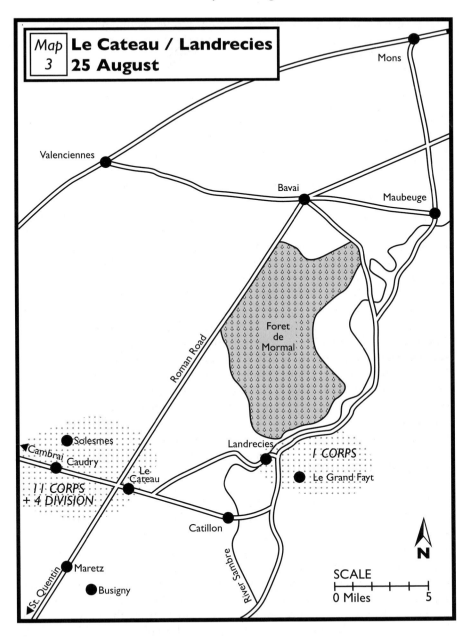

time as Second Corps' greatest trial. Gen Snow on the 24th had been in the same position as Smith-Dorrien had been on the 21st: he knew nothing of the campaign when he arrived at Busigny station but was able to receive a rather pessimistic – if not unrealistic – resume from his old friend Gen Wilson. This briefing confirmed why he had seen full supply wagons going the 'wrong' way as he looked out of his carriage window coming up from the south.

Gen Snow had found time on the 24th, soon after arriving at Busigny and in advance of his division, to inspect the Cambrai/Le Cateau position where he had been told (by whom?) that battle was to be offered to the Germans very shortly. He drove over the ground with his friend Col Bowes and found all quiet among the villagers ('except for a certain amount of excitement'), no sign of any entrenchments, but a generally good position where he expected to fight, with good views towards Cambrai. Of signs of any French troops there were none; he had despatched a staff officer on a fruitless search for them between Cambrai and Esnes. That night he had another briefing at GHQ in the town hall at Le Cateau where everyone was sunk in gloomy pessimism; his own French liaison officer was drunk and useless. He then took up his positions around the south-west of Solesmes.

Gen Snow himself was blessed with a natural optimism ('I always cheer up when other people are downhearted') which the absence of his signals staff and the amateurism of 12th Brigade troops failed to dent ('the British soldier will never dig unless forced to by his officer'). He was quite prepared to fight on the morrow. He received a visit from the commander-in-chief on the 25th, who curiously seemed more concerned about Haig's position at Landrecies than Snow's. The C-in-C was unsurprisingly not taken to the 12 Brigade area.

The 4th Division did not begin to leave Solesmes until after 6.00pm on the 25th, with Gen Snow getting increasingly agitated about the log-jam of traffic, the imminent arrival of the Germans and the need to let the Mons (3rd Div) troops pass through before he could move himself; his division was effectively sheltering the 3rd. 19th Brigade, which passed through his area, was already cleared to fight under Smith-Dorrien. The last columns did not leave Solesmes until midnight; the Iniskillings had already been posted on the Cambrai–Le Cateau road so they were spared the to-ing and fro-ing. Everyone got thoroughly soaked by a thunderstorm, which was not that unwelcome to the dusty troops. His three brigades were ordered to take up positions west of Caudry with the 11th on the right (i.e. as facing the enemy), followed by the 10th and then the 12th, on the ground previously reconnoitred by Snow. These became their fighting positions. But late on the 25th Snow's orders, contained in Operation Order No. 8, were to retreat 'in the general direction of Peronne'.

But the overwhelming consideration in Smith-Dorrien's mind in the early hours of the 26th was the sheer impossibility of getting the scattered units of Second Corps safely away by daylight on the 26th when the Germans were expected to attack. At Bavai on the 24th Smith-Dorrien had been tempted to halt and give his weary troops a rest, but was persuaded to move on, at least according to Haig. But now von Kluck had effectively caught up with Smith-Dorrien; his vanguard was in Le Cateau itself before midnight and in Caudry not long after. There was clearly no question of the luxury of a rest, or of an unmolested retirement at 7.00am. Gen Allenby of the cavalry was adamant that, with his own cavalry brigades spread out and unreachable, he could not be sanguine about his outpost defence. In other words, the fear among the commanders of the corps was that the retreat could turn into a rout.

There is no doubt that a main constraint on the movement of the BEF – all the way from Mons – was the sheer volume of civilian refugee columns on the roads, traffic that bothered the Germans hardly at all since the population that took to the roads obviously did so in advance of the Germans. If 3rd and 4th Divisions had been entirely unhampered by civilians around Solesmes on the evening of the 25th, never mind the remnants of a French territorial regiment getting in the way, the battle to come would probably never have been fought. Solesmes was a military policeman's nightmare: there were at least 40,000 troops, with all their impedimenta, going one way or the other, in the general area of Solesmes on the night of the 25th so that even without the refugees there was going to be congestion and delay. An artillery brigade or a battalion of infantry took up almost a mile of road, it must be remembered. To give one example, 41 Battery of XLII Royal Field Artillery Brigade moved through Le Cateau during the night of the 25/26th; this one battery alone took three hours to get through the streets of the town and out to the south-west.

Haig could point with justification to the same problems of congestion in causing his own slow progress, particularly when having to cross the Sambre, caused mainly by being muddled up with French troops. He later, when the width of the road allowed, got vehicles 'double-banked' and managed to move two divisions on one road. But that was exceptional. Smith-Dorrien himself mentioned the need to allow time for the civilian fugitives and carts to clear off before the scattered units of Second Corps could themselves get away. 'It will be difficult to realize the fog of war that surrounded us that night', he wrote, by which he meant the poor communication with his scattered units as well as their lack of cohesion. All this experience was not lost on the German commanders: in the next war, air attack on refugee columns in the BEF area – a war crime let it be said – was used as an act of war to throw confusion, fear and chaos into the military lines of communications. Such are the perils of a retreat.

In later years, in the acrimonious debate about the decision to fight on this morning, Allenby never wavered from his support for the decision taken. The Germans were expected to resume the attack at dawn and all Smith-Dorrien's military instincts told him that with the proven staunchness (his word) of his troops, both infantry and gunners, it was better to 'stand and fight' than to

Gen Sir Edmund Allenby ('The Bull') of the cavalry.

'turn our backs on them in broad daylight'. Gen Hamilton was in full agreement. Gen Fergusson was not at the 2.00am meeting but Smith-Dorrien met him two hours later as the rearguards were coming in and Fergusson fully concurred with Hamilton and Allenby. Forestier-Walker considered at the time, and never changed his mind, that there was 'a fair prospect' of holding off the enemy, making him suffer 'terribly' and being able to continue the march; it was not a view shared at St Quentin by Gen Wilson. He wrote in his diary for that day that if Second Corps was not destroyed 'it ought to be', in his unhappy phrase. But of course nobody in the BEF had yet had any experience of what prolonged, heavy and accurate shelling could do to exposed troops, although Mons had provided an unpleasant foretaste.

Smith-Dorrien could, and later did, quote *Field Service Regulations* in support of his decision, which explicitly allow the commander on the spot considerable autonomy in situations analogous to this. Smith-Dorrien was also well aware that the choice between fighting or running away was a 'choice of evils' but a slavish adherence to orders is not the mark of a good commander of men, which Sir Horace undoubtedly was. And Sir Horace, awkward at the best of times and bad-tempered at worst, was not of a mind to be slavish toward Sir John. And this time, compared with Mons, the field of battle at least met with his approval. He did not need to be reminded, as Kitchener had put in his Instructions, that he was no longer up against an 'untrained adversary'.

Bertry Town Hall, Second Corps' HQ on 25–26 August.

By this time (say 2.00am) the overall disposition of the troops was clearly demarcated and staff officers got frantically busy drawing up the orders: 5th Division (Fergusson) on the right (nearest the town of Le Cateau), based at Reumont, on the Roman road; 3rd Division (Hamilton) in the centre at Bertry, near Sir Horace's own HQ; and 4th Division (Snow) on the left at Haucourt, having the furthest to march and having to get to their fighting positions in the hours of darkness. These orders to all divisional commands were specific about standing on the ground to fight the enemy when he appeared; they were not specific about the imperative to break off the action. This was to be dependent on further orders, although the divisional generals were fully aware of the need to break off the action when the time came. The sheer impossibility of getting the orders to disengage to the forward troops later in the day was to cause much confusion in the minds of battalion and company commanders.

The cavalry brigades were allocated their traditional position on the flanks and Gen Sordet was further out to the west, having brought more troopers across the BEF's line of march during the night of 25/26th. The bulk of his three divisions had moved west, just south of the Cambrai road, on the evening of the 25th, avoiding the hard surface of the road. There were French territorial troops in Cambrai under Gen d'Amade. The 19th Brigade was to be positioned as reserve near Reumont in the 5th Division area, together with two companies of the 1st Royal Scots Fusiliers who had become detached that night, amid the general confusion. There were one and a half battalions of 14th Brigade (5th Div) holding ground to the north and east of the town: the Duke of Cornwall's Light Infantry and half of the East Surreys.

At 5.00am a message was sent by wire to GHQ asking them to inform Gen Sordet that Second Corps would not be retiring that day and to ask for his co-operation on the left flank; this wire was in reply to GHQ's wire giving approval of the 'stand' decision. It served as Smith-Dorrien's second notice to GHQ of his decision to offer battle. The original lengthy notification, sent by car, arrived at St Quentin at 5.00am; it was this message to which French had replied immediately with his conditional approval. All this time Haig was in complete ignorance about the impending battle and was not included in the signals traffic.

Smith-Dorrien's Force

The die was now cast for what Sir Horace called his 'smashing blow'. First Corps were still thought to be close up on the right, but they were of course under orders to continue the retreat. Smith-Dorrien now had ten brigades of infantry to cover a front of 10 miles (16km) or so, a situation greatly superior to that at Mons three days earlier with a front twice as long, although the canal itself had acted as a barrier to German advance; the Le Cateau position possessed no such natural barrier. The ten brigades, with four battalions each, were arrayed as follows from right to left: 14th, 13th, 15th, 9th, 8th, 7th, 11th, 10th, and 12th; the 19th was in reserve near Reumont. These ten brigades fielded eighty machine guns, each with a crew of a maximum of eight men, an allocation of two per battalion under the command of a lieutenant, the guns usually deployed together. The machine guns were mostly the new Vickers model, based on the Maxim; both Vickers and the Maxim were water-cooled, the water carried in two 1gal (4.55ltr) cans. Everything was man-handled.

Infantry battalions at this stage of the war had a nominal strength of 1,000 men and officers; there were forty of them, including 19th Brigade, each battalion divided into four companies under the command of a captain. We must remember that those battalions that had borne the brunt of the attacks on the 23rd and 24th were by now between 10–20 per cent below strength, the Cheshires with only the rump of a battalion. By pure chance, the battalions that were about to receive the next German attack were not among them.

Smith-Dorrien had a total of 246 guns at his disposal in both the Royal Field Artillery and the Royal Horse Artillery; about a hundred more than Wellington had at Waterloo. The cavalry (RHA) fielded twenty-four 13-pounder guns in four batteries (designated by capital Roman letters).* The Royal Field Artillery 18-pounder field guns and howitzers were organized in four brigades

*The Royal Flying Corps had four squadrons, (2, 3, 4, and 5).

52

per division with four batteries in each brigade. There were eighteen howitzers per division, armed with 4.5in HE and shrapnel shells. The 18-pounder field guns were to be used mainly for infantry support against hostile infantry, as were the howitzers; a battery major's ideal target would be a battalion forming up for an attack. The KOSB *History* states, 'The British gunners, rightly no doubt, preferred the magnificent massed infantry targets to counter-battery work.' As a killing weapon, the 18-pounder was as good as anything in Europe. There were eight heavy 60lb guns in the corps, those of 4th Division being stuck down the line. These heavy batteries were under the command of the Royal Garrison Artillery. All these guns were to be used primarily in the infantry support role in the battle to come, rather than in the counter-battery role, although enemy batteries were fired on when in plain view, especially across the Selle.

The KOSB *History* also states, with an attempt at dry military humour, that the decision not to attempt counter-battery fire 'left the Germans the freer to bombard their own and their infantry comrades' position'. This is the only reference that we have been able to find to support the declaration in the *Official History* that the German gunners kept up a sustained and accurate fire on their own troops advancing on the 14th Brigade position (*see* Chapter 2). It could equally be an attempt not to gloat over an all-too-frequent occurrence that every soldier knows could happen to him in similar circumstances.

Von Kluck's Forces

On the German side, von Kluck had four corps at his disposal (II, III, IV and IV Reserve, the III being on his left and IV Reserve on his right) plus twelve cavalry regiments. A German army corps, like a British one, consisted of two infantry divisions; reserve divisions in reserve corps had half the number of field guns and had no heavy guns. The British cavalry division was about twice the size of its German counterpart in guns, horses and men, and had four times as many machine guns. Von Kluck had more than 600 guns, of which 430 were field guns, and about 240 machine guns which he intended to use aggressively. Gen von der Marwitz was in overall command of the two reserve cavalry divisions on the right flank (7th Reserve and 22nd Reserve), which in the event took some time to get up to the Cambrai road in full strength. German cavalry rode their horses continually while on the march, unlike the British who would for periods walk alongside their mounts, and they arrived with many of their mounts already blown. His 4th Cavalry Division remained in reserve all day, not having recovered from fighting around Solesmes.

The German equivalent to the 18-pounder was the Krupp 77mm field gun, of which the German armies were equipped with 6,000. The German counterparts to the British 4.5in howitzer were the 15cm (5.9in) howitzer, always known to the British by its imperial measurement, although technically it was a heavy weapon with a high rate of fire rather than a field piece, and the 10.5cm light howitzer, highly mobile and fast-firing, for which there was no British equivalent. The 5.9in HE shell produced the black smoke that gave it its nickname of 'Jack Johnson', after the famous black boxer of the time who was also a big hitter. Other names the troops gave the big shells producing black smoke were 'woolly bears', 'black Maria', 'coal box' (which was a mortar), and 'Willie', after the Kaiser. The ratio of field guns to howitzers was roughly the same in each army, but it was the 5.9in howitzers firing high explosive that the BEF was already learning to fear most.

Manpower losses were of less concern to von Kluck than they were to the British. This was the battle he had been devoutly hoping for ever since the 23rd, the battle that would enable him to bring his superior numbers to bear on the British in an enveloping and annihilating action. The road to Paris would then be clear of this elusive, hated and yet dangerous enemy. His soldiers were no less eager for the fight. An aristocratic officer, von Lattorf, later wrote, 'Excitement mounted when we heard that we had the British opposite us, because we were thirsting for the blood of this most hated of all enemies.' (Quoted in Cave and Sheldon.) This sentiment was not shared by the British at the time, at least not with the same ferocity. Von Lattorf's hatred was increased further by his mistaken belief that the British were using snub-nose 'dum-dum' bullets, a belief that was shared by a great many Germans.

The German Army, drawn by conscription from the whole nation, was imbued with offensive spirit and a belief in the interdependence of all arms. In practice this meant that light infantry – Jäger – were included in cavalry regiments and that all attacks were to be supported by artillery and machine-gun fire. The reserve divisions were not necessarily of inferior quality – they consisted of men who had already served three years in active units and hence were over twenty-three years old – but it is safe to assume that the army would pick the best men for service in the active units. Their dense attacking waves seen at Mons and soon to be seen at Le Cateau were not just the result of inexperienced infantry bunching together – although this might have had something to do with it – but the result of carefully thought-out military doctrine. But their dense waves would very soon go to ground when receiving accurate incoming fire.

Preparing for the Battle

It was one thing for a corps commander to allocate divisions and brigades to sectors; it was quite another to get the new fighting orders to battalion officers, but thankfully those further battalions that did not receive the 'stand' order in the event conformed to the movements of those that did. And, on the whole, when the time came to retreat most units also conformed to the movements of others, although there were many examples of individual companies that stood their ground until overwhelmed, orders to retire not having reached them; 'C' Company of the 2nd KOSB was among these. But 4th Division spent the day never knowing that retreat was imperative. Many of the men in all the divisions spent the day not knowing whether they were fighting a rearguard or a last-ditch stand, trusting that their officers had a clear idea of the overall plan. Many of them found it hard enough to pronounce 'Le Cateau' ('Le Catoo'), let alone place it on a map. Frank Richards of the Royal Welch (19th Brigade) was in the usual soldier's muddle:

> We arrived in Le Cateau about midnight, dead-beat to the world. I don't believe any one of us at this time realized that we were retiring, though it was clear that we were not going in the direction of Germany. Of course the officers knew, but they were telling us that we were drawing the enemy into a trap. Le Cateau that night presented a strange sight. Everyone was in a panic, packing up their stuff on carts and barrows to get away south in time. The Royal Welch camped on the square in the centre of the town. We were told to get as much rest as we could. The majority sank down where they were and fell straight asleep. Although dead-beat, Billy, Stevens and I went on the scrounge for food and drink. For three days officers and men had been on short rations. This was the only time during the whole of the war that I saw officers and men buying food and drink in the same café. [A private soldier in those days could not speak unbidden to an officer.] I slept the sleep of the just that night, for about three hours. I could have done with forty-three, but we were roused up at 4am and ordered to leave our packs and greatcoats on the square.
>
> Everyone was glad when that order was issued; the only things we had to carry now, besides rifle and ammunition, were an extra pair of socks and our iron rations which consisted of four army biscuits, a pound tin of bully beef and a small quantity of tea and sugar. Iron rations were carried in case of emergency but were never supposed to be used unless orders came from our superior officers. Haversacks were now strapped on our shoulders and each man was issued with another fifty rounds of ammunition, which made 250 rounds to carry. At dawn we marched out of Le Cateau with fixed bayonets.

Duffy said, 'We'll have a bang at the bastards to-day.' We all hoped the same. We were all fed up with the marching and would have welcomed a scrap to relieve the monotony. But we were even more fed up before the day was over.

Even as Frank Richards and his Welshmen marched out with a light step at dawn to meet the enemy, there were gentlemen in England still abed who on the morrow would write letters to *The Times* as follows:

It is manifestly a war between Christ and the Devil ... The infernal machine which has been scientifically preparing for the last twenty-five years is now on its wild career like one of Mr Wells's inventions, and wherever it goes it will leave desolation behind it and put all material progress back for at least half a century ... There was never anything in the world worthier of extermination, and it is the plain duty of civilized nations to unite to drive it back into its home and exterminate it there.

(from Mr Robert Bridges in *The Times,* 2 September 1914)

This letter – from the Poet Laureate, no less – with its appeal to exterminate the Hun may appear risible today, but it was the case throughout the war that there was more belligerent sentiment at home than among the men at the front, whose songs contained no hint of jingoism. In the very same edition of *The Times* a more poetic call to arms by Rudyard Kipling was also published:

No easy hope or lies
Shall bring us to our goal.
But iron sacrifice
Of body, will and soul.
There is but one task for all –
For each one life to give.
Who stands if freedom fall?
Who dies if England live?

Also on the home front at this time George Bernard Shaw, in the *Daily News* of 11 August, although immune from the 'hypocrisy' of outrage and emotion for neutral Belgium, nevertheless urged 'Let us take our pugnacity to the field ... the field once taken, it is not a practicable reason for betraying your allies and your country by throwing down your arms and kneeling to pray.' And this was from a noted pacifist.

While the Royal Welch just slept where they lay in the square, the 2nd Argyll and Sutherlands grabbed a few hours sleep on the floor of a cotton mill near the station.* They were crammed in, as were the 2nd Suffolks on the floor of a barn on the edge of town, on the road to the south. There were no washing facilities of course, the best part of a thousand unwashed men in an enclosed space after the day's exertions giving off its own particular odour and the khaki serge of their uniforms, wet from the recent downpour, making its own contribution. Their rifles were piled up and their knapsacks were their pillows. But at least they could take their boots off their swollen feet. They all had what little there was from the cookers. The officers were billeted separately, turning in after the men had had supper. The 1st Duke of Cornwalls bivouacked in the open, at the south-east outskirts of the town, wet through, but at least the cookers had managed to get to them.

Frank Richards was not going to have a chance to brew up his ration of tea and sugar for a long time yet, and he was to get separated from his pack and greatcoat for even longer. The fighting had started even as they made their way out of the town, and the Middlesex behind them as rearguard had, as one of their officers later said, 'a lively exit'. The 19th Brigade was under orders to get out to Reumont and not to engage in street fighting. First Corps was expected to hold the right, with the Cavalry Division (part of 1st and 2nd Brigades as well as 3rd Brigade) already ordered to the Selle valley.

This account confirms the official record that the 19th Brigade received their orders for battle around dawn and did not get clear of the town until well after dawn. At the same time, ten miles to the west, battalions of the 4th Division were only now coming back to what was to become their battle positions. Private Ted Gale of the 1st Rifle Brigade, 11th Brigade, 4th Division was at Solesmes as a driver with the battalion transport and was involved in the most frightful muddle as the 2½ miles (4km) of brigade traffic looked for Fontaine in the dark. He has left us this description of a night march around this time:

> All night long, we never stopped all night. The Army Service Corps who had our rations, they couldn't stop. They just threw our rations on the side of the road and left us to pick them up. The drivers were retiring in front of us and they couldn't stop to deliver them to the regiments ... And there were a lot of complaints, people saying, 'Why are we retiring, what are we retiring for? Why don't we turn around and have a scrap with them?'

When 11th Brigade troops did eventually get a couple of hours fitful rest in the abandoned village of Fontaine (the men sleeping in the streets), 1st RB were sent out in front to the west of the village before dawn as an outpost line. It must have been galling for the Riflemen, knowing the Germans would be helping themselves to whatever they could find in the village the next day, to be under orders to leave everything neat and tidy for them. They were to form a rearguard at the end of the day, when it was every man for himself – as an

---

*The Argylls, the 93rd, had arrived at Boulogne on 10 August, making them the first BEF infantry troops to land, their kilts causing wonderment among the citizens of the town. Major Tom Bridges' 4th Dragoons had arrived on the 9th and had been briefly fired upon by a jittery coastal battery.

élite battalion they would expect nothing less. By contrast, Private Roe of 1st East Lancs (11th Brigade, 4th Division) wrote later of arriving on the battlefield as late as 9am, but such are the fortunes of war that he himself never fired his rifle in spite of the fact that his battalion was heavily engaged and his record of this day is just one in an almost seamless retreat. The young Lt B.L. Montgomery of the 1st Royal Warwicks (10th Brigade, 4th Division) was to write in his *Memoirs* years later of how the dawn retreat from the high ground back to their battle positions was a far from orderly affair: the 12th Brigade abandoned the ridge at 5.15am 'in great disorder'. We will come back to him later.

To the west of 5th Division, who were the right of the line, 9th Brigade of 3rd Division took up the line from Troisvilles to Audencourt, having arrived early enough to improve the trenches dug earlier by the helpful, if bullied, French. Not all of the men by any means still had their 'grubbers'; they were lying somewhere on the road from Mons. French farming folk provided some implements, not always willingly. Otherwise men used what was to hand, even their mess tins, which were about as much use as the grubbers. The British infantryman is notoriously reluctant to dig, even when his life depends on it, and junior officers would have had to supervise the digging. Gen Snow himself had been appalled to discover the lack of even elementary digging by his outpost troops on the 25th.

The 3rd Division spread west, south of the Cambrai road, as far as Caudry, which was occupied by 7th Brigade; this formation at dawn found itself to be very weak, many men having lost their way coming from the area of Solesmes in the dark. There was a large gap between the weak 7th Brigade of 3rd Division and the 11th Brigade of 4th Division to their left, which was to become a critical factor as the fighting intensified around Caudry. The 8th Brigade was in the middle of the division line and they also arrived in time to improve their trenches. In general, the 3rd Division was better prepared for action and better posted than its neighbouring divisions. Its RFA brigades were mostly dug in in support of the infantry, with the RGA heavy and RFA howitzer batteries about 1,000yd back from the 18-pounder batteries.

The battalions of 14th Brigade (5th Div) that straddled Le Cateau and that were to suffer so much during the day – 1st Cornwalls, 1st East Surreys (two companies) to the east and 2nd Suffolks, 2nd Manchester (the battalion in which Wilfred Owen later served) and two companies of the East Surreys to the west – were also late in getting their fighting orders, those to the east of the town never receiving them and so fighting where they stood in ill-prepared positions. They were eventually to make their way back to the St Quentin road by early afternoon, when they formed part of the rearguard, being given useful covering fire by the cavalry batteries to the east of the Roman road and having a running battle through the cabbage patches of the town allotments as they got away from the town.

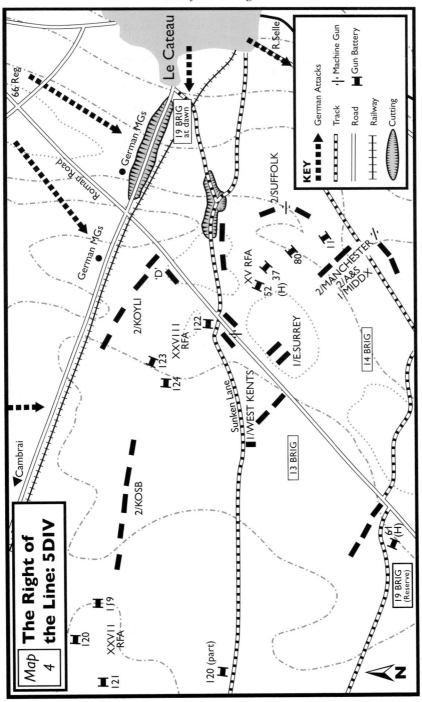

Map 4 **The Right of the Line: 5DIV**

KEY

German Attacks · Machine Gun · Gun Battery · Track · Road · Railway · Cutting

Le Cateau
R.Selle
66:Reg
19 BRIG at dawn
German MGs
Roman Road
German MGs
2/SUFFOLK
XV RFA
80
37
52 (H)
2/MANCHESTER
2/A&S
1/MIDDX
2/KOYLI
'D'
XXVIII RFA
122
123
124
I/E.SURREY
14 BRIG
Cambrai
Sunken Lane
I/WEST KENTS
13 BRIG
2/KOSB
61 (H)
19 BRIG (Reserve)
119
120
XXVII RFA
121
120 (part)

On the left of the 2nd Suffolks of 14th Brigade were the 2nd King's Own Yorkshire Light Infantry of 13th Brigade, and to their right and rear were the Manchesters; these were the battalions that were to bear the brunt of the assault to come, the Manchesters forming the right bend of a horseshoe formation. To their west were spread out the other battalions of the 13th and then 15th Brigades as far as Troisvilles, the 3rd Division taking up the line further west to Caudry. The 4th Division line bent round to the south-west in a horseshoe shape around the village of Esnes, making up the left flank, 10 miles (16km) or so from the right. The horseshoe was complete. The *Field Service Regulations* laid down that as far as possible battalions were to dig in with a firing line and support lines in echelon; the firing line was normally one company strong. The machine guns, kept together, were not normally positioned in the firing line and the transport was sent to the rear. But the haste with which the battalions moved into their positions meant that there was not a continuous line resembling the trench lines that emerged later in the year. 11th Brigade fought throughout the day largely without the benefit of trenches and the KOSB found that their trenches acted as a magnet for enemy fire and they were better off in the open, lying down.

When the shelling started none of the troops would have any knowledge of what was happening to other parts of the line beyond their immediate line of sight. At first light many officers had only the vaguest notion of the position of friendly troops. Major Yate, of the 2nd KOYLI, who we will come across later, sent an NCO, Fred Atkinson, out at first light to look for their neighbours; he returned none the wiser, though staff officers soon appeared with information. But the men knew instinctively that they were to stay in their trenches until an officer told them to go in one direction or the other. They knew this because that was the way the army worked, the way it had always worked. The soldiers also knew instinctively that in a tight spot you stay with your friends, but if it's time to go, you go with your friends. This must count more in a man's reckoning than any threat posed by military law for disobedience. The new 'stand' order, when they received it, meant just that: stand until ordered otherwise.

For most of the officers and men, this day was going to be their first day of battle. For one young officer, 18-year-old Lt Ian Stewart of the Argylls, who was to become laird of Achnacone, and whose brother was a young officer in the Gordons,* it was a time when:

> Only to us was it vouchsafed to experience the finest of all emotions which war engenders in their absolute purity: the chivalry, the spirit of disinterested self-sacrifice, the joyful exaltation of patriotic loyalty, all untarnished by the sordid horrors of war's reality.

*Both were to survive the war: Ian, after being decorated and wounded, on the staff in the Tank Corps and his brother as a prisoner of war.

As he and his battalion marched out of Le Cateau onto the Cambrai Road:

> Some there were among us whose life had been dark and sometimes sordid, many there were of us who would be dead before the evening came, all were tired; yet they marched these men, gay as though to their wedding, leaving behind them their past lives as with the night, out into the dawn.

And continuing the romantic theme, in language that Frank Richards and his mates would have sniggered at: 'No lover went to meet his mistress more eagerly than we of the 93rd went to battle in those lovely days of August 1914.'

The eagerness to enter the fray was expressed by Rupert Brooke at this time, although he explicitly rejected the romantic love analogy:

> Now, God be thanked Who has matched us with His hour,
> And caught our youth, and wakened us from sleeping,
> With hand made sure, clear eye, and sharpened power,
> To turn, as swimmers into cleanness leaping,
> Glad from a world grown old and cold and weary,
> Leave the sick hearts that honour could not move,
> And half-men, and their dirty songs and dreary,
> And all the little emptiness of love.

Haig's Inaction

The decision to fight was Smith-Dorrien's, with tacit approval being given by GHQ and full support from his divisional generals. In other words, if the forthcoming battle went well for Second Corps, Sir John could claim some credit for having approved it and having selected the ground. If it went badly Sir John could quote his earlier retirement order and disclaim responsibility. Curiously, on the 7 September in his despatch to Kitchener he heaped praise (through gritted teeth) on Sir Horace for saving the retreat, claiming reflected credit. But forever after he never missed an opportunity to disparage the corps' achievement – in effect throwing away his credit and forever damaging his reputation. During the actual battle he did nothing within his power as C-in-C to help Smith-Dorrien by summoning help from Haig's nearest brigades. And Haig himself did not march towards the sound of gunfire; his entry in his diary merely confirms the fact that there was no telephone communication possible with St Quentin on the day, at least after 6.00am when he was on the move. When he did manage to get a message to French offering help, it was already getting dark and French did just as well to ignore it. At some stage in the afternoon Haig ordered 5th Cavalry Brigade to patrol to the west 'and ascertain the cause of the heavy gunfire toward Le Cateau', orders which hardly amounted to a serious offensive sortie. His overriding intention was now to reach Etreux with the bulk of his force, having rejected the St Quentin route suggested by GHQ at dawn. The impedimenta were sent to Etreux, which is 12 miles (20km) from the battlefield of Le Cateau, or half a day's march.

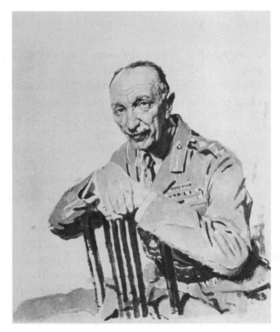

Gen Sir Henry Wilson of GHQ, by Orpen.

Haig gave a further possible reason for his failure to make any contact with Second Corps on the 26th. Apart from the problem of civilian traffic, there was a misunderstanding over orders between Gen Munro (GOC 2nd Div), Brig Haking and Corps HQ. Haking went to 'PONT SUR SAMBRE' instead of where he should have gone which was 'LANDRECIES', i.e. about 5 miles (8km) too far east. But, with this exception, Haig noted with satisfaction that 'all the movements of the corps were successfully carried out'. But this mix-up in orders cannot be taken as a reason for Haig's failure to turn right. We will return to this failure later.

Gen Wilson gave three bizarre reasons in his diary (26 August) for the inability of First Corps to come to the aid of Second Corps. He thought, as it seems did everyone at GHQ, that Haig was still engaged at Landrecies and 'of course is obviously unable to help owing to the Forest of Mormal and to confusion of having same billets as two French Reserve Divisions'. The first is barely excusable and the last two are risible, showing a lamentable inability to read a map. It is noteworthy that Wilson did not say that the distance was too great between the corps for help to be possible from Haig. In fact, at the 6.30am telephone conversation on the morning of the battle between Wilson and Smith-Dorrien (who Wilson privately called 'Smith-Doreen' – he called Gen Snow 'Snowball' to his face), Wilson again advanced the Landrecies action as a reason for Haig being otherwise engaged and attempted to mollify Smith-Dorrien by saying that 'troops fighting Haig cannot fight you'. This last comment managed to be both incorrect and patronising. In fact it was the other way round: the German troops fighting Smith-Dorrien couldn't fight Haig, who was able to continue the Retreat more or less unmolested, the same situation as had obtained after Mons. But, strangely, French's diary, as we have seen, shows that his fears over Haig had now lessened, twenty-four hours after the Landrecies attack. It is also noteworthy that no one at GHQ put forward the overall aim that Second Corps was now acting to shelter First Corps in its withdrawal, although some of the officers in Second Corps assumed this must be the case, which would after all make some military sense and was in effect what happened.

The communications between GHQ and the two corps on the 26th show up clearly the difficulties faced by commanders at this time of emerging technology. At 6.00am a staff officer arrived on horseback from St Quentin to First Corps HQ (still near Landrecies at Le Grand Fayt) with orders to continue the Retreat (which had started at 3.00am with 3rd Brigade) but now giving Haig effectively three choices of route: towards Lanrezac's 5th Army (south-east), towards St Quentin (south-west) or due south. The south-east route meant greater protection from Lanrezac's larger army but would have meant rejoining the rest of the BEF by rail. It was quite clearly not a possibility; in any case the idea of seeking shelter from an Anglophobe French general would have been anathema to Haig. Haig chose the due-south route to Etreux, with potentially dire consequences for Second Corps; but of course at 6.00am he could know nothing of the impending battle. This staff officer must have left St Quentin before GHQ knew that Second Corps was going to offer battle, that is, before 5.00am. It was a distance of 27 miles (43km) or so, a two-hour ride. No subsequent messenger was sent after him to amend the orders when the new situation became known. This is not really surprising; French on the 23rd had given his corps commanders latitude in choosing the details of their retreat routes and was not likely to change that degree of latitude now; his faith in Haig's military abilities was such that he was more than willing to entrust decisions like this to him. But even though only on the previous day, the 25th, Haig had been given Busigny as a direction, in three separate communications post-Landrecies a new urgency seems to have entered Haig's thinking: First Corps must save itself. French appeared, with his new choice of routes, to be complicit in this new outlook. From the morning of the 26th the priority in the Retreat, to conjoin the two corps effectively, now had a new priority superimposed on it: the two corps must save themselves, like ships in a convoy ordered to scatter in the face of a new threat. Safety to Haig clearly meant due south for First Corps; abandoned was the Busigny axis. The southern route was not the move that an instructor at a staff college would recommend in a war-game; it is unfathomable unless the thought had struck both French and Haig that, as Smith-Dorrien had the main body of the BEF under his command, it was his fight and his alone. Both French and Haig had their separate reasons for not wanting to go out of their way to help him: for French, Smith-Dorrien was at best an irritation; for Haig, he was a rival. And Haig and French were bound by their invisible ties. Even after the war, in the battle of the memoirs, when Haig could afford to be magnanimous, he was less than helpful toward Smith-Dorrien.

Changes in orders notoriously can result in confusion and it is no easy matter to turn a corps of 40,000 men. But a detached brigade was all that was needed on the 26th, an action that Haig had been willing to agree to at Mons. In the event, the 5th Cavalry Brigade that Haig did send west on the 26th was ordered only to patrol and report; it was in any case well into the afternoon by this time. Late on the 23rd both Smith-Dorrien and Forestier-Walker had motored to Haig's HQ at Le Bonnet to ask for troops to fill the gap between 3rd and 5th Divisions; Forestier-Walker had pleaded 'the battle is won if you will only send us a battalion or two'. In the event, although three battalions under Brig-Gen Haking were sent, reluctantly, they did not meet the enemy. It is interesting that Smith-Dorrien did not appeal to GHQ for their intervention in seeking help from First Corps on the 23rd, for whatever reason, although this would have been a normal route in the chain of command.

French was of course focused on the Retreat above all other considerations and Haig was definitely moving out of harm's way, although the order to send the scout plane looking for Haig in the morning of the 26th shows that at least someone at GHQ was worried about his whereabouts. In fact for the time being, certainly after 6.00am on the 26th, the truth was that GHQ had again lost touch with almost half its force for the whole day, something that a field marshal is not going to admit to in his memoirs, but a truth that Haig was more than willing to acknowledge. He did so with an exclamation mark in his diary (although he was liberal with exclamation marks). The situation that GHQ was presented with at 6.30am on the 26th was that one half of the BEF, the 'main body', was fighting, against GHQ's better judgement, and the other half, or rather the smaller part of the body, was somewhere over the hill making good its exit. David Ascoli (*see* Bibliography) has called this perverse move of Haig's, on a day when he had the noise of the guns of 5th Division in his ears, a 'defection'. That is an unfortunate choice of word, in as it does that Haig had somehow gone over to the other side. An ext dereliction of duty is nearer the mark, a statement made admittedly with t benefit of hindsight. Buried in Haig's ambitious, stubborn and cautious personality lies the reason for his plodding on to Etreux, with the sound of battle rumbling to the west. Gardner (*see* Bibliography) detects a pattern already emerging in Haig's behaviour *vis-à-vis* Second Corps, starting at Mons and characterized by far more concern for his own force than for the rest of the army. He sees the reason for the abandonment of Second Corps as lying in the machinations of Haig's HQ rather than at St Quentin.

In defence of Haig on that momentous day, Gary Sheffield and John Bourne, the editors of Haig's diaries, find it 'incredible' that he could have been swayed by his ambition and 'professional jealousy' of Smith-Dorrien to risk the destruction of half of the BEF. To support this view, they suggest that he has been somehow the victim of a campaign of innuendo by none other than the official historian John Edmonds (admittedly not partial to Haig) and that any suggestion of a personal motive in his decision is a 'conspiracy theory' that runs counter to his acknowledged conscientiousness as a military commander. He was tired, he was not young and 'he was groping around in the fog of war': that is all. They acknowledge that his corps was not seriously threatened on the 26th and that he had the sound of the battle in his ears. They give him credit for sending two (sic) messages to GHQ offering help, to neither of which he received a reply. And there they leave it, and so shall we for the moment, beyond suggesting that if Haig was 'acutely conscious of his responsibility as a commander', it remains regrettable that he did not interpret those responsibilities as extending beyond the confines of his own corps; and to suggest also that Haig's treatment in his diary of his choice of route is less than satisfactory and that he secretly knew that he had failed to rise to the occasion. Even with the benefit of revision he was not able to make anything other than a poor case for a less than noble action.* He neglected his duty as a commander in the BEF: *that* is all.

The next and sole communication on the 26th from GHQ to both corps commanders and to Allenby, by telegraph signal, was at 1.00pm and urged retreat to St Quentin-Noyon (*not* Peronne). It is noteworthy that only eight hours after sending orders to Haig allowing him to move away from Smith-Dorrien, this new order was designed to bring him closer. Neither Haig nor Smith-Dorrien acknowledged this signal; Haig was on the move and Smith-Dorrien was fighting a battle. Allenby was probably not aware of it. Haig 'despatched an enquiry' at the end of the day (8.30pm) when the battle was over.

---

*Charles Deedes, a staff officer at GHQ, commented, 'I cannot help thinking that the entry made by Haig in his diary for the 26th must have been written some time after the event.'

ertry had a conversation was on the telephone at
time the staff officer was at Haig's HQ and the
econd Corps. There was still no communication
is message-relaying systems were used at different
a familiar to Wellington (horse), General Grant
ntgomery (telephone and aeroplane). Even as late
om Valenciennes to French army commanders by

to Second Corps' 5.00am request for Gen Sordet's
cavalry assistance. He took advantage of Joffre's presence at St Quentin to send a
rather belated telephone message (in cipher) via Huguet at 12.10pm on the 26th
to Sordet as follows:

> General Joffre requests that you will not only cover the left of the British Army,
> but do more and intervene in the battle with all the forces at your disposal.

Sordet responded and the French 75s were clearly heard by Smith-Dorrien
himself at about 4.30pm, much to his relief.*

But that was the extent of GHQ's intervention on the day; keen to summon
French cavalry to British aid but not his own. Was the pilot sent out to look
for Haig bearing an order for his intervention? If he was, we have not been
told; it would be safe to assume not. It was as if Second Corps, more than half
the force, was personified in the square-jawed, prickly, irritating person of Sir
Horace. We have seen, at Landrecies for example, how French could behave
in a perceived crisis, when Haig's corps was involved; he summoned help even
from the unlikely corner of Lanrezac's 5th Army. French's opinion of Haig's
abilities was as high as that of his opinion of Smith-Dorrien's was low, and
French was more than willing to do Haig's bidding. French's military judgement was completely swayed by his judgement of the commander he was
dealing with and he wasn't going to do Smith-Dorrien's bidding.

In this new crisis with Second Corps, French and his staff were to become
sunk in depression and inactivity. The *Official History* even goes so far as to
state, with remarkable frankness, that by 8.30pm on the 26th GHQ 'seems to
have given up Second Corps as lost', citing in support of this astonishing statement Huguet's telegraph to Joffre: '*Battaille perdu*' ('Battle lost'). They certainly
believed for a time that the entire Cavalry Division was lost, whereas in fact it
was hardly directly engaged (its casualties were fifteen on the day), although in
the post-war battle of the memoirs French was to credit it with a major role,
in his attempt to belittle Smith-Dorrien and Second Corps in general. GHQ's
despondent mood is all the more surprising in view of the fact, reported by the
Official History, that they were receiving quite accurate intelligence on the battle

---

*A *Soixante-quinze* was a champagne cocktail served at the Ritz between the wars.

from scout planes. They believed what they wanted to believe, that Smith-Dorrien was wilfully destroying the Second Corps, and they were prepared to sit out the action. It was Smith-Dorrien's battle and he was going to have to fight it on his own, with the French cavalry on his left and Haig's corps somewhere on his right, and GHQ knew as much about its whereabouts as Bertry did. In Gardner's words, GHQ went into 'cognitive closure'.

GHQ shifted down to Noyon even as St Quentin began filling up with the first exhausted troops drifting in from Le Cateau, sheltered by cavalry. The sight of the field marshal's train puffing out of the St Quentin station did nothing to improve the morale of the Le Cateau survivors. French left behind at St Quentin none of his staff officers to help sort out the dazed stragglers from the battlefield, although he attempted to remedy the situation by sending some officers back to St Quentin early on the 27th. It had been the same story at Le Cateau on the 24th; the train bringing in the Rifle Brigade from Le Havre coincided with the GHQ train being got ready to go down to St Quentin. The Riflemen had got stiffly off their train (French trains carried a whole battalion but were very slow) after their long journey knowing nothing about the battle of Mons, saw the GHQ train preparing to go the wrong way, then saw what they took to be a German aeroplane and loosed off some rounds at it, to no avail; it at least made them feel better. The officers were dismayed to find that Le Cateau did not appear on their maps: they had only been issued with maps of Belgium. It was not an auspicious beginning.

GHQ, with its fourteen staff officers, signallers, cooks, drivers, servants, the Artist Rifles guard, liaison officers, translators, and so on, was a nomadic caravan of more than a hundred men; at times the NCOs didn't even have time to unpack. But if the move from Le Cateau on the 25th was prudent, the move from St Quentin smacked of panic. At Dammartin on 1 September there were to be scenes of panic at GHQ when rumours of Uhlans caused the whole caravan to be bundled into lorries, just as Sir William Robertson was sitting down to a roast leg of mutton (he ate it cold the next day).

The cooks were to be severely tested on the 26th when Joffre was at GHQ. His mood brightened after lunch when Lanrezac had left (with the invaluable Spears) and he became positively genial; lunch was a vital part of his war effort and a relief to his system on this day so singularly lacking in other restorative tonics.

It was not of course French's job to get personally involved in the struggle being played out to the north. Only admirals go into battle with their men on equal terms, sharing the dangers with them, as Jellicoe was to do at Jutland. French's successful appeal to Sordet was his one major contribution on the day, although there was an apparent misunderstanding at the Bertry end at one point that the C-in-C was coming up to take charge. We have seen that at Landrecies it was extremely unhelpful to have even the corps commander muddled up with his troops in a small battle; French's presence at Le Cateau would have been unthinkable. But whatever French's failings, excessive meddling in detail, like that of his counterpart Lord Gort in the next war, was not one of them. French's place was at St Quentin; it was at the meeting with Joffre at St Quentin on the day of the battle that French learned of the vital creation of the 6th Army, a rendezvous that follows the clichéd narrative of the war: army commanders in a château twenty miles from the front planning the formation of new armies to throw into battle, while men are being killed during lunch.*

As the BEF expanded so of course did GHQ, so that by the end of 1918 there were 300 staff officers in four branches. In August 1914, even if it had not taken on the rarified atmosphere that it had later, there were already signs of the growing gulf between the staff and the front-line soldier. It is this gulf, with the mud, the barbed wire, the machine guns and the trenches that are the defining characteristics of the war, the gulf in knowledge between the lines on a staff map and the reality of mud and barbed wire on the ground. But all this lay in the future. Le Cateau was a battle without mud, without barbed wire, and where staff colonels and infantry major-generals and brigadiers were at the front on horseback, a battle the like of which would never be seen again.

---

*When the C-in-C later wrote in a supercilious way that 'it is very difficult for the uninitiated to realize the concentration which the direction of an army ... demands from the brain of a commander-in-chief', he did not exactly improve his standing in military history, if that was his aim, although it was more likely to have been a side-swipe at Smith-Dorrien.

2
The Right Flank: Morning, 26 August

An airman flying over the landscape west and south of the town of Le Cateau at dawn, soon after 4.30am, on 26 August would have seen, as the mist rose off the land with the morning sun, the corn in stubble, cut and piled in stooks; beetroot and clover uncut; the straight Roman roads leading roughly to the north-west (to Cambrai) and south-west (towards St Quentin); and a line of intermittent shallow trenches running from the south of the town, skirting the villages of Troisvilles, Audencourt, Beaumont, Caudry, Fontaine-au Pire and then bending left to Esnes in the west. Between Fontaine and Ligny he could see the railway line running east-west in a ravine, the line snaking up from Bertry. Between Inchy and Le Cateau the railway line ran alongside the south side of the road.* The earth was thrown up haphazardly and the trenches were dug in straight lines rather than in the zigzag pattern that was to become universal, constructed so as to minimize lateral blast and enfilade fire. Farmers may be good at digging but the soil, although not a heavy clay, was baked by the August sun; the work of digging the trenches on the 24th, rudimentary as they were, must have contributed to Smith-Dorrien's decision, although he does not mention it. The trenches were not continuous; to the west of Caudry there seemed to be no fortifications for a mile or so. Those constructed on the spur nearest Le Cateau were not meant for British troops, but to protect the crops; they were not much use to the British when the shelling started. The villages, not at all picturesque, presented a solid brick- and stone-built appearance, dominated by their churches and substantial barns; they would be protection against shrapnel but not high explosive. In the villages the roads were cobbled. Perhaps the finest structure in the whole battlefield area was – and still is – the fifteenth-century castle at Esnes, where there was also a large sugar factory.

There were some hobbled cattle near the farmyards. Civilians were still coming out of the town and there was a great deal of movement to be seen all along the line and roads. Frank Richards was very annoyed with the civilians

---

*This bit of railway was not a significant feature; Major Becke, who we shall meet later, does not include it on his map.

who actually accompanied him to his sunken road near Reumont, particularly one who claimed to be an Englishman, but certainly didn't behave like one. Soldiers prefer to have a battlefield free of useless civilians, while they always welcome friendly ones while on the march. But the majority of the citizens of Le Cateau itself stayed in the town, using their cellars as shelter if they had them. Out on the roads to the south and west the cookers were fired up, having as usual come on ahead of the fighting troops, and some of them were at battalion HQs bringing up breakfast. Dawn is of course the time for stand-to in the British Army; there was now less than two hours before the German artillery opened fire.

Le Cateau in 1903, a town of 14,000 souls.

If he had strained his ears above the sound of the engine, our airman would have heard the sound of rifle fire in the town, where the enemy were already fighting the Cornwalls and the East Surreys. Uhlans (lancers) had made a dramatic entrance in the town earlier, their iron-shod hooves throwing up sparks on the cobbles, but had been driven off; Capt Dunn described two ranks of Welch Fusiliers forming up and delivering volleys of fire with the front rank kneeling, in the nineteenth-century manner.

It was not British practice to defend towns with street fighting if the town had no military value. There was in any case no time to prepare the town for defence, which would have meant clearing out the inhabitants, barricading streets and using materials such as mattresses for protection; it was simply not the British way of fighting. By executing a fighting retreat out of the town, the troops of 19th Brigade and 14th Brigade were conforming to standard fighting instructions, although this left the town, with its exit routes to the south

70

and west, free for the enemy to exploit. There was fighting in the streets of Caudry by the 3rd Worcesters, but here not all the men by any means were as steady as their officers would have liked, as we shall see. Street fighting, with shells crashing down on buildings, is an unnerving business and British troops would rather take their chances in the open. To the west of Caudry, German dismounted cavalry were already infiltrating Fontaine from Beauvois.

Le Cateau, seen from the Suffolk position.

From the air the ground is largely treeless and undulating with the highest ground to the east, nearest the town. The trees most visible to the pilot were the poplars lining the road and railway in front of the KOYLI position, which were well spaced out. A lone tree (the *Arbre*) stood out to the south of the Cambrai Road on the sunken lane about 2 miles (3km) or so from Le Cateau and east of Troisvilles; some of the 1st Norfolks were attempting to cut it down (it could have become an artillery aiming point) but they lacked a proper saw and after two hours they gave up. Patches of dead ground, so vital to troops, were not discernible to our airman, but he would have been able to see clearly the partly sunken lane running east-west from Troisvilles to Le Cateau, with troops both to the north and south of it and 13th and 15th Brigade HQs located in it.

He may have been surprised to see the supporting guns of the Royal Field Artillery placed so close to the infantry (Suffolks, Manchesters and KOYLI) to the west of the town: XV Brigade RFA, close up with the Suffolks, with 37 Howitzer Battery RFA, and XXVIII Brigade close up with the KOYLI. In fact Brig Headlam, commanding the 5th Division artillery had deliberately shifted the guns forward. A commander of the old school, his orders were now to fight and not retreat; in his mind that meant up with the infantry, which did in fact conform to standard practice at the time of his initiation. It was to cost his gunners dear. He may have thought that the closeness of the guns to the infantry would boost their morale. This is at best doubtful; guns attract counter-battery fire which the troops would not wish to share. But both infantry and gunners were to be full of admiration for each other's professionalism and stoicism; in fact the next day, survivors from the 5th Division infantry 'stepped out of the ranks to give a silent pat to the guns drawn up beside the road'.

LIEUTENANT-COLONEL C. A. H. BRETT, D.S.O.

Lt-Col C. Brett of the 2nd Suffolks, who was killed at Le Cateau.

The spur or knoll on which the Suffolks, the Manchesters and the XV RFA Brigade had established themselves before dawn revealed some alarming weaknesses at first light. There was concealed ground to the front only about 300yd away from the sunken lane, where the Cambrai road goes into a cutting, although the KOYLI had a good line of sight from the left. There was concealed access to the sunken lane from the town. The dead ground to the right, the Selle valley, was also barely 300yd away from the right of the Suffolks and Manchesters. The church clock-tower in the town, clearly visible, was later used by the Germans as a machine-gun position; an 18-pounder was turned on it later in the morning. In fact, the town of Le Cateau formed a concealed concentration area for enemy troops to assemble and filter out to the battlefield. But there they were and there they were staying: 'We will fight it out here and there will be no retreat', in the words of Lt-Col C.F. Stevens, the commander of XV Brigade RFA, at 6.00am; he was to be wounded an hour later along with Major Jones of 37 (Howitzer) Battery, both struck by the same HE shell at the brigade observation post. They stayed at their posts. His order was then passed on in turn to his men by Major Nutt of 52 Battery. The Suffolks at the apex were to be well supported by the KOYLI on their left and the Manchesters on their right, their line bent round to the right forming a horseshoe shape, the form laid down by *Field Service Regulations*; it was the twentieth-century version of the square adopted in the days of muskets against cavalry.*

The Heavy Battery (108) was positioned just to the north of Reumont, 3,000yd back from the firing line and 61 Howitzer Battery was a little closer, just off the Roman road. These batteries were intended for the long-range counter-battery work. The smaller 13-pounders of the RHA were positioned on the flank to the south-east of the Roman road that leads down to St Quentin. These were E and L Batteries, which had been in action at Elouges, the latter to achieve ever-lasting fame at Nery on 1 September.

To the west our airman would be able to see, north of the ravine, higher ground to the north of the village of Haucourt, where British troops of the 4th Division were taking up positions between this ravine (the Warnelle Ravine, which is also a railway embankment) and the Roman road to Cambrai. The biggest settlement, about 5 miles (8km) from Le Cateau, lying just south of the Roman road, was Caudry, an unlovely lace-making town of 13,000 people; the battle to come could equally well be called the Battle of Caudry. The Cambrai road, which in part was lined with poplars, was in effect the defining feature dividing the assembled forces. Before dawn the Germans were mostly to the north of it, and by afternoon they were everywhere to the south of it. The villages to the south, of which Bertry was the largest, were linked by roads, which were only partly cobbled and not metalled.

Each battery of six 18-pounders (three batteries per brigade) was lined up mathematically to bring concentrated salvoes of fuze-timed shrapnel shells

---

*There are documented accounts of infantry officers in the 1920s being taught to form square against cavalry.

down on their targets, each gun capable of firing up to six rounds per minute at over 5 miles (8km) range when fully elevated, each shell filled with 300 balls designed to tear through flesh and bone. The 18-pounder shells were in effect giant shotgun cartridges, but with one potential weakness: their effectiveness depended on the gunners setting the fuze correctly, to achieve an air-burst at the correct height. The guns could also theoretically fire high explosive shells using yellow-bursting Lyddite explosive, which burst on impact, but these were not supplied at this stage of the war; only the heavy batteries of 60-pounders and howitzers could fire HE, intended for counter-battery fire. The 18-pounders were the British equivalent of the famed French 75mm field gun, by which French tacticians set such store.* The 75mm, an elegant gun with a pneumatic recoil system, had a rate of fire more than four times that of the 18-pounder; it was still being used in an anti-tank role as late as 1940. The field howitzer batteries, designed to throw shells over hills, were accustomed from Boer War days to having an officer well forward as an observer, although on this day they had no one forward. But nor were they firing over a hill; they were on the hill.

Their horse teams, up to 150 mounts for each battery when at full war strength, were well back from the guns, using what dead ground they could find. The war establishment of each battery was five officers and 198 NCOs and men, under the command of a major, although only half this total would actually be in the firing line. Most of the drivers, batmen, shoe-smiths and other support personnel were with the horses in the rear. With all the support troops an RFA Brigade, commanded by a Lt-Col, mustered close on 320 men and eighteen officers.

This was to be much more of a gunner's battle than Mons, where the fields of fire were so poor. The gunners, a technical arm with arcane skills in fuze setting and range finding, were fiercely proud of their hundred-year history** and they were viscerally attached to their guns, although officers would know their *Field Training Manual,* which stated that the loss of guns was justified 'when ensuring the safe withdrawal of the main body'. All the gunnery officers had attended the two-year course at the Woolwich Academy (abbreviated during the war to six months), where entry was by examination and fees were paid, thus ensuring an exclusively middle-class intake. The course was harsh and exacting; one graduate said that 'the exertions of the war were mild by comparison'. The gunners were imbued with the doctrine that they were to serve the infantry ('their infantry') and in doing so any risk must be taken. But

---

*British field guns were designated by weight of ordnance; howitzers by diameter of breech, even though howitzers are also field guns. German and French guns were designated by diameter of breech.
**Gunnery officers, unlike infantry and cavalry officers, had never purchased their commissions.

for now the British guns were blind in the mist, waiting, camouflaged with stooks of corn, only the XXVII RFA to the east of Troisvilles having had time to dig in adequately. They did what they could to improve their protection in the time they had and some of the gun crews got what little rest they could. Each gun had a wagon-load of just over 100 shells as its initial allocation, covered by tarpaulin.

Lt Rory Macleod of 80 Battery, RFA 5th Division, a junior subaltern of four years' service, was up with the guns. Not long after dawn a staff officer (Capt Bartholomew) had ridden up and told the whole crew that there was going to be a big battle and that there would be no retreat. The young Rory does not record his reaction to this piece of news; it is tempting to think that thoughts of his Irish fiancée, Colleen Honner, passed through his mind; he had just bought her an engagement ring from the £75 that the Army had paid him for bringing his own mare to France. A fellow subaltern of Macleod's, Lt C.F. Hodgson (122 Battery), some seventy years later recorded his feelings on hearing Capt Bartholomew's pep talk:

> I felt terribly elated. I was terribly young and quite inexperienced and I felt this was something really exciting, that something was really going to happen in my life. I wasn't scared or apprehensive at all. Oddly enough I thought more about my brother – my twin brother Victor. He was in 124 Battery and I hadn't seen him at all though their battery position wasn't far away from us.

The night before he had listened to the corps commander giving a pep talk and ending with the words 'It is do or die' (though this seems unlikely and he may have mis-remembered). He was to remember later the pair of Zeiss binoculars that he acquired from a dead German gunner on the Retreat; in this war as in the next, German binoculars, so superior to British-made ones, were a much-prized trophy.

At about this time (6.30am) Gen Wilson at St Quentin managed to get through to Gen Smith-Dorrien on the telephone at Bertry railway station. Sir Horace strained to hear through the static and the station noise: 'If you stand and fight, there will be another Sedan.'* Like his chief, Wilson's mood was oscillating between despair and hope. Smith-Dorrien merely replied, according to one account, 'It's already started.' According to his own account, he left the little railway station with Wilson's words of encouragement ringing in his ear: 'Good luck to you; yours is the first cheerful voice I have heard for three days.' Wilson always did have his ebullient moments but this comment could be taken as showing less than full confidence in the decision to offer battle.

---

*The decisive battle, in 1870, of the Franco-Prussian War in which the French, commanded by Napoleon III, were bottled up and forced to surrender by von Moltke.

German Atrocities

All along the British line at dawn (about 4.30am) the men had stood to arms, in the time-honoured tradition, but it was on both flanks that von Kluck was starting his battle. He was clearly following classic military tactics: drive in the flanks and the centre will collapse of its own accord. This is in fact what nearly happened in the battle to come. Alexander von Kluck, sixty-eight years old, a veteran of the War of 1870, a professional soldier born without the *von*, was an old man in a hurry. His saturnine looks curiously resembled the actor James Mason. He was not the archetypal monocled Prussian (he was born in Westphalia) but he was certainly capable of acting with all the ruthlessness with which that warrior tribe is associated. In Belgium he was implicated in the systematic murder of civilians at Vise, to name but one example, and he shared the universal German view that any act of armed resistance by civilians put them beyond the protection of civilized law.

In fact, in Belgium only a week before von Kluck had gone beyond even what the German Army laid down as appropriate: not only death for civilians firing on soldiers, but even for approaching within 200m of an aeroplane or balloon post. Farmers were shot for being found in possession of a rook rifle in a barn; individuals were shot merely for looking 'suspicious'. Hostages were taken and shot in the ratio of ten for every German 'casualty' or simply to force the surrender of a town; in fact 'atrocities' by Belgians were largely a figment of the fevered German imagination, and frequently the result of drunken German troops firing at random.* Even while the war was still in progress it was established by the Bryce Report that unofficial Belgian resistance was negligible, and had no appreciable effect on the movement of the German First and Second Armies. There was no official civilian resistance of course. But such was the fear of guerrilla attack in Belgium that von Kluck's HQ had a guard of a full battalion, complete with machine guns and even a 77mm field gun.

The Bryce Committee on Alleged Outrages, set up by Prime Minister Asquith in September 1914, found compelling evidence not just from Belgian refugees but from the diaries of German troops directly involved of both systematic and isolated outrages against the civilian population. 'Murder, rape, arson and pillage began from the moment the German Army crossed the frontier', the area around Liège being the first to suffer. The report recounted in incontrovertible detail, with eyewitness accounts, the killing under orders of defenceless old men, children and women. The killing of civilians was part of a deliberate plan to cower the Belgian population; there was no repression of individual acts of murder committed by German soldiers. In the measured

*Although Lt Johnston on the 22nd recorded a lone German soldier beaten to death by Belgians.

Kaiser Wilheim II; he revelled in gory deeds from the front and likened his troops to Huns.

words of the Committee, which included both lawyers and a historian (H.A.L. Fisher), individual acts 'are more numerous and shocking than would be expected between civilized powers'. In a chilling foretaste of events a generation later, some German officers went on record to say that they were reluctantly carrying out orders, and the committee expressed the hope that 'sanctions can be devised to prevent the reoccurrence of such horrors as our generation is now witnessing'. Another tactic employed officially by German troops, and banned by the Hague Convention, was the use of civilians as cover in attacks, a tactic which was seen at Mons, used opposite the 4th Royal Fusiliers.

Von Kluck complained that these measures were 'slow in remedying the evil practices of the Belgian population, which are eating into the very vitals of our army'. The Schlieffen timetable was everything and yet Belgian hostages were still being transported to Germany (and shot) a month after the First Army had completed its march through that unfortunate country. Altogether 6,500 civilians were killed, 20,000 buildings destroyed and the priceless university library at Louvain 'wilfully and systematically burned', in the words of the American diplomat Brand Whitlock, who was an eyewitness. He saw German soldiers smashing windows with their rifle butts to fan the flames created by the incendiaries they had placed there. The news of these atrocities went ahead of the German armies, reported in American newspapers, and sowed fear into the towns that lay in their path; we shall see their effect on St Quentin on the 26th. Both von Kluck and von Bulow were war criminals, in breach of the Hague

Convention, and the perpetrators of a form of warfare more akin to civil war than war between professional armies conducted by a nation that prided itself on its *Kultur*. It was perhaps for this reason that many people thought that allied propaganda which made much of German atrocities was not totally believable. But without doubt the German armies of von Kluck and von Bulow had rampaged their way through Belgium and were not about to turn into models of civilized behaviour now that they were on French soil. The towns of northern France received the invaders ('an army delirious and drunk with victory and wine' in the words of St Quentin resident Yves Flamand, quoted by Hilary Spurling) with empty streets and closed shutters, as they had done in 1871.

Even Capt Bloem of the 12th Grenadiers, 1st Army, who we will come across again, in his march through Belgium, which he called without irony a 'free, bright and happy country', and who was undoubtedly a civilized and humane man, thought it was 'monstrous' when a few shots were fired harmlessly at his column by no more than a handful of civilians from the edge of a wood. His men were kept in column 'by the thought of the reported tortures awaiting them at the hands of marauding bands of armed civilians at night'. The burning of villages and the shooting of civilians he considered a 'suitable revenge and a just punishment' for firing on German troops. German newspapers published daily atrocity stories of the unspeakable things done to the leading troops by Belgian soldiers and, much worse, civilians. The newspapers seemed incapable of grasping the fact that the invasion of their small neutral country might make the Belgians very angry.

Allied propaganda poster (Peronne Museum).

It is important to bear in mind that in the clash of arms to come soon after dawn on this late summer day, the fight would be between on the one hand an army that had in the last few weeks murdered thousands of Belgian civilians as an act of state terror, and on the other hand an army that had strict rules against picking apples that belonged to civilians and making love to girls who might have easy virtue. These are not idle considerations; they go to the heart of a conflict that many serious historians and probably most interested individuals still consider to have been futile. But that is another debate altogether.

Battle is Joined

As previously stated, von Kluck's advantage in guns over the British Second Corps was nearly three to one and he fully intended to take advantage of this, although his intelligence officers were telling him that it was the whole of the BEF that he was up against: so much the better. His machine guns, although not more liberally supplied to the infantry regiments than the British, were used in German tactics in attacking groupings. His conscript soldiers were required to serve for three years; behind him he had an army, an autocratic militarized regime and a society that was accustomed to fighting and winning European wars and was equipped for that purpose, although admittedly they had not fought a European war for more than a generation. He did not suffer the agonizing doubts of his superior von Moltke. He was the right of the line of the Schlieffen-inspired plan to defeat France before the Russians could deploy and he wasn't going to be put off by the 'contemptible' BEF, although the Kaiser's adjective was not one that von Kluck would have used himself ('contemptible' should in any case be taken to refer to its size rather than its fighting ability; 'insignificant' is nearer the mark). Germany had a population twice the size of Great Britain's and her steel production was nearly twice as large. For von Moltke as much as for Lt Bloem Germany's hour had come, the world was ready for German *Kultur* and a Germanic peace and order would be imposed upon Europe. It was von Kluck's greatest ambition to enter Paris in triumph.

Allied propaganda was not slow in graphically pointing out the ironic juxtaposition of the words *Gott mit uns* (God with us) engraved on the buckles of the belts of German soldiers who were simultaneously committing atrocities against Belgian women. *Gott mit uns* became for the British 'Got mittens'.

Very soon after 6.00am, as the mist was lifting, German batteries began firing on the position held by the Suffolks to the west of the town, although the target of the guns was XV Brigade RFA. The Suffolks like their neighbours, the King's Own Yorkshire Light Infantry and the Manchesters, had had a relatively quiet time at Mons; artillery fire such as they were now experiencing

Gen von Kluck, commander of the German 1st Army, French's opposite number.

was a horrifyingly new experience. It is no insult to say that there was nothing exceptional about the Suffolks; they were one of the older county regiments with 200 years of tradition behind them, but they were not the Guards and nor could they lay claim to a specialist tradition such as the Rifle Brigade. The men of the Suffolk towns like Ipswich do not have a particularly martial tradition. Many of the men were part of 'that mysterious army of horsemen, ploughmen and field workers who fled the wretchedness of the land', in the words of Ronald Blythe. For these men, the call of the plover and the jangle of harness were as much part of the natural order of things as the squire in his manor and the fear of the workhouse: there was nothing romantic or picturesque about rural poverty to them. The Suffolk Regiment were the 12th in the line. And that was good enough for them.

Attached all day to the 2nd Suffolks during the whole action – and sharing its fate – was a mixed bag of details who had become separated from their units the previous night: twenty-six men of the 1st Dorsets, two men of the 1st Bedfords and six men, unarmed, of the artillery. They had been handed over to Lt-Col Brett by Brig Rolt and placed on the right of the line.

The German batteries were firing from high ground at least 3,000yd north-north-east of the town so that their shells were arcing across the western outskirts of Le Cateau, from positions masked from XV Brigade's guns. This was quite an achievement of deployment and target identification so early in the day. It could only have been facilitated by putting observers well forward equipped with telephone cable. German infantry were already in the town. They were using the church tower as a machine gun position later in the day, with deadly effect on the gunners; it was now being used to control the fire of their batteries firing on XV Brigade at a range of 5,000yd. The German battery commanders had without doubt put an observer up the tower at first light, anticipating the battle to come and linked with his guns by cable. But the original location of the RA batteries was made by a *Taube* that flew high over the position at 6.00am as the mist cleared off and, although it dropped no markers, it reported back to the III Corps artillery. The BEF in August 1914 had only small arms to fire at enemy planes. Later in the morning a field gun was turned on the tower and a hit was achieved that got the intended result; the machine-gunners and observer must have scampered down the spiral stairs.

The Suffolk men now frantically tried to get extra depth in their scrapings, using their 'grubbers', wishing they had done just that little bit more digging before the shelling started. The little entrenching tools carried as part of the men's kit had not all survived the retreat to Le Cateau, but the adjutant had thoughtfully sent back to the transport for spares. Fred Petch of the Suffolks later said, 'The thing was, to throw up a sort of parapet and to keep your head and your bum down.' The XV Brigade gunners fired back at enemy batteries to the north, engaging the gun flashes at ranges of about 5,000yd; two batteries were temporarily silenced. The Reserve Artillery back at Reumont joined in the action against enemy batteries, 108th Heavy Battery guided by its OP as the light improved and 61st Battery's howitzers searching, using the map.

The only guns in the brigade able to fire back at the enemy batteries to the north-east of Le Cateau at this time were 123 and 124 Batteries (XXVIII Brigade RFA), to the west of the Roman road. 124 had dug itself in as far as possible and was facing north-west; the men now manhandled the guns 45 degrees to face north-east and started firing directly over 123. Such was the concentration of the officers that the major of 123 was not even aware of 124's shells passing directly over his head. Both 123 and 124 were receiving accurate shell-fire from 6.15am, but for some reason 122 near the road escaped detection by enemy artillery observers throughout the day. The effect of the British counter-battery firing at this stage was minimal; the mist was still hanging about and it has to be said that in this work the Germans seemed to possess all the advantages of observation and deployment and a greater proportion of HE shell-fire as well as the advantage of sheer numbers of guns. The British gunners instinctively knew that more profitable targets would present themselves before long. As early as 6.15am German infantry were spotted to the north at 5,000yd and fired at, causing them to spread out.

At this stage the fight on the British right was going very much in favour of the attackers. The British 5th Division gunners had been able to put an OP forward but only a couple of hundred yards at most. They had flags to signal to their batteries if and when the lines were cut. In the static war to come these were seldom, if ever, used. It was extremely dangerous, and on this occasion suicidal, to stand up and signal, for obvious reasons. Later, when the lines were cut, chains of orderlies lying in the open were used to maintain contact between the guns and the OP. Major Becke, the authority on the artillery at Le Cateau, states that officers did reconnoitre the ground the previous night, especially the hostile terrain, but the rain and poor visibility hindered them and in any case they did not know of the 'stand' order until 4.30am. They were still (and throughout the morning) under the impression that First Corps was somewhere on their right, although in fact German infantry was slowly exploiting the gap, using the town as a concentration area. Two guns began firing at 11 Battery from the east at 10.00am and its commander – Major Henning – hesitated to return fire from fear of First Corps troops, but soon realized that he had no choice. He turned his guns around and succeeded in temporarily silencing the guns, and was then wounded himself. His guns then engaged enemy troops at fuze zero emerging from the valley, together with the rifles and machine guns of the Manchesters. For the time being the enemy came no further.

Fresh German batteries from south-east of the town began dropping shells on to British infantry south of the Cambrai road as far as 2 miles (3km) west of Le Cateau; once again the troops had to stick it. 'There was a continual roar of fire', both from the crash of the incoming HE and the firing of the 18-pounders. It was not until about 8am that the Suffolks had any targets to fire at when skirmishers appeared on the high ground to the north and a machine gun was detected emerging from the dead ground, or cutting, to the front, in the Cambrai road. A machine-gun detachment this far forward at this early stage (8.00am) should have been a worrying sign for the British. The forward company of the KOYLI, in particular Lt Wynne with his platoon of 'D' Company, was able to bring diagonal fire on the cutting as well as firing to their front. The XV Brigade gunners were just out of the direct fire of the machine gun, which was much more troublesome to the infantry 150yd to their front. 122 Battery came under both rifle and machine gun fire from the Roman road/Cambrai road junction (Pont des Quatre Vaux), as well as from sniper fire from the high ground to its right front, the place where the cemetery lies today. The layer of No. 1 gun was shot in the head by a sniper from this commanding position, another crew member stepping up to the breach, getting shot through the head in his turn. Re-supply of the remaining guns of 123 and 124 Batteries was out of the question, but three wagons set off from the lines to replenish 80 Battery from the sheltered lee of the hill.

The 2nd KOYLI to the left of the Suffolks had dug in before dawn and had received their new orders at 6.00am by runner from Brig Cuthbert, whose 13th Brigade HQ was in the sunken lane leading to Troisvilles. The order read, 'Orders have been changed. There will be NO retirement for the fighting troops; fill up your trenches with water, food and ammunition, as far as you can.'

13-pounder gun at Nery on 1 Sept 1914; this was the cavalry version of the 18-pounder field gun.

Col Romer of Second Corps HQ and Capt Ackroyd, the adjutant of the KOYLI, rode up to the trenches and were there while more ammunition was brought up at the canter by cart from battalion HQ back down the Roman road. The buglers distributed the ammunition to the companies within reach. Within minutes, in the words of the regimental history:

> The air was being torn and ripped by the whistling shells; intercommunication became impossible; telephone wires were rent and scattered; a tornado of shrapnel and high explosive burst over and around our guns. The weak spots of a position taken up in a half-light, and only half-prepared, were soon only too apparent.

From the vantage point of the KOYLI, until about 10.30am most of the Yorkshiremen were spectators to the fight on the knoll to their right, only 'D' Company being directly engaged, although the machine guns under Lt Unett, which had a good line of fire straight up the road, had opened fire at 8.30am. They had been placed near Battalion HQ on the Roman road and remained in action until 2.30pm, by which time one gun was knocked out and several men wounded; the other gun was then disabled. But from 11.00am onwards the battalion was firing to its front and both east and west as the enemy tried to establish themselves on the near side of the Cambrai road.

To the left of the Yorkshiremen, the 2nd Scottish Borderers had bivouacked overnight and dug in at dawn with their grubbers, their NCOs having managed to get the men to retain them on the retreat from Mons. The Borderers found that the freshly turned earth of their trenches made them a conspicuous artillery target and they moved out into the open and lay down.

The Suffolk machine guns had fields of fire of about 650yd, but the folds in the ground and the bank to their front meant that many of the men were not able to fire their rifles to any great extent and were thus denied the satisfaction of being able to hit back at their foe. By 9.00am the garrison to the south-west of the town was under fire from artillery, machine guns and rifle fire, although for now the German infantry to the north of the road were holding back, hoping that the gunners would do their work for them and perhaps waiting for their troops to move up the Selle valley on the flank in greater strength. The German attempt to build up a firing line of infantry to the north of the Suffolks in the cutting was brought to a stop by the marksmanship of the Suffoks firing from the sunken lane and the forward 'D' Company of the KOYLI; Major Doughty (2nd i/c Suffolks), through his binoculars, counted 'from twelve to fifteen corpses'. The range was less than 400yd from the forward Suffolk trenches. Capt E.E. Orford, on the left of the Suffolks' line, noticed the enemy bringing up machine guns to the west of the Pont des Quatre Vaux and fired at them. Neither the Manchester machine guns, on their right flank, facing east, nor the Suffolk guns, in the middle of their line, but facing north-east toward the town, could fire at the Pont des Quatre Vaux. The bank of the sunken lane hid the road, which was why the guns had been faced north-east.

Quite early in the morning, according to Lt Hodgson, the gunners received the order 'Prepare to repel cavalry!' He remembered, in later years, the Prussian lancers charging in to the point where the gunners opened up at six rounds per minute at fuze zero. What survivors there were withdrew, only to regroup for another charge. Hodgson's account is not supported by any other accounts, although one dead Uhlan was found in front of the Suffolks' position early in the morning by Brigadier Rolt, who had ridden up to see what all the fuss was about; presumably part of the squadron seen and fired at in the town in the early morning by the Welch.

Von Kluck now brought up the artillery of three divisions (108 guns) onto the ground to the north of the town and more salvoes of high-explosive shells began to crash down on the exposed batteries of XV and XXVIII Brigades RFA. 11 Battery was the worst hit; only two guns were able to return fire. It was an unequal gunnery contest, but the British gunners still had some fight in them. The Suffolks and their neighbours the KOYLI got their full share of this hail of shrapnel and high explosive and, like the gunners, held on, losses mounting. They had never before been exposed to such prolonged shelling. Its assault on all the senses was enough to make a man shake uncontrollably, the shock-wave or blast alone from high explosive being enough to kill a man at close quarters; to unprotected troops a 77mm shell could be lethal at up to 50yd. In 1914 shell-shock was not even recognized by the War Office as a medical condition. But it was the 5.9in HE that was doing the most damage. Before long the ground on the knoll, particularly in front of the sunken lane, was pitted with craters, or in the words of Major Becke, 'shell-smitten'.

The Mass Infantry Attack

Major 'Cal' Yate, B Company commander with the Yorkshiremen, was to win one of the five VCs won on this day. For now, like his men, he could do nothing but endure the relentless bombardment. The knoll was becoming the Spion Kop of 1914: there were more than 2,000 men in the garrison and so far the infantry had had little to fire at with any profit. It was soon after 10.00am that the situation became desperate: German infantry now entered the battle, possibly as many as four battalions from the 7th Division. They came forward in thick masses along a front of 2 miles (3km) from the woods next to the town, to Rambourlieux Farm, north of the Cambrai road. Their commanders must have reckoned that the British were no longer capable of resisting a determined infantry attack; they were wrong. Great gaps were opened up in their ranks by the last remaining gun that 11th Battery could now bring to bear, by the other remaining guns of XV Brigade and by the guns of XXVIII Brigade. It was a sight that the surviving Yorkshiremen would never forget: to their front at between 1,300–2,400yd German infantry was advancing in four waves, the men in each line being but a pace apart, with 50yd between each wave. It was a target that gunners dream of and one for which the gunners had been waiting; one round was sufficient for the destruction of a platoon of enemy infantry. It was 'like a target at practice camp' and 'each gathering line of Germans was laid low'. Both 123

MAJOR C. A. L. YATE LEADING THE NINETEEN SURVIVORS OF HIS COMPANY IN A CHARGE AT THE BATTLE OF LE CATEAU.

Major 'Cal' Yate leads the KOYLI rearguard survivors in the last charge.

An unknown soldier of the BEF.

and 124 began to run low on ammunition; four of their wagons were on fire and three guns received direct hits. Remarkably, there were no explosions of ammunition in the wagons. An attempt at getting more wagons up, at about midday, had to be abandoned.

For the attackers of the 66 Regiment (13th Brigade, 7th Division, IV Corps) it was the stuff of nightmares; they had to cross 2,000yd of open ground, in view of the British guns, without being able to fire back effectively and with no alternative but to push on, reduce the range, and try to reach dead ground in the Cambrai road. But that lay only 500yd from the all-but-invisible British. The enemy did not come further than the Cambrai road for the time being, where they already had their outpost in the cutting; this outpost of machine guns was far more dangerous to the 14th and 15th Brigades for the moment than the infantry on the slope across the road to the north. But the 66th Regiment was by noon probing for the gaps in the British line, particularly between the Scottish Borderers and the Yorkshiremen, and beginning to add their 1,500 rifles to the volume of fire coming from north of the road. Many of the leading German infantry fired their rifles from the hip as they advanced.

The firing line on the right was reinforced in the late morning by the Argyll and Sutherland Highlanders, ordered forward from reserve near Reumont, who provided much-needed rifles now that there were good targets for them.

German troops on the Marne with rifle grenades; these weapons were not used at Le Cateau.

The guns of 108 Heavy Battery back at Reumont joined in and achieved remarkable accuracy; the *Official History* records the ground being strewn with German killed and wounded and a gunner back at Bertry recalled Lyddite smoke overhanging the Montay spur to the north of the Cambrai road. The machine guns of the KOYLI continued to do wonderful work from their position on the St Quentin road; they seemed to lead a charmed life, as did those of the Suffolks, and the British needed more of them. At this stage on the right and as far west as Inchy the tide of battle was if anything with the British, although to the men in the scrapings it would not have seemed that way.

The 18-pounder field gun, firing fuzed shrapnel, had now come into its own as the main British weapon for killing and wounding exposed troops. Even though in the balmy days of peace gun crews were only allowed one week per year of live firing on the ranges, and their officers spent four days per week on the hunting field, somehow the men and their guns at Le Cateau exulted in being able to find their infantry targets, something that had largely been denied them at Mons. The social gulf between officers and men may have been unbridgeable in the old army of 1914 – as it was in the wider society – but in battle they fought and died together, as of course they always have.

Lt Rory Macleod has given us a vivid account of this early part of the German onslaught:

> We opened fire at about 6.00am and registered a few targets including the railway embankment. When the mist lifted, we saw that the high ground on the opposite side of the valley beyond the embankment [to the east] was crowded with Germans. We opened on them with battery fire 20 seconds [i.e. eighteen shells per minute in three salvoes of six] at 4,000yd, gradually reducing the range as the Germans advanced, and for two hours we kept up battery fire 5 seconds at a range of 2,400yd on the line of the embankment they were trying to cross. They suffered severely.
>
> The German artillery soon opened frontally on the trench in front of us. The fire became hotter and hotter and several 'overs' fell among our batteries. One of our first casualties was Lt Coghlan of 11 Battery on our right. He was killed, and I saw his body being taken to the rear on a stretcher along the back of our position to a sunken lane. We continued to fire at the German infantry. Some of them came within rifle fire of our infantry and were wiped out.
>
> More and more German batteries came into action, a big concentration of them at Rambourlieux Farm which was now visible on our left flank (it had been concealed by the early morning mist) and from there they could enfilade our position. A German aeroplane came overhead about 9.00am and started dropping stuff like streamers of silver paper over our trenches. Whenever he did this the German guns opened up on the spot he was flying over. He came over our brigade and did the same. A ranging round fell near 11 Battery from a German battery enfilading from the left. Salvoes began to fall on 11 Battery, and their casualties started mounting up; we could hear them calling for stretchers, and many shells also fell on 37 Battery on our left knocking out some guns and detachments. We, behind our low ridge, were more fortunate and had only comparatively few shells on the position. Wounded infantry and gunners began to trickle past us on their way back to the dressing station in Reumont.
>
> Our infantry were splendid. They had only scratchings in the ground made with their entrenching tools, which didn't give them much cover, but they stuck it out and returned a good rate of fire. German infantry fired from the hip as they advanced, but the fire was very inaccurate.

The infantry were grateful for the calm professionalism of the gunners who even in the most frantic moments never caused a single premature explosion from faulty fuze-setting.

Lt Roupell, the platoon commander with A Company of the 1st East Surreys, was lying in his shallow trench just back from the Suffolks and the Manchesters, with the KOYLI on his left front, and actually behind the gunners of

52, 37(Howitzers), 80 and 11 Batteries, in the same small patch of ground to the east of the Roman road. The other half of his battalion was on the other side of the Selle valley. The Royal West Kents were to his left. He wrote:

> Got into position about 7.00am, dug 1ft trenches (graves). Had to borrow another man's entrenching tool when he had finished, so did not get a deep trench by 9.00am when the enemy opened fire on us ... A section of artillery just in front of us and a battery on the hill on our right. 'Woolley bears' [i.e. 5.9s] came over with great regularity from 9.00am onwards and we could see the German artillery coming into action on a distant hill in front of us. The battery on our right [probably 11 Battery] got hell and suffered heavy casualties.
>
> Mine was the front platoon of A company so we got a good view. The Suffolks had a bad time on our right front and the A and S Highlanders shared the same fate when they went forward to support the Suffolks.

The remarkable feature of these accounts, written at different times and from different viewpoints, is that they differ only with regard to the timing of the main events, although the gunners seemed to think that the infantry were the targets of the enemy artillery and the infantry thought it was the other way round. Either way it made little difference: the gun lines and the second-line infantry trenches were 100–200yd apart in the XV Brigade area.

Late Morning

At this stage, say until midday, the enemy was being held back, although he was pushing on in strength on two sides, both up the valley to the right and in front up to the Cambrai road, and up the lane from the town. But the tide was to turn all too soon; the German infantry of 1914 was fired with a zeal that was not to be extinguished by losses such as they had already suffered. The gaps in their ranks caused by the earlier RA shelling were 'instantly filled'. Now they were beginning to come on in small parties, using concealed access from the town, and to bring up more machine guns. Major Peebles, now second in command of the Suffolks, later reckoned that the Germans brought up as many as eight more machine guns to the lip of the embanked road from where they had earlier tried to form an infantry firing line. From this range of less than 500yd they swept the forward British trenches with fire; only the trenches on the Suffolks' hill behind the mound were safe from this direct fire, as were the XVth's guns. The British forward positions were quite simply being overwhelmed with fire to which they could not respond in anything like the same measure; of all the machine guns, only the KOYLI guns back at Battalion HQ could fire at the crossroads cutting.

Soon after 11.00am, on the right, Lt-Col H.L. James of the Manchesters, on his own initiative, brought up two companies of his battalion to the firing line of the Suffolks. Not all of the men by any means reached the line; some accounts say less than half. It was at 11.30am that all four companies of the Argylls came up the Roman road to reinforce the British front, making use of a slight valley running parallel to the road. Major Maclean took four platoons of B and C Companies, and went through the corn stubble straight to the Suffolks' front where all were 'annihilated'. The rest of B Company, under Capt Hyslop, joining the right firing line of the Suffolks, faced a terrible storm of fire from the German guns but the 'men of the 93rd advanced through it without a falter' which made Hyslop 'very proud'. It was an action 'beyond all praise', in the words of Major Peebles. A Company went up the slope on the left of the line in support, lost their company commander, were ordered back in error and then went back up again, after Col Moulton-Barrett's intervention. D Company were up with C.

At the time, in fact, Capt Hyslop had serious doubts about the wisdom of his orders to 'reinforce the firing line'. The *Official History* writes that his company came up to the firing line 'on their own initiative'. This was hardly the case. To Hyslop, this seemed 'an extraordinary order'; at 11.30am he was in the relative shelter of the valley, the men had dug some scrapings 'to give them something to do', there were some Manchesters nearby and a number of artillery horses were in a nearby hollow. There were no German infantry visible, although he was getting some casualties from long-range machine-gun fire from the north. It was on the higher ground that the storm of steel was descending and it was on to this ridge that he was now ordered to go. As far as Hyslop could see, a forward move up to the firing line would only expose his men to fire without 'any compensating advantage'. He consulted Major Maclean and his platoon commanders as to how best to obey the order; the result was that the major went north up the valley, through the Suffolk lines, and then straight towards the enemy on the Cambrai road, while Hyslop went to his right, up the slope, through the already shattered shallow gun-pits of 52 Battery and at once received the fire of enemy guns from every direction. He went to ground, the men seeking what shelter they could find; he never saw Major Maclean again. We will never know what was in the minds of Major Maclean and his men as they made their charge, but some at least of his men were taken prisoner with the Suffolks at the end; their testimony is lost. Major Maclean was 'blotted out', in a phrase current at the time and used on the headstones of graves in the Gallipoli peninsula.* All we know is that Maclean chose for himself the longest and most dangerous route to the front line, and then went straight through it and into no man's land from where he never returned. The KOYLI, from only a few hundred yards away, had earlier witnessed an attempt at a counter-attack by the Manchesters into the low ground towards the town, but the ground lay 'strewn with their dead and wounded'.

*'Their glory shall not be blotted out.' Ecclesiastes, Ch.44, v.13.

On the ridge Hyslop found very little shelter, no enemy visible and fire from machine guns and artillery that seemed to come from everywhere. His best sergeant, Maclaren, was killed lying alongside him while they were talking. The Argyll machine guns were knocked out. Some Argylls (A Company) came back from the firing line and went back when ordered to do so. He then witnessed the effect of the heavy guns firing from Reumont on advancing German infantry: they were doing 'excellent work'. During a lull in the artillery fire, and to get out of some troublesome machine-gun fire from the flank, he moved his men a short way down the gentle slope to the east. From this new position, at 1.00pm or so Hyslop could at last direct the fire of his own men onto some good targets: German infantry at 800yd emerging from the town. He checked his fire when a Red Cross flag appeared but it was quite clearly a ruse; who would carry a Red Cross flag into battle in an infantry attack, if not to deceive? Hyslop merely wrote that the Germans went behind a wall and did not re-emerge.

Out of Hyslop's sight, the cavalry 13-pounder guns to the east, in the Selle valley, were also engaging the enemy, as were the big guns of 108 Battery, so at one time or another the enemy on this flank were fired on by every gun in the British armoury.

Lt-Col Moulton-Barrett was at this time at his HQ north of Reumont; both he and Lt-Col James were to bring back the remnants of their battalions at the end of the day. It was Lt-Col Brett of the Suffolks who elected to be up with the fighting companies, and he paid for it with his life, killed early in the day. Two other Lt-Colonels were also killed on this day, Lt-Col A. Dykes of the King's Own and Lt-Col Panter-Downes of the 2nd Royal Irish Regiment. In the KOYLI trenches officers from the second-line support positions rushed forward with small groups of men to reinforce the firing line of A and D companies and to bring up more ammunition; Lt Patterson, promoted to lieutenant on this very morning, was killed in the firing line of D Company, having come up from B Company trenches. A German veteran later recalled of this stage of the attack:

> I did not think it possible that flesh and blood could survive so great an on-slaught. Our men attacked with the utmost determination, but again and again they were driven back by those incomparable soldiers. Regardless of loss, the English artillery came forward to protect their infantrymen and in full view of our own guns kept up a devastating fire.

From the Suffolk trenches, Fred Petch later wrote:

> I was firing away at some Germans trying to creep up a little gully to my right when I was hit by two machine-gun bullets. One ricocheted off the stock of my rifle but the other went through my left hip and out my right leg, which left me pretty much paralysed. There was no way anyone could move me, and I was picked up later that evening by the Germans.

Private Charles Ditcham of the Argylls, a bugler, wrote that,

> ... the company was put in a cornfield and we were told to dig ourselves in. So
> we just made a bit of a hole in the ground with the entrenching tool and then
> took up a position. Then the party started when the Hun came along. It was
> what made me realize what war was about. We just lined up in the cornfield,
> one company on the right, one company on the left, Middlesex and other
> people all mixed up. And these Germans came in their hordes and were just
> shot down. But they still kept coming. There were sufficient of them to shove
> us out of the field eventually. And then the realization what war meant – when
> I saw my company sergeant-major for instance, a fellow called Sim, who was
> wounded in the mouth. He was going back dripping blood. There were vari-
> ous people getting killed and wounded.

Private Ditcham got back to St Quentin on the back of an artillery horse; he
never did blow his bugle.

About 11.30am the Suffolks still had their two Vickers machine guns firing
but at 11.45am the ammunition began to run out – each bandolier of 250 rounds
of .303 ammunition could lay down in thirty seconds the same volume of fire as
a company of infantry, although not with the same accuracy as aimed rifle fire.
The appropriately named Major E.C. Doughty, who had now assumed command of the Suffolks, gathered a small party of men, including the CSM, and
leading them across the bullet-swept stubble, he managed to collect a number
of bandoliers of ammunition from the Manchesters, he himself collapsing from
three wounds just as he reached the gunners with the ammunition. The intrepid
Major Doughty survived to be taken prisoner and was awarded the DSO.

It was now about noon. The heavy German howitzers were taking their
toll, and succeeded in knocking out the last gun still firing in 11 Battery. The
Suffolks and Manchesters, now with the more recently arrived Highlanders,
with the KOYLI on their left, and the two companies of East Surreys just
behind, together with the close-up gunners, had been under fire for six hours
from German infantry, machine-gunners, field guns and the dreaded 5.9in
howitzer, both firing HE. Word passed around the men that First Corps was
coming, or even the French. But it was not to be. Major Peebles thought at
the time that they were being sacrificed as the rearguard for the whole division. There were no friendly troops to be seen on their right and enemy troops
were infiltrating down the valley, but for now keeping their distance. In fact
it was not until about 1.00pm that the enemy was established in strength on
the right flank, infiltrating surprisingly slowly up the Selle valley, troops that
Capt Hyslop was able to fire at as they came up the near side. The *Official
History* confirms that after 10.00am the high ground across the Selle was clear
of British troops (the DCLI and the East Surreys) and the German gunners
and infantry had been able to take advantage.

But the garrison was not to yield until ordered back by Gen Fergusson, and that was still hours away. The line held. Some wounded went back, assisted by their mates, only too happy for a genuine reason to get back, itself no mean feat. Towards the end of the morning the 1st Middlesex, who had been last out of Le Cateau, moved up to the right of the line, a position from which they could bring fire to bear to the east. The other two battalions of the 19th Brigade remained in reserve to the west of Reumont; they were the only division reserve.

But now came some blessed relief which was not of British making: one of those battlefield events, arising out of the inevitable confusion of warfare and exacerbated by the crude nature of battlefield communications: German guns put down a heavy and sustained fire on their troops attacking from the north. It does not seem to have been noticed by any of the men on the knoll, although the KOSB witnessed it from their position; but it is clearly stated in the *Official History*. There was a simple system operating in the German Army whereby troops held up painted screens to indicate their position to their own artillery. But the infantry of two corps and different divisions were muddled up, and III Corps artillery fired on IV Corps troops, not seeing any marking screens. They also could not believe that the infantry could have got so far forward; in any event the German infantry went to ground. The German Army has never published separate casualty figures for Le Cateau (indeed, von Kluck was reticent on Le Cateau in his memoir; both he and French had their separate reasons for a selective memory, but *see* Chapter 7) and we cannot know the full extent of casualties on this occasion but they must have been heavy. At Gerbevillier on 31 August a French reserve regiment fell victim to fire from their own artillery and suffered 'several hundred' casualties.

At noon, which coincided with a lull in the firing, Smith-Dorrien paid a visit to Fergusson at Reumont and they agreed to postpone for the moment the retirement of 5th Division. The brigades to the left of the Scottish Borderers were hardly engaged for this period and could only observe distant movements of troops, but had the satisfaction of seeing them caught by 5th Division gunfire.

By about 1.30pm 11 Battery in the Manchester lines was out of action. 80 had two guns firing, two wagons having reached the firing line from the rear carrying a resupply of ammunition, Major Birley 'giving his orders as if it were an ordinary field day'. 52 Battery, firing in the open, had two flank guns firing and had received three more ammunition wagons. 37 (Howitzers) was still in action as a battery but was out of ammunition, as were the battalion machine guns. But the combined effect of the much reduced and now-ragged salvoes of the batteries kept the enemy from coming across the Cambrai road. The lack of howitzers was very serious: the howitzer, armed with HE, was the only weapon available to engage the machine guns in the cutting at short range, although the field guns had been firing 'at point blank range' (fuze zero) to the east since 10.30am, which was 'disheartening' to the enemy; it could be a very effective short-range weapon against exposed troops. The officer in the OP of 52 Battery (Major Nutt) was still controlling the fire of his battery although shot through the throat; he was only able to whisper his fire orders. His battery by the end of the day achieved the highest expenditure of ammunition in the whole division, at 183 rounds per gun, a remarkable feat of resupply. Two ammunition wagons were on fire in XXVIII Brigade; 122,123 and 124 Batteries (west of the Roman road) all kept firing against infantry attacks from the north-west, albeit at less than half their full strength. 122 Battery alone remained undetected by the enemy artillery, although at the end of the day it was only able to get two guns away.

It was during the frantic action at late morning that one advantage of having the guns up with the infantry was used: some of the Manchesters helped the gunners manhandle the guns to face about and engage the enemy on the right flank. When they had not guns to fire, gunners took the rifles of wounded and dead infantrymen and joined them in their trenches. And the gunners still firing could see what the infantry could see, just like their forebears at Waterloo.

Even the teams and wagon lines of XV Brigade were not safe from the shelling. German artillery, with the luxury of plentiful ammunition and guns, constantly searched for them as far back as Reumont and the teams changed positions to evade the fire. Men and horses were hit. A Royal Engineer major said later that it was 'one of the saddest things I have seen: the wounded horses trying to keep themselves on their legs by leaning against the stooks of corn'. Lt Roupell wrote of this stage of the battle, about 1.30pm:

> We didn't get any good shooting until the Germans got into the Suffolks' position; it was the first time that day that we had seen the enemy close enough to shoot at and I woke up my company to do some firing; before, they had been so tired that a great many of them had been asleep, in spite of the noise of bursting shells. Earlier in the morning we had seen the German column deploying on the far hill and coming down the hill in large square; our 60-pounders made good shooting on these squares and must have caused a number of casualties.

From the KOYLI position the fight for the ridge was watched anxiously for most of the morning, those watching helplessly as the fight went on, seeing it towards the end in the hands of the Germans and then in the hands of the Suffolks, at 500yd it being perfectly possible to tell friend from foe but too far to be confident of shooting without hitting friends. The German machine-gunners in the cutting also held their fire when khaki and field grey from the east flank became too close. The massed enemy to their front was initially a target for the guns of XVIII Brigade rather than the rifles of the Yorkshiremen; but their trial was about to come as the enemy worked their way forward on both sides of them, bringing machine guns up to the Cambrai road directly to their front, the guns that Capt Orford of the Suffolks was able to fire at from his position on the left of the Suffolk line. Von Kluck was using all his arms in the attacks and several different manuals; mass formations reminiscent of Waterloo, and infiltration presaging the attacks of 1918. What he did not attempt, and could not attempt, was an encircling movement so beloved of pre-war war games.

3
The Left Flank: Morning

Von Kluck, as has been said, launched his attack on the British Second Corps by probing forward in the classic manner on the two flanks. The 4th Division held the left of the line around Harcourt and was to hold this position until further orders. They were opposed initially by the German 2nd Cavalry Division plus two light infantry *Jäger* battalions. On the British side, the 12th Brigade was on the left of the line with the 11th on their right, with 10th Brigade around Haucourt. On paper, at least, the two sides were not unevenly matched, to begin with anyway, although as we shall see the Germans had a vast superiority in machine guns.

By 5.00am most of the brigades had got to their fighting positions to the south of the Cambrai road, although not without some hot fire being exchanged on the way with dismounted German cavalry and *Jäger* infantry (who operated as cavalry support). The 1st Rifle Brigade (a historical misnomer; it was in fact a battalion) was acting as outpost for the 11th Brigade south of Beauvois, near Fontaine-au-Pire; they had had two hours sleep in the main street of Fontaine, leaving the deserted houses of the inhabitants unviolated. Before dawn the Riflemen took up a position in the field west of the village* and made out in the mist a body of enemy cavalry and guns moving across the stubble off to their left which they didn't fire on; they were presumably part of von Kluck's flank attack. They could well have been the same cavalry that caused such damage to the King's Own (*see* page 98). The transport was got away at dawn, even as the enemy were pushing down through Beauvois. There was an exchange of shots between the East Lancs under Major Lambert and leading German dismounted cavalry in the streets of Fontaine. The East Lancs were then split into two, both north and south of the ravine, the machine guns being sent back to a hollow in the rear, rather than up in the firing line in the quarry, the position to the south-west of Fontaine; the tactical deployment of these guns reflected a nervousness about their vulnerability

---

*The *Infantry Training Manual* of 1914 decreed that troops should be sited in front of a village to escape artillery fire. Both guns and troops were not to fight from buildings in villages; this remained the Field Training Instruction throughout the next war.

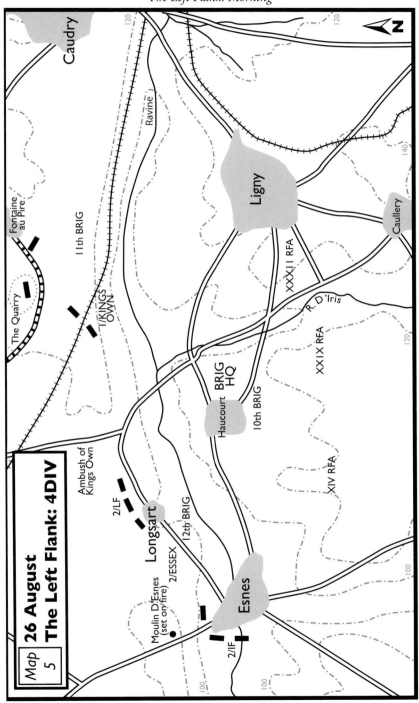

Map 5

26 August
The Left Flank: 4DIV

Caudry

120

120

N

Ravine

140

Ligny

Caullery

The Quarry

Fontaine au Pire

11th BRIG

1/KING'S OWN

XXXII RFA

R. D'Iris

120

XXIX RFA

BRIG HQ

Haucourt

10th BRIG

XIV RFA

Ambush of Kings Own

2/LF

Longsart

12th BRIG

2/ESSEX

Esnes

Moulin D'Esnes (set on fire)

2/IF

100

100

100

rather than exploitation of their fire-power. There was an awareness that the exposed quarry position was only going to be a very temporary forward line. In the event, with the Hampshires on the left and the Somersets on the right, 11th Brigade were to hang on to the position for more than eight hours.

If the 4th Division had the advantage of being relatively fresh, they were still without most of their supporting arms and equipment: what military men call 'impedimenta'. They were lacking their RAMC ambulance support, their signalling engineers, and in particular their own cavalry and cyclists. Their heavy battery was not to arrive at the front until 7 September.

Relying on French cavalry patrols turned out to be a disaster. Soon after dawn on the Haucourt–Cattanieres road, to the west of the quarry position, the Kings Own (Royal Lancaster Regiment) – believing the front to be clear from French reports – were behaving as if they were still in England and were taken by surprise by German cavalry. Things could not have been worse, as the following account from a young officer makes all too clear:

> The battalion was ordered to form close column facing the enemy's direction. Companies were dressed by the right, piled arms and placed equipment at their feet. There was a big stir because some of the arms were out of alignment and the equipment did not in all cases show a true line. A full 7 to 10 minutes was spent in adjusting these errors. The brigade commander [Wilson] rode up to the commanding officer [Dykes] and shortly afterwards we were told to remain where we were, as breakfast would shortly be up. Everyone was very tired and hungry, having had nothing to eat since dinner [lunch] the day before. A remark was passed as regards our safety. My company commander replied the French cavalry were out in front and the enemy could not possibly worry us for at least three hours ... about this time some cavalry, about a troop, rode within 500yd of us, looked at us and trotted off again. I saw their uniforms quite distinctly and mentioned that these were not Frenchmen. I was told not to talk nonsense and reminded that I was very young. It was very early in the morning and nobody felt very talkative, least of all my company commander. The cavalry appeared again in the distance and brought up wheeled vehicles; this was all done very peaceably and exposed to full view. We could now hear the wheeled transport on the cobbled road and a shout went up, 'Here's the cooker!' New life came to the men and mess tins were hurriedly sought. Then came the fire. The field we were in was a cornfield. The corn had been cut. Bullets were mostly about 4ft high, just hitting the top of the cornstooks. Temporary panic ensued. Some tried to reach the valley behind, others chewed the cud. Of those who got up most were hit. The MG fire only lasted about 2 minutes and caused about 400 casualties. The fourth company moving off to the left was caught in columns of fours. Shell-fire now started and did considerable damage to the transport, the cooker being the first vehicle to go.

> The CO was killed by the first burst and the second-in-command rallied the battalion, several of us taking up positions to the right of the point where we had suffered so heavily. An attack was organized at once, we retook our arms and got in most of the wounded. The others were left and taken prisoner later at Harcourt church that night.

The fact that the battalion – now reduced in strength by 40 per cent – was able to fight on throughout the day is remarkable. But this disaster was entirely preventable. The obsession with neatly piled arms was unfortunate when every weapon could be needed at a moment's notice.

On the left flank north of the Warnelle ravine the battle had already started before dawn; or rather there was continuous firing throughout the night as the 12th Brigade moved off from Solesmes, firing that confronted Gen Snow as he toured the outposts with Col Bowes. In fact to Snow it had looked as if the whole countryside around Solesmes was on fire, which he soon discovered was due to the troops lighting fires to dry themselves out and to cook. He found a state of affairs on his tour of Cattenières and Esnes at first light that sorely tested his optimism – he did not get as far as Cattanières because of the battle that was already in progress with the King's Own, with shells landing around his HQ at Haucourt. He found the lack of forward observers put out by the gunners a disastrous continuation of the old peacetime habits; the Germans seemed much more active at daybreak, with their machine guns in particular, while 'our battalions were comparatively slow in getting in to fighting formation', as we have seen with the King's Own; 12th Brigade was only saved from disintegration by the actions of a few officers; and a Capt Allfrey said that he (Snow) had been reported killed. He had no divisional cavalry to guard his flanks, but cheered himself up with the thought that at least the enemy were not expected in large numbers of infantry. He then encountered machine-gunners in rear areas looking for positions to set up their guns; how different from the way the Germans do things, he thought. He was also greatly impressed with German artillery range finding and target spotting. On this subject he wrote:

> At one time I and a good many of my staff were dismounted in the open and our horses were being led about nearby. We were spotted and had fire opened on us very quickly. No damage resulted although the shells were all around us. We galloped away as quickly as possible and were followed by shrapnel till we took refuge in a fold of the ground. Even then the hollow we had disappeared into was searched up and down. The way the Germans picked up targets seemed to me at the time almost uncanny, but really it was because they made use of aeroplanes.

What emerged over the next few hours on this western flank was a battle of movement over ground of several square miles fought by the battalions of 4th

Division, with their supporting artillery, in a way that would be inconceivable during the long years of static trench warfare that followed. Artillery batteries on both sides galloped on and off the field, battalions fired and charged and withdrew and stood again, but the British were able to make an orderly withdrawal at the end of the day. It was in many ways a textbook example of how to carry out a fighting withdrawal; but not entirely, as we shall see.

Still early in the day, about 6.30am, the Germans shifted their attention to their right where they found the 2nd Lancashire Fusiliers and two companies of Inniskilling Fusiliers in their inadequate trenches. The 2nd Essex were hard by, both they and the Lancashires having arrived from their night march only two hours or so before. They were facing north-west at the edge of the British horseshoe, with a good field of fire toward Wambaix, from where the Germans were to mount their attack. It was nothing short of a miracle that they had found their allotted positions in the dark; their first view of the battlefield was at first light. Mounted German cavalry appeared, followed by large numbers of infantry. Six companies of 1914 vintage BEF infantry could easily hold off six battalions of advancing infantry, even under hostile shellfire. But in this case the enemy brought up a large number of machine guns and used this barrage of fire (later estimated at twenty-three guns) to creep away to the left flank and enfilade the Lancashires, with deadly effect. Two batteries of 77mm field guns galloped up and unlimbered 1,200yd from the Lancashire trenches; these fired off all their ammunition and withdrew from the field. One of the Lancashire's two machine guns jammed at once, which was rare for the normally robust Vickers (although it may have been an earlier Maxim). *Jäger* infantry actually got up to the parapet of the Essex trench. Further German attacks built up on the extreme left of the British line at Esnes held by two companies of the Inniskillings, who caught them in a stubble field with no shelter but the stooks. During a lull in the fight an Iniskilling major, with remarkable insouciance, came out to count the enemy dead. He counted forty-seven and calmly walked back to his trench without being fired on. Later in the battle, in the centre, the Dorsets similarly held fire when they saw what they took to be stretchers but were in fact machine gun carts.*

The situation by about 8.45am, after an hour and a half of battle, was that, at a cost, the 12th Brigade had held off the equivalent of a division of German infantry and dismounted cavalry (cavalry divisions are smaller than infantry ones and German cavalry were reluctant infantry). But it was time to think of retirement. Part of the line about the Moulin d'Esnes, which was on fire, the most westerly part of the Corps lines, had been abandoned by 10.00am in

---

*Lt Roupell had earlier witnessed a German soldier taking careful aim and firing on a wounded British officer lying on the ground by the Mons Canal. The officer survived when the bullet ricocheted off his sword.

what was probably a premature move (Gen Snow thought so), although the War Office later wrote that 'it had to be given up'; the men would have agreed. It was not helpful to 11th Brigade on their right, but there was no exploitation of this gap in the line by the Germans. The attacking cavalry and *Jäger* infantry on this left flank had no sheltered concentration area like the town of Le Cateau to the east that had been used to such advantage by III and IV Corps.

The two machine guns of the Lancashire Fusiliers were lost on their way back to Haucourt and the battalion was to be without guns for four weeks. 10th Brigade was in reserve near Haucourt under Brig-Gen Haldane, who used 1st Royal Irish Fusiliers and 2nd Seaforth Highlanders to support 12th Brigade as they came back. The 2nd Dublins and the 1st Warwicks were kept back and formed the rearguard at 6.00pm. Haldane admitted later that communications with his lieutenant-colonels was almost impossible; in this form of mobile warfare the initiative of battalion commanders became paramount. But when the enemy came on they didn't need to be told to fight.

By about 7.00am Brig-Gen H.F.M. Wilson of 12th Brigade had recovered his grip on the battle; at any rate he seems to have recovered from his 'great disorder' at 5.15am (Lt B.L. Montgomery's words, a platoon commander with the 1st Warwicks); he may not even have known about the full seriousness of the disaster to the King's Own, in which he almost became embroiled himself, although German shells fired at the King's Own were landing around Haucourt, wounding an ADC. We must remember that, though they were professional soldiers, almost all of these 4th Division troops were experiencing their first action; Gen Snow had been appalled to discover 12th Brigade troops on outpost on the 25th behaving as if they were still on the Essex marshes.

Lt Bernard Montgomery of the Warwickshire Regiment.

The problem as Wilson saw it was, first, to bring the depleted King's Own on the right of the 12 Brigade line back to the south side of the Warnelle ravine. To cover this movement two companies of the Warwickshires (10th Brigade) were ordered to counter-attack from Harcourt on to the ridge north of Longsart. The 1st Hampshires (11th Brigade) in turn pushed two platoons forward to protect the Warwickshires' right.

The reality of the Warwicks' counter-attack was that it was a suicidal charge up a bullet-swept hill. The needless slaughter of these young men, ordered in to an impossible attack by an incompetent lieutenant-colonel, made a lasting impression on the 27-year-old Montgomery, one that would mould his later generalship. The absolute need for careful preparation in attack to avoid unnecessary loss of life was something that never left him. His later account amplifies the battalion diary, which records a casualty figure of seven officers and forty men for this action:

> Our battalion was deployed in two lines; my company and one other were forward, with the remaining two companies out of sight some 100yd to the rear. The CO galloped up to us forward companies and shouted to us to attack the enemy on the forward hill at once. This was the only order; there was no reconnaissance, no plan, no covering fire ... waving my sword I ran forward in front of my platoon, but unfortunately I had only gone six paces when I tripped over my scabbard, the sword fell from my hand (I hadn't wound that sword strap round my wrist in the approved fashion) and I fell flat on my face on very hard ground. By the time I had picked myself up and rushed after my men I found that most of them had been killed ... Nobody knew what to do so we returned to the original position from which we had begun the attack.

In fact the young Monty found himself one of only two officers left standing in the two companies.

This was by no means the end of the ordeal for the Warwicks. So far they had been ordered to help extricate troops in trouble through no fault of the Warwicks, now they were abandoned to their fate by their CO, Lt-Col Elkington, who promptly took off for St Quentin, to become involved in the infamous surrender debacle.* We will return later to Montgomery's escape from the German envelopment, his 'Retreat from Moscow', as he called it.

At about the time that the 1st Warwicks made their near-suicidal attack, a German battery galloped up to a position a 1,000yd away, south of Catteniers, near the railway station, unlimbered and prepared to fire. The Hampshire officers took the range and ordered fire at 1,500yd. It was a superb piece of long-range marksmanship and the battery swiftly moved off. The

---

*Elkington was an odd man, to say the least. He had had all his hair shaved off before coming to France, and he had told Montgomery that he wouldn't be needing any money while on campaign.

surviving King's Own got back although, as we have seen, at heavy cost to the Warwicks. The Lancashire Fusiliers were helped back by the covering fire of two companies of the Essex, pulling back within full view of German infantry 300yd away. The Inniskillings withdrew with the Essex and the Lancashire Fusiliers, leaving one platoon on the left which remained where it had fought. With not a single man unwounded, this handful of Inniskillings sacrificed themselves for the withdrawal and lay down their arms amid a circle of German dead. The withdrawal of 12th Brigade across the valley to a new line, Ligny–Esnes, was accomplished soon after 10.00am, greatly helped by the gunners of 4th Division RFA. Some of the Essex and Inniskillings went back to collect their wounded at about 3.00pm before coming back to Selvigny at 4.30pm.

The Quarry

All this time the Field Artillery was active in support of 12th Brigade and the more isolated 11th Brigade, which was holding on to the north of the Warnelle ravine in the quarry; they had moved just 100yd or so south into this good position from their earlier exposed position to the west of Fontaine. There also the East Lancashires had been forced back off the northern slope by shell-fire and found temporary shelter on the reverse slope in a sunken lane, which became in effect the reserve trench for the firing line in the quarry. At the quarry 11th Brigade, with, initially, three companies of Hampshires on the left, the 1st Rifle Brigade in the centre and two companies of the Somerset Light Infantry on the right, though heavily shelled, held on and was able to cut down German infantry advancing over the stubble, although after their early enthusiasm the German infantry settled down into a firefight. This position was to be their temporary home until later in the afternoon; it was purely by chance that the landscape afforded them such an advantageous position, although officers had been able to do a reconnoitre at first light. The quarry, although horribly exposed, afforded some cover from its broken ground and to their front an attacking force had no cover at all; in military parlance it was a 'glacis'. The German cavalry did, however, get machine guns into Fontaine, which became more troublesome throughout the day, particularly for the Somersets; that was the price of abandoning the village. Brigade HQ was in the ravine to the south of the firing line.

There was a lull in enemy activity in the late morning, as there was all along the middle of the line, and 12th Brigade on the left looked as if they were about to make a counter-attack. Col Biddulph of the Rifle Brigade was still up with the battalion at this stage and the four brigade colonels met at Hunter-Weston's HQ to decide what to do. Hunter-Weston himself was up in the quarry; he used his horse to get about the field, in fact having two horses shot under him during the day. It seemed the moment for a counter-attack.* Mercifully this was cancelled when the Germans were seen to be in considerable strength; an attack would surely have increased the brigade's casualties beyond the 1,180 it suffered on the day (thirty officers and 1,150 other ranks). A counter-attack seems to contradict all notions of military sense; the Riflemen, with the East Lancs, the Hampshires and the Somersets had a good defensive position; they were holding the enemy off; the enemy were in uncertain number, although obviously numerous.**

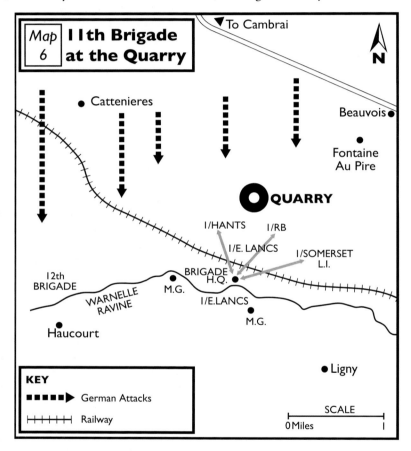

*The relevant section of *Field Service Regulations*, 1909, is of interest here: 'The guiding principle in all delaying action must be that where an enemy has liberty to manoeuvre the passive occupation of a position, however strong, can rarely be justified and always involves the risk of crushing defeat; under these circumstances a delaying force must manoeuvre, so as to force the enemy to deploy as often as possible, but should rarely accept battle.'

**Although there is no denying his personal bravery on this occasion, Hunter-Weston nearly did for the grandfather of this author by his plan of attack in the Dardenelles on 4 June 1915 when commanding 29th Division.

To the great relief of the troops in the sunken lane, German artillery shelled a line of poplar trees behind them for quite a time. But the quarry position was clearly to become untenable very soon, when the enemy superiority in numbers became clear and his artillery started to find the range and location of the Riflemen, and when friendly troops on the right fell back, thereby exposing 11th Brigade to fire from that flank. Earlier in the morning some of the 'other troops' (according to the Rifle Brigade *History*) had left the firing line for the relative shelter of the sunken lane and the quarry line was reinforced by Major Salmon and two captains who led C Company of the RB up to it, through heavy fire, to fill the gap; the 'other troops' holding the flanks of the firing line were clearly not as steady under fire as the Riflemen, but the evacuation of the line 'afforded an opportunity to re-establish the line', in the tactful words of the RB *History*. There C Company stayed until the end of the action, under Capt Prittie.

Throughout the morning 11 Brigade suffered from a lack of close support from their field artillery, XXIX and XXXII RFA Brigades. Brig-Gen Milne had ordered these brigades to position themselves for the close defence of the key village of Ligny, so that as far as the infantry in the quarry were concerned the guns only came into their own when they fell back to Ligny. Before that the gunners were engaged in a prolonged artillery duel that did have the happy result, from the 11 Brigade point of view, of drawing enemy fire onto the batteries rather than the infantry; in fact at one point an infantry brigade major came up to a battery commander and said he was doing just what the infantry wanted. The tactics used here were very different from those employed in 5th Division by Brig-Gen Headlam, but here again the gunners were dependent on direct visual acquisition of targets. The Germans made the error of forming up a battery on the skyline to the north and quickly received an accurate salvo from the howitzers of Lt-Col Battiscombe's battery. Before that 27 and 134 Batteries had used searching fire to try to locate the enemy batteries, which had used up all 27's ammunition; it then withdrew. Officers of 27 Battery also examined the fuzes of enemy shells landing on their position to work out the range of their batteries; there were no forward observers with 11th Brigade in the quarry.

Hunter-Weston was less reticent, at least in private, about naming the wavering troops and his own role in restoring the line. In a letter to his wife, he wrote, 'On three occasions [the Hampshires] retired from their positions and on each occasion by personally leading them forward and explaining to the young soldiers that it was essential they hold this position we were able to maintain the position without due cost.' (quoted in Gardner). It is of course more than possible that both actions happened; the RB restored the line with C Company under Major Salmon and Capt Prittie and the brigadier led back the Hampshires. The Hampshires were indeed fulsome in their praise of the brigadier, saying that on one occasion he intervened to bring back two companies who were counter-attacking to help out 12th Brigade on their left and coming under heavy fire. There is no doubt that the forward company of the Hampshires (D) included some very fine shots, who distinguished themselves by bringing down German machine-gunners and artillerymen at long range, as well as picking out officers with drawn swords. The two companies of the Somersets on the right had gone back to the railway embankment soon after 8.00am, save for one platoon under Lt Taylor, none of whom were present at roll-call that night. A little later in the morning Major Collins of the East Lancs led back his company from the firing line to the embankment, also leaving one platoon behind. Two platoons of D Company, East Lancashires went back up to the left of the quarry line to reinforce the Hampshires soon after noon. These two platoons went back again to the railway and moved along it, 'clearing the scrub through which the enemy were advancing', as if on a rabbit shoot. Major Collins was badly wounded getting back to Ligny and was captured. There was therefore a good deal of movement in and out of the firing line all day, but the three companies of Riflemen in the centre felt rather bereft of support at times. Their fear of losing the machine guns had precluded their use in the front line, and without support from field guns the position rapidly became untenable.

Brig-Gen Hunter-Weston ('Hunter-Bunter' to the troops), who spent the entire day in and out of the firing line (his HQ was in the little railwayman's house by the Arret) later wrote of the heroic stand of the 11th Brigade, and the Riflemen in particular, at the quarry, a position where the right flank of the Rifle Brigade and the Somersets was very much 'in the air', the 7th Brigade being a mile to the east. Caudry itself was fought over in a confusing series of attacks and counter-attacks by the 3rd Worcesters; the battles at Caudry and the quarry were fought entirely separately from each other. In Hunter-Weston's words:

> If this position [the quarry] which was unsupported by the fire of other troops, had been evacuated early in the day, the results of the consequent advance of the German enveloping attack from the north-west [the attack which had hurled the 12th Brigade across the Warnelle Ravine at nine o'clock in the morning] could not have been other than disastrous for the remainder of our army.

Snow wrote later that the Ligny position was the key to the battle as far as he was concerned.

When the Riflemen at last fell back upon the Ligny position, at about 3.00pm, using the church as a rallying point, 'the German infantrymen sprang up from their concealed positions and rushed in pursuit', in the words of the *Official History*. There is no doubt that in this sector at least the German infantry was learning from the disasters they suffered in their earlier massed attacks at Mons; it is inexperienced troops that tend to bunch together for the false sense of protection it offers. At the end three *Jäger* battalions and a cavalry brigade had been held at bay by three shattered companies of British Riflemen. Throughout the day the Riflemen had no dug-in positions: they took advantage of natural cover and folds in the land, as well as the sunken road, to provide positions to fight from. After their initial attack the Germans had held back because 'the deadly rapid fire of the Riflemen was too suggestive of their own machine guns'; in fact the Rifle Brigade guns and the East Lancs guns were the other side of the ravine. At the end, Major Salmon,* who had assumed command, and without orders, realized it was time to go; the enemy had crept up to within 100yd of the Riflemen and were already across the railway on either side. The other 11th Brigade troops were already in the ravine or making their way up to Ligny. Covered by 'five rounds rapid' of the forward C Company under Capt Prittie, they ran back across the lane and down into the ravine; Capt Prittie and the rearguard also got away. Their wounded were left at the quarry in the care of the Medical Officer, Capt F.J. Garland RAMC who became one of the two RB officers captured; the other was Capt G.E. Lane who evaded capture overnight until being captured on the 27th.** The walking wounded were given nips of brandy from the flasks of two RB officers – Capt Morgan-Grenville and Capt Sutton-Nelthorpe – to help them on their way; these two officers 'acted like whippers-in', urging the tired men across the valley and back to Ligny. The RB suffered 35 per cent casualties on the day, the highest in the brigade, but miraculously only one officer was killed: Major Rickman, the second-in-command, who lies buried in a named grave in Fontaine municipal cemetery. This was the old BEF at its best.

In getting back to Ligny the Riflemen, like the rest of 11 Brigade, having got into the dead ground of the ravine, had to sprint up the Ligny slope where they were exposed to the advancing German infantry who had taken up the vacated position and were not far behind. Here, thanks to foresight at division, were two field guns (135 Battery) which fired over open sights at the Germans who were now faced with shrapnel, rifle-fire from the other two Somerset companies and a cavalry machine gun as well as the machine guns of the 1st RB, which had been placed between Ligny and Haucourt. It was too much for them; they faltered, attempted to rally and then went back. Rifleman George Cox said later:

> They came at us in what looked their thousands but despite losing a lot of men
> we managed to hold them off and our gunners, catching them in the open,
> gave them a real pasting.

*Major Salmon's son Hugo also became a Rifle Brigade officer and was killed at El Alamein in October 1942.
**Capt Bloem of the 12th Grenadiers, 1st Army, captured a British doctor on 30 August who had stayed behind to care for his dying colonel; he was not treated as an ordinary prisoner but kept with Bloem's unit until a suitable moment arrived to send him back down the German lines with some wounded British prisoners.

11th Brigade was in possession of Ligny, battered but triumphant. Major Salmon was awarded the DSO for his actions on this day; he had saved the battalion from encirclement and capture. The 1st RB was less fortunate in the next war: it was sacrificed and captured at the defence of Calais on 26 May 1940, along with the 2nd Battalion 60th Rifles and the QVR.

In the dash back to Ligny the Riflemen got split up into two groups and were not reunited until they got back to Noyon two days later. Col Biddulph and about forty men, together with some of the 1st Somersets, had previously retired in a separate group to Walincourt from where Col Biddulph rejoined the main body of his battalion at Ligny; each group thought for a time that they were the sole survivors of the battalion. (Col Biddulph's move to Walincourt with I Company at least ensured that there would be a nucleus of survivors if the battalion was overwhelmed.) The retirement from Ligny, covered by guns, did not start until 5.00pm and was not seriously molested by enemy infantry. Some of the Hampshires, under their CO, stayed in Ligny until 7.00pm. From the Ligny position, 11 Brigade machine-gunners 'did a good deal of shooting' in the direction of Caudry at Germans advancing through the gap, the machine-gunners being among the last to leave; the Hampshire guns, due to a series of mishaps in the gathering gloom, were lost on the way back to the Roman road. The slowness of the Germans to come on through this gap remains a mystery; it could simply be due to the fact that, at the end of an exhausting day, they were fought to a standstill. The British had to get back; the *Jäger* infantry and the dismounted cavalry could rest on their laurels and tend their wounded. But nowhere on this part of the line was the German attack pressed with the same vigour as on the right.

Remarkably, due to what must have been a superhuman effort by the engineers, by midday 4th Division HQ at Harcourt was connected by signal-cable to Bertry. This was all the more impressive because the 4th Division Signal Company RE was still stuck down the railway line with the rest of 4th Division units. The Rifle Brigade *History* merely states that the divisional units had been 'impounded' at St Quentin by order of GHQ; the retreat had priority.

In the centre of the line 3rd Division held everywhere, although villages changed hands and they faced a terrible storm of shell-fire. Both Caudry and Audencourt were subjected to a prolonged attack of HE shells from 5.9in artillery and Caudry was on fire by noon. A British plane flew over the ground to the north of the Cambrai road and the pilot threw some bombs out of the cockpit of his plane at troop and vehicle concentrations; this is the first recorded instance of aerial attack and Major Becke of the RA considered it a 'very proper' action. German infantry got into the village of Inchy at 1.30pm and were promptly shelled by howitzers using HE; they came no further. At 1.00pm Snow got a wire through to Bertry appealing for help in plugging the gap between Caudry and 11th Brigade but no battalions could be spared. But at 2.00pm the retirement order came from Bertry.

4
The Right Flank –
Afternoon

For much of the morning Sir Charles Fergusson, 5th Division's commander, had been pinned to Reumont from where he did at least have a view of parts of the field of battle through his binoculars. Runners came and went. He had seen Sir Horace in person at noon. A little earlier he had ridden out among the bursting shells exhorting the men to stand firm, many considering him lucky to have survived this part of the battle. Some men of the King's Own Scottish Borderers, to the left of the KOYLI, thinking a retirement had started, began to go back but were restrained by their CO, Lt-Col Stephenson, who was later wounded, as well as by Gen Fergusson himself. These men, probably reservists, may have been those later referred to as 'dribbling away'; troops on the right were also seen coming back at around 1.30pm. The reservists in this early period of the war were less amenable to army discipline, both on the march and in the trenches. Earlier, Lt-Col Stephenson had rushed from his trench, with one man, to bring in a wounded gunner, the only surviving officer of a battery that had received a direct hit. In the words of their regimental history, it was a 'most gallant action in full view of the enemy'.

Fergusson knew by 1.00pm that a whole enemy division was working round to his right on the high ground south of Le Cateau and in the valley (actually the 165th Regiment of the 7th Division of IV Corps). In fact the Duke of Cornwall's Light Infantry and two companies of the East Surreys had been doing useful work all morning to the east of the valley, delaying the outflanking movement of the German IV Corps; this fighting would cost the DCLI 10 per cent of their strength. In the confusion of their exit from the town Major J.H.T. Cornish-Bowden of the Cornwalls, with some men, became separated from A and D Companies while B and C Companies made their own separate way back to Reumont under Capt Trelawny. Cornish-Bowden has recorded what must have been a rare instance of bugles being usefully employed on the Western Front:

> How the men under my command became separated from those with the colonel was and remains to this day a mystery. When I received orders to fall back from the first position among the cabbages in the allotment field I carried out

the retirement by successive parties from the right of the line under the fire of those that remained ... Arriving at what seemed to be the crest of a hill we were astonished to find ourselves again under fire. Somebody expressed the opinion that the whistle of the bullets denoted that they were British and that therefore we were under the fire of our own side ... so I ordered the bugler to sound the regimental call. Of course I was unaware at the time that the colonel had resorted to a similar expedient to attract my attention. The fire continued just the same as ever, but the bugle call produced Capt Oliver, who presently appeared on the scene with a considerable number of his company, and also the OC East Surrey Regiment and some men of that regiment. The result was that I had with me the greater part of Capt Romilly's and Capt Olivier's companies.

The clarion call of the bugle brought another visitor to the major. Private Phillips, the CO's groom, came to Cornish-Bowen with the news that the colonel's horse had been hit. He was told to take more care. He then returned with the news that the colonel's spare horse was also hit. He was sent away with a flea in his ear. He returned a third time; 'What is it this time, Private?' 'Beg pardon, sir, but I'm hit myself!'

The East Surreys and the DCLI came back to the main body without any help from the cavalry, who they never saw. Half of A and D Companies of the Argylls, led by Capt Henderson, with some of the Middlesex, were also active in the afternoon in the valley, but were ordered back up to the ridge by the OC Middlesex, Lt-Col Ward (who would be killed near Fromelles in October).

Fergusson knew of the state of his shattered guns and infantry. Finally at 1.20pm he 'suggested' (a rather non-military word but used by the *Official History*) to Smith-Dorrien that he had better begin retiring. Back at the firing line of the guns at about this time, or shortly before, as Lt Rory Macleod of 80 Battery RFA was later to write:

> The German infantry began advancing again, and we shortened our range to 1,200yd and increased our fire. We could see them dropping down, taking shelter behind corn stooks.
>
> We had to go easy now as our ammunition was beginning to run out, so Captain Higgon ordered up three ammunition wagons, one for each section. The first two for the right and centre sections came up and the teams got away, but the team of the wagon for my section got caught up in the brigade telephone wire, which ran through the standing corn behind the battery. We ran to get them out, but the horses were plunging and struggling. Some men ran to them, and tried to unhook them, while I and some others ran to the wagon body to start unloading the ammunition so that we could go on firing. The Germans spotted us and a salvo burst almost on top of us. All the horses and men at the wagon were killed or wounded.

> I was just pulling a shell out of the wagon body when I was hit by shrapnel bullets in the head and arm and knocked to the ground. Several of the rest of the battery came running to help us. Reay Mirrlees put field dressings on my head and arm, and they helped us back into the shallow pits we had dug behind the guns. I think I must have passed out for a short time.

By 1.40pm Smith-Dorrien had responded to Fergusson's 'suggestion'. He ordered the Royal Welch and the Scottish Rifles back to Bertry from where they had been shifted to the west; Fergusson was to begin the withdrawal of 5th Division as soon as he saw fit; 3rd and 4th were to follow in that order; 19th Brigade to go with the 5th Division; the cavalry to find their way west of 4th Division; the divisions to follow broadly parallel roads. (Fergusson himself came out with the rearguard.) But the men in the trenches still had somehow to make good their escape, the most dangerous moment when they had to expose themselves and turn their backs on the enemy. Or stick it out and hope that the enemy would accept their surrender. Many of the lightly wounded had been hit again on their way back to the dressing station in Reumont.

Lt Roupell wrote of what he saw at about this time:

> From one o'clock onwards the situation was distinctly trying [allow for British understatement]. We had only a few troops on our right and these started to retire about 1.30pm. Soon after 2pm we had no one on our right on the ridge which ran at right angles to our line. The men were very worn out and wanted to go but behaved well. At last, much to my relief, Schomberg [a fellow platoon leader] came up from behind and lay down with me in the front line. He told me that as his orderlies had failed to get through to me he had come himself. We saw a number of the A & S Highlanders in trouble, surrounded by Germans, and could not fire for fear of hitting our own men.

By now the German machine guns were up in strength on the sunken road. The British guns, one of which in 123 Battery was being served by the battery commander and his sergeant-major, were being fired at by advancing German infantry. The enemy machine-gunners were not a target that the gunners could with profit engage with shrapnel. Lt Rory Macleod of 80 Battery, just out of the direct fire of the machine guns in the cutting, had now recovered consciousness:

> When No. 3 gun was hit, Mirrlees moved to No. 2 and we now had two guns and eight men left in action firing away as hard as they could go, with salvoes bursting all around them. It was passed down that Hewson had been hit in the shoulder by a shrapnel bullet, but Mirrlees standing up behind No. 2 gun seemed to bear a charmed life. Suddenly someone called out, 'The major's hit!'

About 2.30 pm I saw all the brigade teams racing up at a gallop from the wagon lines led by Major Taylour, the brigade major, and ours by Captain Higgon. Shells were bursting all around them. It was a magnificent sight! Now and again a man or horse or whole team would go down. It was like Balaclava all over again.

All along the line the cry went up, 'Stand fast! Cease fire! You are firing on friends!' Even as the horse teams thundered up to the guns, the firing line over the crest was being rounded up by the Germans. The last guns still capable of being fired, two guns of 52 Battery being served by Capt Starkey and a sergeant, both wounded, got off a couple of last shots: 'the Battery was in its death-throes'.

Lt Hodgson, the signals officer with 122 Battery, has also given us a vivid account of the rescue of the guns, which the *Official History* has called a feat 'that redounds to the eternal honour of the officers and men of the 5th Division artillery':

> The Germans kept moving forward, forward, until they were actually shooting at us with their rifles. Then the order came down, 'Save the guns!' And the gun teams came dashing down, over the hill, right through the middle of all this carnage. And then the Hun opened up on them – artillery, machine guns, rifles, everything! The horses were silhouetted against the skyline and they made a perfect target. It was absolute slaughter! Men and horses were just blown to pieces. One team of four horses and a limber managed to reach one of the guns, limber up and drag it over the high ground behind us. We were still in position, doing what we could, although we were practically cut off by the Hun and we realized our position was hopeless. Our colonel, the adjutant and two battery commanders had been killed, and many of the men, and the place was a shambles. Then, to our intense relief came the order – 'Every man for himself. Destroy the guns.'
>
> I ran to one of the guns and I yelled to Gunner Major, an Irish chap who was the limber gunner. The orthodox way to destroy the guns was to put a round down the muzzle and one in the breech and then fire it from a safe distance by using a lanyard. But there was no time for that. All we could do was smash the sights and remove the breech, which would at least put it out of action. So that's what we did. Major took the breech and we started to run up the hill behind us.

Gunner Major was shot as they ran for safety.* Hodgson retrieved the breach and flung it into the cesspit of a farm. His next instinct was to look for something to eat in the farmhouse. There was nothing.

---

*He was taken back and recovered from his wound. He was killed in December in the Salient.

As the 122 Battery teams, led by Capt R.A. Jones and teams of volunteers, galloped through the trenches of the West Kent, who were 600yd behind the front lines in reserve, the men of Kent stood up and cheered them loudly. When they reached the gun lines Capt Jones and seven others were killed and fifteen were wounded, including Lt Macleod (not to be confused with the Lt Macleod in 80 Battery). Macleod rallied; twenty horses were dead and dying in the teams. With superhuman effort, and with the help of the surviving team, he unhooked the dead lead-horses, hooked in others, got up on the leading horse and galloped away, being wounded again before getting clear of the battery. Two guns were saved, yet he received no medal. What is equally remarkable is that these two guns were in action within an hour or so as part of the rearguard at Honnechy, having found an ammunition wagon belonging to another battery. Twelve rounds were fired at an enemy column, which was driven off.

All the guns that Brigade had to abandon – the sixteen guns of 123, 124 and 122 – were disabled, with their breech blocks removed and their sights smashed, although two guns were already unserviceable having received direct hits. Captain Gillman of 123 fired off the last sixteen rounds on the wagon before disabling his gun and then carried back a wounded KOYLI infantryman. The teams of 124 had been turned back at the sunken road from their attempt to rescue the guns, the sergeant in charge, clearly frustrated, calmly stopping, dismounting and adjusting the girths on the other horses which seemed to his quartermaster's eye to need attention. He turned back reluctantly. The senior officers of 122 and 124 were the last to leave the position; by this time 14th Infantry Brigade had been rolled up, but the enemy were still on the north of the Cambrai road in front of 13th Brigade. It was about 3.00pm. The 15th Infantry Brigade and XXVII Brigade RFA to the left had yet to retire.

Major Hastings of the West Kents, hard up by the Roman road near 108 Battery, was an enthralled witness to all these events. He kept a diary at the time:

> Sometimes we got a spell of machine-gun fire but it was no doubt aimed at something in front. The noise was like a whip being swished backwards and forwards. Fortunately we escaped most of the howitzer fire, which burst beyond us while trying to get the 60-pounders. The ordinary shrapnel from guns did not get into our trenches, but splinters and bullets fell all around us.

During lulls he went around the trenches giving words of encouragement to the men. He could see wounded gunners going back across the road to his right. He had a little sleep and then read the *Daily Mail*. Then:

> We saw the limbers galloping forward to try and get the guns back. One battery galloped past our trench within a few yards. The captain was leading and shouting 'Come on boys!' at the top of his voice. Another lot went forward to

the battery to our right and another passed the left of our trenches, but I did not see the others. After a bit they came back, but it was a sad sight. Very few returned and these had the greatest difficulty in moving the horses. I saw one gun from our right front coming back at a slow walk, dragged by four horses. The two drivers were flogging for their lives, and shells were bursting all over them. A few gunners were hanging on to the limbers and others were struggling back wounded ... There was a good deal of fire, but I could not keep down as it was all so exciting.

Major Hastings was killed on 1 September.

Out of the thirty-eight guns lost at Le Cateau, twenty-five were lost in this part of the field. Bullets were coming through the gun-shields at the end. At the very last, when the German infantry was within 200yd, and being kept at bay by the Manchesters, Captain D. Reynolds with Lt E.G. Earle and Lt W.D. Morgan of 37 Howitzer Battery came galloping down with two teams – all volunteers – to rescue the two remaining guns. British infantry ceased firing, for fear of hitting friends. The distance from the guns to the wagon-teams was 2,000yd. One team was shot down but Capt Reynolds and Drivers Luke and Drain brought one gun safely away; all three were awarded the Victoria Cross. Lt Earle, who was wounded, received the DSO.

CAPTAIN DOUGLAS REYNOLDS AND DRIVERS DRAIN AND LUKE WINNING THE V.C. FOR SAVING A GUN AT LE CATEAU

Capt D. Reynolds rescuing the guns.

Lt H. Clark of the Argylls was a witness to the rescue of the guns of 37 Battery. The gun teams galloped back through his lines, 'just as we had read about in war books of earlier days', and the Highlanders raised a ragged cheer. He noticed,

> ... through the flash and smoke of bursting shell we could see the figure of an officer taking the necessary steps to render the remaining guns unserviceable before moving quietly to the rear to rejoin the remnants of his battery.

One young gunnery officer, Lt Lionel Lutyens, got away on a horse and as he galloped away looked back to see,

> ... an extraordinary sight, a wild scene of galloping and falling horses, then everyone gone, dead horses and dead men everywhere, four guns left solitary on the position [122 Battery], a few wagon limbers lying about, and one standing on the skyline with its pole straight up in the air. *Voila tout.*

The scene was now set for the final acts of heroic defiance. At about 2.45pm the Germans sprang up from the Cambrai road and other points on the right flank and fell upon the Suffolks, the Manchesters and the Argylls from three sides. The Suffolks in the firing line had already been overwhelmed. The officers urged the men to keep firing, two officers of the Highlanders, Capt Maclean and Capt Bruce, in particular counting out the score of field grey targets they were hitting; Bruce (a direct descendent of the Scottish patriot) was killed but Maclean survived.* The Germans attempted to induce the British to surrender by blowing the British cease-fire notes on their bugles. (At the other end of the British line, in front of the Somerset Light Infantry, a white flag was waved in an attempt to induce a surrender; the Germans were fired on.) In the end, all the survivors were overwhelmed and their surrender was accepted. They had fought to the last, covering themselves with undying glory on what a later poet has called the 'fields of praise'. It had been the emergence of the enemy in their right rear that had made it impossible for the Suffolks and Argylls to get away. When the surviving Suffolks and the triumphant Germans were all mixed up, German planes flew over dropping smoke markers to tell their gunners to cease fire or lengthen their range. Major Peebles wrote later that 'with the exception of some wounded and stretcher-bearers, no-one of the 2nd left the trenches after the action began nine hours before'. There are those today who still call this spot 'Suffolk Hill'.

---

*There were three Macleans amongst the officers of the Argylls: Major A.H. Maclean of C Company who was killed, Capt A.J.H. Maclean, firing to the end (POW) and Lt A.K. Maclean (killed).

BEF dead 1914, precise location unknown

Just a few moments before, Lt Roupell had given the order to his platoon to retire and:

> The whole battlefield appeared to be alive with running men and the enemy opened up with every gun at his disposal. A great deal of shrapnel burst over us and practically every man in my company was hit, but very few were wounded. The shrapnel pellets were very ineffective and bounced off us. One pellet hit my cap at the back and my cap shot off in front; I picked it up as I went on. Torrens [the company commander] fell into a ditch but was not hurt. I caught up Jimmy Tew and we went on together for a bit. When we got to the outskirts of a village [Reumont], a staff officer stopped me and told me to collect some men and hold the front edge of the village, as it was anticipated that the enemy cavalry would follow us, and in that case anything might have happened.
>
> I stopped the next twenty men that came along; they belonged to all sorts of regiments, and we lay down on either side of the road and let the rest go through, a streaming mass with no formation, no orders, no idea where they were going to or where their units were.
>
> When no one else was in sight we waited a few minutes longer and then joined in at the rear of the column.

At about 3.00pm when the surviving infantry, including Lt Roupell, were running for their lives, 61 Howitzer Battery back toward Reumont fired off all its ammunition on the advancing German hordes, which were now in an attacking line eight deep. It was using Lyddite which had the 'happiest results' on the enemy. It was ordered to retire, picking up two wagons of ammunition, which had been ordered up to 37 Battery, on the way. One of the two 60-pounders got a lucky Lyddite shot at crowded German infantry at 3,200yd, and then trotted out of the action.

At roll-call in St Quentin the next morning 111 men and two officers of the 2nd Suffolks reported, most of them non-combatants from the transport lines, including a number of footsore men who had been left with the transport. There were about 500 officers and men taken prisoner, many of them wounded. Eighty men and officers were killed on the knoll of ground on which they fought. At the end of the day the survivors were taken into Le Cateau, the men and officers were separated and the officers were asked to give their word that they would not attempt to escape; they refused. They were then told that if only one officer attempted escape the rest would be shot. By the evening of the 28th, however, more men drifted back in, swelling the remnant to 229, which now became a company of the 1st East Surreys; they later became GHQ troops. Their total casualties at the battle were 720. The senior surviving officer was a junior officer, Lt N.B. Oakes.

The 2nd Manchesters losses were four officers killed, wounded and captured, including their doctor, Capt C. Morley RAMC* and 350 of their men. The Argylls were much scattered and indeed were not reunited until 5 September but the reckoning was 160 killed or wounded and 300 officially missing. Of the eleven officers missing only two were taken into prison unhurt; eight were killed. Lt Stirling of the Argylls Machine Gun Section, wounded in four places, was carried back by Capt Hyslop himself, with others, to the temporary hospital in Reumont Church. The Germans took prisoner all the wounded lying there who the RAMC had been unable to move again; one doctor remained behind. Lt Stirling recovered from his wounds in prison.

It was Capt Hyslop, who had been so reluctant to go up to the forward slope, who had directed the fire of his company at the moment the enemy appeared on his front and who at the end, being the senior officer left standing, had brought them out. He did not leave the knoll until 5.00pm according to his own account, although this seems later than one would expect; it is almost two hours later than the pell-mell escape of the other troops to his north on the knoll. In fact his account of how he made good his escape smacks slightly of British understatement. He merely says that 'we were becoming distinctly isolated ... I determined therefore to withdraw to a spur running north-east from Reumont and where I still saw some troops'. Perhaps the Germans somehow overlooked his band of less than 100 men; he was, after all, well

---

*The frequency with which MOs were captured with the fighting troops shows that that is where they saw their place.

back from the front line of the Suffolks at this stage, having come back from the high ground of the knoll at 1.00pm to a point where he had a good field of fire to the east and north-east. His subaltern, Henry Clark, confirmed the time of their withdrawal in his memoir, writing that:

> … touch had been lost with the forward platoons of B and C Companies, which had disappeared in the smoke of the battle as though swallowed up in a London fog, nor could reconnaissance parties make contact with them … the CO now decided to commence our withdrawal, it being evident that the lost platoons had been overwhelmed in the German advance.

Before leaving their outpost they had a satisfactory shoot against some marching German troops on the far side of the valley, at extreme range of 1,000yd. E and L Batteries of the RHA were in action in the valley to the south. None of Major Maclean's party was ever seen again; the artillery horses in their hollow in the valley had long since bolted.

The KOYLI up by the Cambrai Road had stood alone, or rather five platoons had stood alone at the end. The rest of the battalion had either got away, were dead or otherwise *hors de combat*; officers had got word to their men in the forward positions that they could take their chance of getting back to the column. Many made the attempt but only a few got through to bring back their evidence of what had taken place in the trenches in the last phase of the action. Those still in the trenches responded to the British cease-fire notes played on the German bugles by bursts of fire. At the end, about 4.30pm, in the words of his VC citation:

> Major Charles Allix Lavington Yate (deceased), 2nd Battalion The Kings Own Yorkshire Light Infantry, commanded one of the two companies that remained to the end in the trenches at Le Cateau on August 26, and when all other officers were killed or wounded and ammunition exhausted, led his nineteen survivors against the enemy in a bayonet charge in which he was severely wounded. He was picked up by the enemy and he subsequently died as a prisoner of war.

One of Major Yate's NCOs, Fred Atkinson, recorded later of how when the Germans were coming on 'shoulder to shoulder', he was unable to work the bolt of his rifle, so hot had it become. At the end he prayed to God for 'wisdom, guidance and protection' and told his men, 'we may as well die charging', but was spared from death, living to an old age. He received no medal.

At the end the Germans were on all sides and the struggle was soon over. As a KOYLI officer later wrote, 'To the honour of the German soldier most of the unwounded were made prisoners and the wounded were respected.' The *Regimental History* declares with pride, 'There was no surrender. The occupants of the trenches were mobbed and swamped by the rising tide of grey-coated Germans.'

In fact the circumstances of Yate's death remain a mystery. He appears to have recovered from his wounds while in prison. He then escaped and was found near Berlin in 1917 with his throat cut. He was a vicar's son. Over the years there have been appeals for information that might throw light on his death.

Before the final sacrifice of Major Yate's band of Yorkshiremen, Corporal Holmes carried a wounded man to safety for almost a mile (1.5km), then went back to rescue a gun team with its gun, which he found all limbered up but with its detachment all killed. He was helped, at first by a trumpeter, but then brought the team out single-handed. He too was awarded the VC; he survived the war and died in 1969.

The survivors of his battalion mustered 320 men and eight officers at roll-call that night, a loss of 600 men, of whom 310 were later reported to be prisoners in Germany. The last stand of Major Yate's men had without doubt given the rest of 5th Division a clear start in their retirement. The position had been attacked by nine German regiments. Fifteen of their officers were captured, nearly all wounded, including their Colonel, R.C. Bond,* Major 'CAL' Yate and Capt K.R. Keppel, who had been with Major Yate at the end. This very high proportion of dead to wounded, almost 50 per cent, is accounted for, in Col Bond's view, by those men reinforcing the front trenches or changing position over the open, bullet-swept ground, who when wounded 'continued to suffer from a rain of bullets until they died'. More than three times as many of the Yorkshiremen had died than the Suffolks, which must be due to the contour of the land. On the knoll where the Suffolks stood all day the slight slope meant that only the forward part of the position was exposed to the German machine-gun fire from the Cambrai road cutting; the whole of the KOYLI was exposed. The likelihood is that the Suffolks in the forward trenches were killed in the same proportion as the Yorkshiremen. But both positions were equally exposed to artillery fire.

To the left of the KOYLI the Scottish Borderers received their orders to retire at 3.00pm but their furthest outpost, C Company, were out of sight and held on until the last, only one platoon under Lt Harvey getting away. The rest of the battalion made towards Maurois, getting shelled along the way. A Company made a stand at the lone Tree for an hour, keeping the enemy away. It was at this point that Col Stephenson was wounded. He would have been got away but for a disgraceful act. There was an ambulance in the sunken lane, not far from the Tree, but its horse team had been stolen by French

*He wrote the history of the regiment.

civilians; the Frenchmen had been seen unyoking the horses while the driver was attending to the wounded. The colonel and six other wounded were put into the horseless ambulance and an attempt was made to manhandle it away to the Roman road. It was not possible; German cavalry were upon them and the ambulance team only just managed to get away. The wounded were taken prisoner. Another officer taken prisoner at this time was Lt Sherwin of B Company who, as the KOSB *History* reported,

> ... was made unconscious and delirious by the close passage of a shell. On coming round, a confused idea that a medical armlet might help him to escape, induced him to put one on. This might have earned him a bullet, but the Germans took the sensible view that he was not in his sound senses.

5

The Centre and Left

On the left of the 5th Division line, which followed the line of the Cambrai road, that is to say around the right centre of the BEF line, was the 15th Brigade with the Bedfordshire and the Dorsets up in the firing line. Troisvilles was to their west where 3rd Div took up the line. The Bedfords and the Dorsets were between the sunken lane and the Cambrai road. Their position was a good one; the Cambrai road 600yd to their front was exposed and offered no shelter to the enemy except for one small wayside house. The lack of natural features on most of the road in the 3rd Div area explains why it was not chosen as a place to fight from by the British. Its prominence in the landscape in any case made it a highly visible target for enemy gunners, and it was best avoided. The ridge to the south of the road, running east-west, with the Warnelle Ravine behind it, and the lanes linking the villages forming natural shelters, combined with the obvious fact that being in the middle of the line meant that the division did not have to worry about its flanks, all combined to make the ground a good position to fight from. The problem was the villages; once infiltrated by the enemy it would be difficult to prevent him getting on to the ridge and once in the villages he would have some protection from shrapnel. There was no time to prepare the villages for defence.

The 1st Beds had bivouacked east of Troisvilles overnight, having been in the van of 5th Division and had arrived on the battlefield at 3.30pm on the 25th. They had a meal, watched three brigade of French cavalry ride west, improved their trenches, and expected to form a rearguard the next morning and resume the retreat. It was not until 9.00am on the 26th that they learned from a staff officer that there was to be no retirement; Lt Davenport overheard him say to the adjutant that they were to be sacrificed to save First Corps. A battery of field guns (121) then unlimbered 250yd behind his trench and he knew that they were going to be in for a hot time – which they were. When the order finally came to fall back, the men perforce came back in gradual driblets and bit by bit. The grass on the crest of the sunken lane was being cut by machine gun bullets 'just as if by a mowing machine'. Most of the men got back to the sunken lane, but their ordeal was far from over. It was a long way back to the Roman road and longer still before they could sleep.

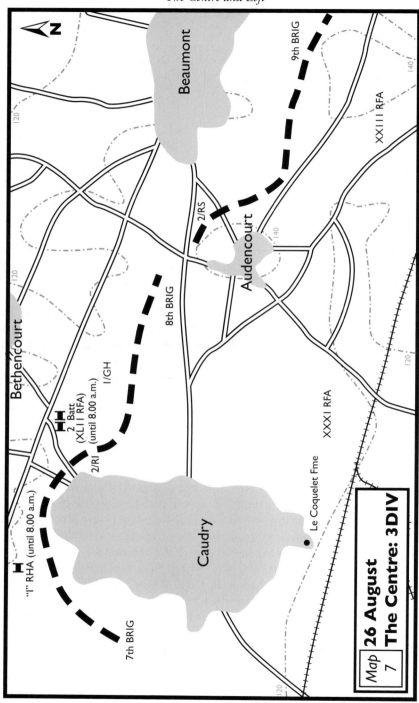

Map 7 — 26 August — The Centre: 3DIV

15th Brigade's experience of fighting in the afternoon, in a prolonged south-east movement toward the St Quentin road, is a good example of infantry and gunners working together. Around noon the Dorsets had a successful shoot against some German machine guns on the Cambrai road – the ones that at first they thought were stretchers. Later both battalions, before breaking off the action, together with their supporting XXVII Brigade RFA, kept up such a hot fire on an enemy formation emerging in regiment strength from Rambourlieux Farm that the enemy came on no further. So far they had not been bothered unduly by the artillery of the German III Division.

The 15th Brigade received their retreat order at about 3.00pm. 119 Battery RFA was the first to go, moving back to just south of the lone Tree in the sunken road. The next to go was 121 Battery together with the bulk of the two battalions, using the two machine guns of the Dorsets to cover them. They went back to Troisvilles where they faced about to the enemy. The German artillery took note of all these manoeuvres and put down heavy fire on Troisvilles, firing from the north and north-east. They put down what would later be called a box barrage to the south of the village, guided by a German spotter plane dropping smoke signals. In the event the Bedfords and Dorsets, together with most of the Scottish Borderers and collecting the rump of the Cheshires on their way, split up into small parties and made their way across country to the St Quentin road between Reumont and Maurois. The 15th Brigade entered the Roman road more or less as a formed body at about 4.30pm, which is a staff officer's dream, the Dorsets coming in last, reaching the road at about 6.30pm. They joined the mass of men and vehicles on the long, weary march of 15 miles (24km) to St Quentin. It soon began to rain. At 11.00pm the Dorsets found a sugar refinery, bedded down and had 'four hours blessed rest'.

Soon after dawn, further to the west, north of Caudry, two batteries of XLII Brigade RFA had established themselves right on the Cambrai road verge, from where they were able to beat off the first attacks of the morning, in support of 7th Infantry Brigade. Here they were perhaps unwittingly following the tactics of Brig Headlam of 5th Division by being up with the infantry; they soon realized that this exposed position was going to avail them nothing. Mounted orderlies appeared thankfully from the commander RA with orders to pull back, which they did at about 8.00am. They had been joined in their early morning shoot by two guns of the RHA (I Battery), firing at exposed infantry to the north-west, which they successfully drove off after twenty shots. The cavalry guns then made off in the direction of Montigny; its 'brief intervention had been as valuable as it was timely'.

By this time the situation to the north of Caudry was critical and it was tacitly agreed that the north of Caudry was not defensible. Both sides in the centre had the greatest difficulty locating each others' gun positions; the German planes were not active here, apart from one that located the Heavy Battery, which thankfully received no direct hits. Even so, the commander of XLII Battery was already learning to be wary of planes; he concealed the battery on the edge of a copse while reconnoitring near Caudry.

Earlier, at Brig-Gen Count Gleichen's* 15th Brigade HQ in the sunken lane near Troisvilles, the veterinary officer had helped out with the crush of wounded coming in, most suffering from shrapnel wounds:

> One man I remember lying across a pony; I took him for a Frenchman for his trousers were drenched in blood, and not a patch of khaki showing. Another man had the whole of the back of his thigh torn away; yet after being bandaged he hobbled gaily off, smoking a pipe ... One would see men apparently at their last gasp with gruesome wounds on them and no more stretchers available, and yet within five minutes they had disappeared.

The vet speculated that the more serious cases were less movable and so tended not to be brought in to the aid post. We could speculate that the urgency of even badly wounded men to return to their units is indicative of extremely high morale.

Coming out south-east to the Roman road, Count Gleichen's brigade staff were shelled by shrapnel, 'which seemed to do extraordinarily little damage ... again and again, why none of this shrapnel hit us was most extraordinary; there we were, seven or eight of us mounted and close together and the shells bursting beautifully with terrific and damnable cracks – yet not one of the brigade staff was touched.' Smith-Dorrien later wrote of Gleichen 'He is quite undisturbed by the heaviest shell-fire.'

To the left of 15th Brigade, in the 3rd Division ground, was the 9th Brigade whose Brigadier, F.C. Shaw, received the retreat order at 3.30pm. He, too, brought his battalions out in succession, covered by the field artillery. Curiously, and the *Official History* makes no critical judgement, both 107 and 108 Batteries disabled and abandoned their guns, having fired off all 1,200 rounds of ammunition. Major Becke merely says that it was impossible to withdraw them; but they had achieved wonderful results from their forward entrenched positions with their shoot against enemy formations emerging from Inchy. The enemy had made the mistake of massing his troops; earlier, north of Inchy, he had attacked in what the British call 'artillery formation'. When he got his troops into Inchy, which the 1st Lincolns had abandoned soon after dawn, he was unable to get out, with the gunners (107 and 108 Batteries) and 9th Brigade infantry firing on all the exit points. The village itself was shelled with HE by 65 Battery. As elsewhere the British chose not to

---

*Gleichen was the only son of Prince Victor of Hohenlohe-Langenburg (1833–91), the fashionable sculptor and artist, who was also an admiral in the Royal Navy.

fight in the villages; Inchy was in any case indefensible, being forward of the British line. Gen Snow himself had earlier witnessed the guns in action to the west of this brigade:

> I was watching one of our batteries near Caudry. It was under fire from some twelve guns. The enemy were firing salvoes and each salvo looked as if it must have annihilated our battery. Directly, however, the last shell burst, BANG BANG went the guns of the battery and you could see lanes being driven through the dense masses advancing on Ligny. Nothing could shake the defence of Ligny, whose garrison mowed down the attacking Germans in thousands.

He was referring to the retirement to Ligny of 11th Brigade, covered by XXXII Brigade RFA.

In the Caudry area the *Official History* admits to some confusion; to the men on the ground that is the normal state of events. Private Roe of the East Lancs, to the west of Caudry, as we know marched in the dark back from Solesmes; he sat in a hole in the ground, got fired at, moved forward, moved back, got shelled, was told to retreat, went up a hill, and never knew that he'd been in the biggest British battle since Waterloo; to him it was all part of the Retreat and it was not his job to know about strategic withdrawals or rows between his corps commander and his field marshal. All he knew was that a religious keepsake given to him by an old lady in Le Cateau was keeping him out of harm's way. Lt Johnston, a signals officer of the 3rd Worcesters, was still in doubt at 9.00am whether or not his battalion was to make a stand in Caudry.

We must remember that this was not a battle to hold or take ground; it was everywhere a battle where the British were trying to extricate themselves while at the same time dealing a stopping blow to the enemy. It has often been said that the British Army is better at dogged defence than operations where attacking flair is required and this would seem to be the case on 26 August 1914, although the defence and evacuation of northern Caudry was not exactly dogged. The Worcesters' *History* put it thus:

> In falling back from the northern to the southern side of the town several units became disordered and there were many stragglers. Lt Johnston rallied stragglers of all units in the main square of the town, organizing them hastily as a fighting force, and led them out to a new position on a spur to the westward.

Lt Johnson was later wounded in several parts of his body and was taken at the end of the action by ambulance back to a dressing station, an evacuation he only allowed after ensuring that all the other wounded had been got away. His account of fighting in Caudry itself and in the fields outside the town is another quite remarkable piece of military literature to come out of this day, and it is quoted extensively in Cave and Sheldon's book.

The day had started badly for Johnston. Up before dawn in the town, he could find only half his men, his sergeant was still missing from the day before, the section cart and his personal kit were God knows where, his horse and groom were gone and 'in spite of the crush in the town nothing much seemed to be doing and as far as one could see no arrangements made for settling on a scheme for defence ... There were a lot of men making their way back in a disgraceful manner, even NCOs.' The gunners somehow had to get out of the streets and into firing positions. Transport men were muddled up with the infantry, who were from several regiments. Everything was blocked with civilians making it as bad as at Solesmes where the confusion had been 'appalling'. It was not clear whether the retirement order was still in force; it became an academic matter anyway. The 2nd Royal Irish, who Johnston had been detailed to locate, still seemed to be lost somewhere between Solesmes and Caudry. The Germans 'were coming on quick all round us'; it is not surprising that there was confusion. The Germans were showing a remarkable ability to deploy all their arms, cavalry, guns and infantry, and to get them into action at first light. The Worcesters on the north of the town had 'slackened off their digging and were dozing over their rifles' when the enemy field guns opened fire close at hand. Two RFA field guns appeared from the town and returned fire, according to Johnston, although these were more likely to have been XLII Battery, which had been there since 5.30am.

The professionalism of the old BEF asserted itself; transport men were put into the line together with Johnston's section of signallers; Johnston issued ammunition; the quartermaster of the 1st Wilts formed a line on the outskirts of the buildings. But the Germans 'showed no inclination to assault', relying on their ample howitzers to do the work of forcing the British from the town, which is more or less what happened. Johnston moved out to a field of turnips, was machine-gunned, moved back into the town and moved back out to the south under direct orders from Gen Hamilton; by the time he got into the ambulance he had pieces of shrapnel and spent bullets in his battledress and a chunk taken out of his leg. He had been fired at by rifle, by machine gun and by artillery. His only bit of luck was finding his horse, which had bolted with the groom. He still thought 'I feel that we ought to have stuck on to the town somehow, although of course one does not know what is happening elsewhere.'

At about 2.00pm, in the centre, when Gen Fergusson was contemplating withdrawal on the British right, von Kluck brought up fresh infantry and simultaneously started shelling Caudry again, with heavy 5.9in howitzers. German infantry also attacked the Royal Scots and Gordon Highlanders of 8th Brigade, 3rd Division just north and west of Audencourt. The battle this day was very much more than a battle for the flanks; von Kluck had enough troops, both cavalry and infantry, to be strong everywhere.

Brig-Gen McCracken of 7th Brigade was an early casualty of the shelling of Caudry when he was stunned and his brigade major wounded by a heavy shell. The 3rd Worcesters HQ in Caudry was also hit; Gen Hamilton was up in Caudry and was lucky to survive a near-miss. McCracken was heard to mutter before he passed out 'we must retire', or words to that effect. Caudry was evacuated and German infantry moved in. The 3rd Worcesters' CO, Col Stuart, had been away from his HQ when it was shelled. He now re-occupied the southern part of the town in a counter-attack, the bayonet being put to its purpose. The guns of Third Division fired all their initial allocation of shells in support of the infantry in the Caudry/Audencourt/Inchy sector, and then fired off all the ammunition brought up in replenishment.

At 3.00pm Gen Hamilton rode out again from Bertry and found Lt-Col W.D. Bird of the Irish Rifles. He put him in command of 7th Brigade since Brig McCracken was still knocked out, and ordered him to get the remaining troops out of Caudry (there was confusion over what troops were in the town) and the whole brigade out on the road south. 7th Brigade came out in tandem, as it were, with part of 8th Brigade. The Royal Scots and Gordon Highlanders stayed behind, doing great execution as rearguard at about 5.00pm: one subaltern of the Royal Scots reckoned he hit thirty or forty enemy at a range of 400–600yd. Col Bird was among the last to leave the position, coming out on the road to Montigny at about 5.00pm. The bulk of the Gordons and two companies of the Royal Irish, with some Royal Scots, having received no orders to move, remained in their positions. The *Official History* records that this rearguard made the impression on the advancing Germans that they were much stronger in men and machine guns than they actually were. The guns had gone, but for more than an hour the German infantry, using a field of beetroot as cover, 'swayed backwards and forwards, completely at a loss how to clear them [the Gordons] out of the way'. The Germans were to become the masters of the fighting retreat in August–November 1918, but today the Gordons unquestionably saved the retreat in the Caudry/Audencourt area; the Worcesters counterattack also had the effect of keeping the Germans paralyzed.

Lt Johnston, realizing that if he stayed in the dressing station he would become a prisoner, there being no ambulances left, became part of the trail of walking wounded back to the Roman road, which they reached at midnight, 'thoroughly dead beat having been fighting and marching all day without any food whatever'. Although he doesn't mention it in his diary, he must have led his horse along, because he rode part of the way along the road to Noyon. The 3rd Worcesters suffered an incredibly light 100 casualties. What is clear, again, is that British troops were not at this time fighting well in the towns; the German HE fire was very unnerving and a firing line was difficult to form. But there was exceptional leadership from Gen Hamilton himself, Col Stuart, Lt Johnson and his friend Lt E. De Salis (later Lt-Col, 9th Worcesters).

The Gordons' action east of Caudry is the subject of Lt M.V. Hay's memoir, which is not only a valuable source, but also a remarkable addition to the literature of war. The battalion was 350yd south of the Cambrai road and a series of range marks were established by the range-finders for sighting the Lee-Enfields. To their front was the village of Bethencourt, at 900yd across the Roman road. To the right front was a line of telegraph poles at 1,200yd, extreme range for a rifle. The road to the front had an embankment that the enemy were to make use of, in a way similar to the one opposite the Suffolks near Le Cateau. The British gunners opened up early in the morning with ranging shots at Bethencourt, whose church was suspected of harbouring German artillery spotters. Hay wrote:

> At the corner of the village of Bethencourt there stands (or stood that morning) a farmhouse. In the adjacent paddock two cows were peacefully browsing. The first shell burst right above them. They plunged and kicked and galloped about, but soon settled down again to graze. Several shells hit the church tower; the fifth or sixth set fire to a large, square, white house near the church on the right. Our gunners made good practice at the two cows and shell after shell burst over or near their paddock, from which they finally escaped to gallop clumsily along the ridge of the hill and disappear into the wood, no doubt carrying bits of shrapnel with them.
>
> About 9.00am the German artillery got to work. Many attempts have been made to describe the situation in a trench when an artillery duel is in progress, but really no words can give any idea of the intensity of the confusion. On both our flanks machine guns maintained a steady staccato. All other sounds were sudden and nerve-straining, especially the sudden rush of the large German shell followed by the roar of its explosion in Audencourt, where dust and debris rose up like smoke from a volcano, showing the enemy that the target had been hit.

Earlier, Lt Johnston had described the experience of being under rifle fire for the first time, an experience that had been a novel one for most of the BEF since the 23rd: 'It is not as bad as one expected, one just realizes that the bullet has just missed one.' Lt Hay continued:

> The Huns evidently suspected that the little wood on our right rear was being used to conceal artillery, for they dropped dozens of shells into it, doing no harm to anything except the trees. The noise of the shells bursting among the branches just behind us was most disturbing. Sometimes these shells pitched short of the wood; they were then less noisy but far more unpleasant in other respects. Just when the uproar was at its highest a scared face appeared over the back of my

trench and stated that four ammunition boxes lay at the far corner of the wood at our disposal please. The owner of the face, having delivered his message, rose up and returned whence he had come, doubled up yet running at great speed.

Gradually the number of our own shells grew less and less as our batteries were silenced or forced, or perhaps ordered, to retire. As this went on it became evident – far more evident than at Mons – that we were up against overwhelming odds. The rush of shells reached a maximum, and then for a short space there was silence. Pipes and cigarettes, up to now smoked only by the fearless ones, for a short time appeared on every side, and conversational remarks were shouted from one trench to another.

The lull was only short-lived. A spotter plane appeared and the German gunnery improved its accuracy, supporting an infantry attack.

It was not long before we had the chance of getting rid of some ammunition. German troops, debouching from the little wood where the cows had taken refuge earlier in the day, now advanced across the stubble field on top of the hill, moving to their left flank across our front. My glasses showed that they were extended to not more than two paces, keeping a very bad line, evidently very weary and marching in the hot sun with manifest disgust.

The command 'Five rounds rapid at the stubble field, 900yd', produced a cinematic picture in my field glasses. The Germans hopped into cover like rabbits. Some threw themselves flat behind the corn stooks and when the firing ceased got up and bolted back to the wood. Two or three who had also appeared to fling themselves down remained motionless.

The enemy, having discovered that we could be dangerous at even 900yd, then successfully crossed the stubble field in two short rushes without losing a man, and reinforced their men who were advancing through the beetroot fields on our right.

Great numbers of troops now began to appear on the ridge between Bethencourt and the little wood. They advanced in three or four lines of sections of ten or fifteen men extended to two paces. Their line of advance was directed on to the village of Audencourt and on to the low plateau on our right, so that we were able to pour on them an enfilade fire. They were advancing in short rushes across pasture-land which provided no cover whatever, and they offered a clearly visible target even when lying down. Although our men were nearly all first-class shots, they did not often hit the target. This was owing to the unpleasant fact that the German gunners kept up a steady stream of shrapnel which burst just in front of our trenches and broke over the top like a wave. Shooting at the enemy had to be timed by the bursting shell.

We adopted the plan of firing two rounds and then ducking down at intervals, which were determined as far as could be arranged by the arrival of the shell. But the shooting of the battalion was good enough to delay the enemy's advance. From the 900yd mark they took more than an hour to reach their first objective, which was the *Route Nationale* (Cambrai road), 400yd from our nearest trench. Here they were able to concentrate in great numbers, as the road runs along an embankment behind which nothing but artillery could reach them. This was the situation on our front at about three o'clock in the afternoon. I happened to look down the line and saw Captain Lumsden looking rather anxiously to the rear. I then saw that a number of our people were retiring. There was not much time to think what this might mean as the enemy were beginning to cross the road; we had fixed bayonets and I thought we would have little chance against the large number of Germans who had concentrated behind the embankment. For a long time, for nearly an hour, the British guns had been silent, but they had not all retired. With a white star-shaped flash two shells burst right over the road behind which the Germans were massed. These two shells must have knocked out forty or fifty men. The enemy fled right back up the hill up to the 900yd mark followed by rapid fire and loud cheering from all along the line.

This respite did not last long. It was at this time that the battalions of 7th and 9th Brigades began to retire on both sides of the Gordons, leaving them in an exposed salient. They were not of course aware of this. The Gordons were soon pinned down and more or less abandoned by the gunners. A machine gun began to 'play up and down the trench'. 48 Heavy Battery, which had done much useful infantry support and counter-battery work, and which was right up with the field guns, was gone by 4.30pm. Hay continued

> The bullets began to spray too close to my left ear, and laying my glasses on the parapet I was about to sit down for a few minutes rest, and indeed had got half-way down to the sitting position, when the machine gun found its target. Recollections of what passed through my mind are very clear. I knew instantly what had happened. The blow might have come from a sledge-hammer, except that it seemed to carry with it an impression of speed. I saw for one instant in my mind's eye the battlefield at which I had been gazing through my glasses the whole day. Then the vision was hidden by a scarlet circle and a voice said, 'Mr H has got it.' Through the red mist of the scarlet circle I looked at my watch (the movement to do so had begun in my mind before I was hit); it was spattered with blood; the hands showed five minutes to four. The voice which had spoken before said, 'Mr H. is killed.'

He lay in the trench for the next eight hours and for the whole of this time, as dusk turned into night, the Germans made no attempt to close with them. Presumably they went to sleep.

He remembered being lifted out of the trench in the dark – it was now midnight but there was still firing – and being carried in a greatcoat in great discomfort for what seemed like hours until eventually perforce abandoned to his fate. A Private Sinclair – probably the voice he had heard when hit – stayed with him until he realized he could do no more. Sinclair then, showing great initiative, evaded the Germans who were now everywhere on the field of battle, made his way into Caudry, found some French people who shielded him, and eventually found his way back to friendly territory. He ended the war as a sergeant. The Gordons' bandsmen/stretcher-bearers – whose forebears had played at the Duchess of Richmond's ball before rushing off to the Battle of Waterloo – were doing all they could on their doomed march to Clary. We will come across Lt Hay later. In his wounded state he was of course unaware of the stand-off between the two colonels of his battalion (*see* Chapter 6).

8th Brigade officers came out to Montigny on foot, all their transport having been lost in the furious German howitzer bombardment of Audencourt. The 4th Middlesex, who had won lasting glory three days before, received the full force of this bombardment, their wounded suffering twice when the church they were sheltering in caught fire. Three gun teams of 6 Battery, XL Brigade RFA were lost to a single lucky German salvo when getting ready to move out. The mangled horses and shattered guns and limbers were a distressing sight to even the oldest veterans.

The 4th Division was immeasurably helped at this time by the French cavalry on their left, although Gen Snow was not exactly generous in his praise of them; at any rate the Germans appear to have believed that there was an unbroken line stretching to Cambrai in the west, which was very far from being the case. General Sordet's three brigades had had a torrid time for the previous twenty-four hours, wearing their horses out during the night of the 25th/26th crossing east–west across the transport lines of the BEF. Once again, all Second Corps HQs were in the dark all day concerning Sordet's whereabouts, which was why it was such a relief to Smith-Dorrien to hear the reassuring sound of the 75s at 4.30pm.

6

Late Afternoon and Night

At about the time that the Suffolks were being overwhelmed and those that could in 14th Brigade were running for their lives, Capt Jack of the Cameronians was at 5th Division HQ at Reumont. Two battalions of his brigade (19th) were up in the firing line and even now the survivors were making their way back: the 1st Middlesex and the Argylls. The other two battalions of his brigade, the Royal Welch and the Cameronians (Scottish Rifles) were coming back from Montigny to join the rest of 5th Division on the Roman road. Smith-Dorrien personally intercepted the Royal Welch, found a junior officer and ordered them to form a rearguard north of Reumont. They were joined by the Scottish Rifles, straddling the Roman road, and faced north-east.

At the same time Capt Jack was walking (his horse and groom had gone missing) towards Le Cateau with orders from Gen Drummond of 19th Brigade* to 'try and get some infantry to hold their ground for a little longer and cover it'. He had two men with him. These orders were going to be difficult to carry out; for a captain to order a senior officer of another battalion to turn about and face the enemy after just managing to extricate himself and his men from a disaster is a tall order, even if it does come straight from the general.

The first battalion, or part of a battalion, he came across was retiring in extended order; Capt Jack duly delivered Gen Drummond's request to the senior officer (Jack does not name the officer or the battalion). He was met with 'an incredulous stare, as if it were a demand for a money subscription'. He was told that the orders were to withdraw, the leading troops had been obliterated and nothing would stop the enemy. There was no panic; the troops merely passed on without stopping.

He then came upon two companies of the Argyll and Sutherland Highlanders, led by their 'tall, handsome' Lt-Col Moulton-Barrett. They were the main body of the survivors of their battalion from the battle just to the north. Jack again delivered the request to turn about and oppose the enemy a little longer. The colonel thought for a moment and then called out '93rd [their old regimental number] about turn', a movement 'executed on the spot with

---

*He was wounded later in the day.

almost parade ground exactitude'. The Argylls took up a position on the east side of Reumont. Jack then rounded up a variety of stragglers, who all seemed surprisingly willing to serve as rearguards: a company of 1st Norfolks, some 1st Scots Fusiliers, and some Royal Engineers who were more than willing to act as infantry. This is what the Germans would have faced if they had come on. Later some of the Cornwalls joined this group, the group led out from the other side of the Selle by Capt Trelawny. Trelawny had earlier come across Lt-Col James of the Manchesters near Reumont, who was at the edge of collapse from exhaustion; the colonel merely said that 'its hot back there'. Trelawny then took part in a rearguard action against 'swarms' of Germans near Honnechy, firing at them at 800yd range.

A little later, about 5.30pm, and very close by, another small column of Argyll survivors was also making its way back south to Reumont; this was Capt Hyslop's gallant band of B Company men, with a few men from other companies collected on the way; about a hundred in all. They were intercepted by Gen Fergusson himself, who ordered them to take up a covering position a little to the east until fresh troops came up. This Hyslop duly did; when the 'fresh troops' turned up Hyslop hurried on to join the main body, believing Moulton-Barrett and the rest of the battalion to be ahead of him, although in fact he was still on rearguard near Reumont. Darkness was setting in. Lt H. Clark, with Hyslop's survivors, was told to collect up any miscellaneous men he could find and take them into his command; this proved to be a difficult task for a junior Highland officer and he handed over to another officer who had a formed body of men under him. Large motor lorries, with the names of their civilian owners on their sides, were scattered about, either overturned or stuck from lack of petrol. These civilian lorries impressed Lt Bloem the next day; he reasoned that if the British were going to war with removal vans that must be some indication of their seriousness.

And so Hyslop pressed on towards St Quentin, collecting more men on the way to his column and then losing them in the darkness and confusion. At one time his party consisted of ten officers and 250 men, finally arriving at St Quentin at 3.30am on the 27th, 'absolutely footsore and weary, having marched over 30 miles and fought a battle all within 24 hours and with practically nothing to eat all the time'. Staff officers would not let him into the town, so they slept beside the road until daybreak.

When Capt Jack got back to Reumont at 4.30pm everyone at divisional HQ had gone. He decided to visit the outposts, feeling somewhat responsible for them. He found the Argylls under Moulton-Barrett still on the south-east edge of town, lined up on the bank of a road, from where they were having a lively battle with some German troops emerging from the Selle to the east. These were the (reserve) troops of 7th Division, III Corps who had been making their way down the flank all day. They were now bold enough to emerge into the open and from 500yd were keeping up an accurate fire on the Argylls; both Jack and the handsome Moulton-Barrett thought it was time to go (there seemed to be no other British troops about) and they brought all the men back to Honnechy without loss. The Germans did not pursue them.*

Captain J.C. Dunn of the 2nd Royal Welch recorded an incident from this period of the day, or a little later, on the Roman road south of Maurois. The enemy were not pursuing the British, although 'the line had given way somewhere on the right', and there were still occasional shells falling in Bertry, Reumont and Maurois. The Royal Welch had pulled back from their earlier position north of Reumont:

> At twilight I stopped to talk to [Capt] Williams, when suddenly a cavalry officer appeared, and, coming up to him, asked in great excitement if he did not 'see that enemy patrol', and why he did not fire at it. The patrol was about 500yd away on our right front; it looked uncommonly like our own people as I saw them through my glasses, and I said as much. The rain and the bad light made it difficult to be sure, the waterproof sheets or capes they wore made it more difficult, but Solly-Flood [afterwards a major-general] was sure they were Germans; 'It's the chance of a lifetime', he said. So an order for rapid independent fire was given. There was a clatter of hooves, and at least a troop galloped across our front amid a hail of bullets. The men were excited and the estimation of the range was as bad as the light, but we certainly knocked over several horses. They were our people right enough, 19th Hussars, although we didn't know it for certain for an hour or more.

This regrettable little action was also witnessed by Major Rob Money, a machine-gun officer of the Cameronians.

In fact, German infantry of III Corps did get as far as Honnechy that night, as we have seen, but no further. To be fair to the Royal Welch, the *Official History* states that: 'Small parties of (enemy) cavalry now hovered about the front, feeling their way forward and provoking constant little bursts of fire from the British rear guards, which in the meanwhile continued to fall back in succession as the Roman road gradually became clear for them.' By 6.00pm the whole of the 5th Division and the 19th Brigade were in retreat along the Roman road, with no threat to their flanks.

The most dangerous moment for 5th Division and the whole corps had passed. If the enemy attack on the British right had been vigorously pursued to the point where he could attack the retreating columns, the whole stopping, smashing blow would have been in vain. It is probable that the German troops on the ground at this point succumbed to their tiredness and instinctively realized that the British were not a beaten enemy; the vigorous actions of the many small rearguard groups were ample testimony to that.

*Capt Jack was awarded the *Légion d'Honeur* for his actions during Le Cateau, on the recommendation of Col Moulton-Barrett.

At this time, a little more than 2 miles (3km) to the north-west, the bulk of the 7th and 8th Brigades were in orderly retreat to Montigny; this was made possible by the 9th Brigade in a covering position astride the line Bertry–Montigny but above all by the left-behind 1,000-strong detachments from the Royal Irish, the Royal Scots and the Gordon Highlanders. They were still occupying their original ground in front of Audencourt, they had received no definite orders and they were resisting all German attempts to advance. Between 5.00 and 6.00pm the German infantry tried to break through the Gordons' front; they then tried to work round the Royal Scots' right. A further bombardment of Audencourt by howitzers followed at 6.45pm and again at 8.30pm, watched from 6 miles (10km) away by their more fortunate 3rd Division comrades, who would not have been aware for the most part that there were still British troops up there. German artillery continued to bombard vacated 4th Division positions until well after 5.00pm, with 'typical Prussian thoroughness'. What was remarkable about the stand taken by the left-behind Scots and Irish was that they appear to have had plenty of opportunity to slip away when darkness fell. There were lulls in the infantry and artillery attacks when a discrete withdrawal could have attracted no criticism from any quarter. We will return to them shortly.

In the 4th Division the infantry brigadiers received their orders to retreat about 5.00pm, the 10th Brigade being detailed as rear-guard, together with the 4th Cavalry Brigade near Selvigny. At the same time Brig Milne made arrangements for the artillery to retire to a succession of covering positions. At Ligny this was not possible; the closeness of the guns to the infantry fighting and the exposure of their position resulted in an order to Maj C.H. Liveing of 135 Battery, XXXII Brigade RFA to abandon his guns. Most men would have obeyed this order; but the gallant major decided to do otherwise. With just a few men, he manhandled the six guns and their wagons and brought them all but one wagon out to safety. His neighbour, 27 Battery, was in an equally perilous position but its major, H.E. Vallentin, with two sergeants and five gunners, ran back four of the guns with their limbers to the sunken road in their rear, where the horses were being kept. During a lull in the shelling he made a dash to the south-west and safety; by this time it was well after 5.00pm. Both majors received the DSO and the NCOs the DCM.

Other gunners in 4th Division, not having received orders to abandon their guns, 'sat in gloomy groups round the guns which they had neither the shells to work, nor the heart to abandon', in the words of Arthur Conan Doyle (*see* Bibliography).

The fighting continued around Ligny until after 5.00pm, Maj C.B. Prowse of the Somerset Light Infantry staying to the bitter end with two companies of the battalion; five of their officers became prisoners, although Maj Prowse himself got away as did Col Swayne of the Somersets. Col Biddulph of the

Rifle Brigade led out a composite group from three 11th Brigade battalions. The East Lancs came back to Clary and the main body of 1st Rifle Brigade to Selvigny where it took up a covering position at around 6.30pm. There it was later joined by Brig Hunter-Weston, who arrived with a scattering of men from other regiments. There they bivouacked, within 2 miles (3km) of the battlefield; the Irish Fusiliers and Seaforths were to the east of them.

Half of the Warwickshires, with Lt Montgomery and Maj Poole, the surviving officers from the earlier debacle, and a good number of the Dublin Fusiliers, were still in Haucourt at this hour. We will let Bernard Montgomery of the Warwicks, who was classed a 'straggler' at this time, take up the story of his escapades during the next two days:

> About 10.00pm we realized that we were alone and we could hear the Germans advancing in large numbers. So we hastily formed up and retired ... I shall never forget that march; we called it the 'Retreat from Moscow'. We were behind our own army and in front of the Germans; we had several very narrow escapes from being cut up and at times had to hide in woods to escape being seen by Uhlan patrols. We had no food and no sleep, and it rained most of the time. We were dead tired when we started so you can imagine what we were like when we finished it. Our men fell out by the dozens and we had to leave them; lots were probably captured by the Germans, some have since rejoined. The chocolate Mother had sent me was invaluable, as of course we had no rations all the time and there was no food in the villages. The villagers were all fleeing before the advancing Germans. All our kit was burnt to make room in the wagons for wounded etc, so we had only what we stood up in. We had passed our kit burning on the wayside; altogether the outlook was black and we were in low spirits. When we retired on the 26th we had got split into two parties, it was a very dark night and somehow we got separated. There were 300 of us in the party I was in and about 300 in the other party ... at 10.00pm on the 28th we caught up our division ...

There followed baths and rest at Le Mans. Altogether, 670 stragglers came in during the days following the 26th, although other estimates put the figure as high as 1,000. Perhaps uncharacteristically Montgomery did give full credit to Maj Poole: 'It was entirely to him that we finally got back to the BEF.'

Monty's battalion was of course in the 4th Division; the sacrifice of the Suffolks and KOYLI on the right was in the 5th Division area. The fortunes of war, as the *Official History* calls it, were now particularly hard on the 1st Gordons, 3rd Division, together with about 300 men and officers of the Royal Irish and Royal Scots. We left them as darkness was falling a little to the east of Audencourt not far south of the Cambrai road which throughout the day was the defining feature of no-man's-land. At 7.45pm Brevet-Col W.E. Gordon vc of the Gordon Highlanders assumed command, mainly on the grounds that their force was a composite battalion. This was entirely proper: he had the distinguished name, the age seniority, the Boer War VC and he was also an honorary ADC to the King; but brevet rank confers seniority in the Army but not in one's own regiment. Gordon was for going south, which was exactly what the men wanted of course, while Lt-Col Neish, the actual commander of the Gordons, would not move without orders; Gordon conceded. In fact, staff officers had ridden up earlier with verbal orders (and two platoons had gone back after receiving them) but this was not good enough for Neish. At 9.20pm Lt-Col Neish sent the adjutant to Troisvilles (brigade HQ) with two men in search of orders. It was a journey of 4 miles (6.5km) round trip and two hours were allotted. At 12.30am, when the three had still not returned (it was presumed they had been captured), the two colonels finally agreed on the need to retire and marched their men through Audencourt and south to Montigny, which they duly reached at 1.30am. The column of the composite battalion was strung out along half a mile of track. A light was seen in a cottage and the occupant reported that British troops had all departed to the east; that is, between Bertry and Maurois. Gordon decided to take this road and, guided by the friendly Frenchman, reached a crossroads to the south-west of Bertry at 2.00am. Here their troubles began.

The crossroads were guarded by a sentry post which turned out to be German and fired on the head of the column. There was an exchange of fire and orders were given to go back to Montigny, but in the dark and without the guide the column found itself in Clary, also now firmly in German hands. Once again a fierce firefight ensued, in the streets of Clary itself and in the fields. Remarkably, in spite of all the hue and cry, a group of officers crept up on an estaminet crowded with Germans, and drawing their revolvers shot the lot; the bullet holes were still visible twenty years later. There were hundreds of dead and wounded on both sides in and around Clary but after an hour 500 Gordons, Royal Irish and Royal Scots laid down their arms. A handful escaped into the night, some even making it to that part of Belgium still in friendly hands; most of these would-be escapers were rounded up by the Germans in the morning; fourteen officers of the Gordons were to sit out the war years in Torgau.

These were not the only lethal nocturnal encounters in the 3rd and 4th Division areas. We know that Maj Poole of the Warwicks was leading a composite party of 600 that split up into two groups at about this time. Also about in the unfriendly dark were at least two other detachments: Majors H.M. Shewan of the Dublin Fusiliers and R.G. Parker of the King's Own, from an area around Haucourt and Ligny. They turned southwards in the dark and, after many ordeals that tested the courage and resourcefulness of the men and officers, about 1,000 of them reached British lines. They acted like paratroops behind enemy lines in a later war, sowing confusion in a greater proportion than their numbers. Maj Parker made good his escape, but Maj Sherwin was not so fortunate.

One example of this nocturnal warfare tells the story well. Lt R.F.H. Massy-Westropp of the Dublin Fusiliers led his platoon from their trench near Haucourt at dusk and started off for Ligny. He came across some Germans in a farm, attacked them, drove them off and got into Ligny at 2.00am. They had a feed and a sleep (the men could not be roused) and started off for Clary, the scene of the Gordons' fight, and by this time in German hands. On the way he met up with Maj Poole and then promptly lost him again. They then fell victim to a German trick when the Dubliners were induced to come into a village, and then fired on. The survivors staggered back to Ligny, where about 300 men from every battalion in the corps were sheltering, under the command of Maj Shewan, also of the Dubliners. Massey-Westropp got through with seventy-eight of these men to Boulogne; the rest were killed or captured, the latter including Maj Shewan and seven of his officers (including the doctor). They were to endure years of imprisonment in Torgau; it was mainly the well-connected and the incapacitated who were repatriated.

The German penalty later imposed for British soldiers found in German-held territory and living of necessity under cover was death, and death for those sheltering them. A handful of men who found themselves behind the lines during the Retreat managed to live out the whole war in occupied territory, showing astonishing resourcefulness. One man, Tpr Fowler of the 11th Hussars, cut off on the 26th, lived for the rest of the war hidden for long stretches of time in a wardrobe, sheltered by a brave woman called Mme Belmont-Gobert. Lt Roupell, by then a lieutenant-colonel, was to live in German-occupied France in the next war for many months after being cut off in May 1940.

7
Aftermath

Historians on the whole have been kind to Smith-Dorrien, not least the *Official History*. It states as a matter of fact:

> Smith-Dorrien's troops had done what GHQ feared was impossible. With both flanks more or less in the air, they had turned upon an enemy of at least twice their strength; had struck him hard, and had withdrawn, except on the right front of the 5th Division, practically without interference, with neither flank enveloped, having suffered losses certainly severe, but, considering the circumstances, by no means extravagant.'

Major Becke wrote:

> By the end of the day the attackers had been beaten to a standstill, and so mauled that their only desire was to allow the Second Corps to continue its withdrawal from the field unmolested, save by the sullen boom of the German guns; and their unsupported fire at this moment was the sure proof of the discomfiture suffered by the German host.

On the 28th the field marshal addressed the 2nd Suffolks survivors and told them that they had 'saved the left wing of the army'.

This is in marked contrast to French's later comments in his memoir that the battle rendered the Retreat more difficult and arduous, and that Second Corps was saved by Allenby, Sordet and d'Amade in Cambrai. Sir John, unlike the Duke of Wellington, was always eager to praise cavalry commanders. French also tried to show that Second Corps was not seriously threatened on the night of the 25th in his attempt to justify the order to continue the retreat at first light. In fact, Smith-Dorrien was generous in his tribute on the 29th to the French cavalry under Sordet on his left, but praised above all the discipline and fighting valour of his own troops. Gen Snow took very much this Smith-Dorrien line after the war, writing in his unpublished memoir that all credit for the battle should go to the troops and the regimental officers; Gen Sordet on his left did little more than offer a token presence and 'left us to our fate to save the skin of his men and horses'. The reason the Germans did not get round the right flank of 4th Division was that they had reserve divisions on this flank that did not come on with the vigour of their active front-line units; German cavalry did not fight willingly as infantry. Snow had a very poor view of French cavalry, who were hard on their mounts and tended to leave the battlefield at the first blast of shrapnel. Major Bridges also tended to a less-than-enthusiastic view of his French opposite numbers, saying they would be reckless in taking a position and then abandon it for no reason. He also said that they tended to be more punctilious in observing *l'heure du dejeuner* than more strictly military timetables.

This is where Sir John is reprehensible: that in his spite against his personal *bête noire* he chose to belittle the sacrifice of his own men, who laid down their lives for their friends and their country; he would rather praise the dubious achievements of French cavalry than his own men. It would be charitable to say that his insistence on the continual retreat at all costs, even on 1 September when all was safely gathered in, was justified to save lives and to obtain a more favourable time and place for the eventual counter-attack; but such a view is not really tenable in view of the strategic situation that presented itself at that time. By September he was over-cautious, misread the strategic situation, and pusillanimous; exactly what he accused Smith-Dorrien of being at different times. He was also, in his communications with London, inconsistent, petulant and child-like: he wanted to fight but was afraid to strike. One can only assume that Wilson did not have the major hand in writing the telegram on 31 August; its jejune style is anyway not his. But, to be fair to Sir John, few at GHQ were mentally prepared in August 1914 for the human and material cost of modern warfare.

His real failure – and Haig's – was to keep the two corps capable of mutual support in the BEF's hour of crisis. That alone should have ensured his sacking in 1914. This failure cannot be laid solely at the door of poor communications.

What is puzzling in the light of his continued belief in the broken state of Second Corps is that Sir John did in fact sit on his horse watching Second Corps soldiers march past him on the road south on the 28th and had a chance to mingle with the men, which always gave his spirits a lift. He wrote:

> I had a most agreeable surprise. I met the men and talked to them as they were lying about resting. I told them how much I appreciated their work and what the country thought of them. I told them also of Joffre's telegram [of congratulation and thanks for Le Cateau] and its publication in England. The wonderful spirit and bearing they showed was beyond all praise – half a million of them would walk over Europe!

He went on to write that the men – heroes every one of them – listened to his few words 'with the confidence of children', showing abiding evidence of the 'instinctive sympathy between officer and men'. It would be interesting to read a reaction from any of the men present at this road-side gathering to their C-in-C's words of encouragement. At best it would be something along the lines of Sassoon's 'The General': 'He's a cheery old card.' Meeting the troops was one thing that Sir John prided himself on. This was August 1914, after all, before the horror of the Ypres Salient had broken the spirit of the BEF, and many officers and men wrote in later years of being genuinely bucked up by informal encounters with senior officers.

Sir John French's mercurial personality was a mixture of martial pride, misty-eyed sentimentality and simmering resentful bitterness against those he perceived as his enemies, in particular Kitchener, Smith-Dorrien and Lanrezac, and he allowed this bitterness to sway his military judgement. He was quite capable of holding contrary opinions in his mind at the same time: that his men, the finest troops in Europe, should fight, and that they should be kept from harm's way. Yet he was also quick, by September, to appreciate the new realities of trench warfare. In many instances he has been unfairly criticized; for instance, that he was optimistic on the 23rd and gloomy on the 26th. He had a right to be; what is harsh is that commanders-in-chief are not allowed by the judgement of history to have mood swings, or if they do, they are meant to keep them to themselves. Haig let off steam in his diary and letters to his wife; he was in any case an extremely reserved man. French was not; but that is not a failing in itself, any more than his mistresses could be considered relevant to the handling of the Battle of Le Cateau, or indeed than Kitchener's repressed homosexuality could have influenced the outcome of the Gallipoli campaign.

But one thing that all historians would agree on is that from Mons to the Marne French's luck held, and luck is an essential ingredient in successful generals. He had the luck, if it can be called that, to be was blessed – as was Smith-Dorrien of course – with the BEF of 1914 that was trained and equipped for the type of small-scale actions fought at Le Cateau. Smith-Dorrien instinctively understood this. It is often said that the BEF was sent off to a European war for which it was not equipped; Kipling's bitter comment in 1922 that Britain's unpreparedness was 'proof of the purity of this country's ideals' is often quoted in this context. But no one could seriously suggest that Britain could have prepared an army in the years of Edwardian peace for a four-year war involving 20 million men. The battle of Le Cateau was exactly the sort of encounter that Wilson and Foch had envisaged in their many discussions before the war, and for which the BEF was prepared.

As von Kluck fed his troops into the 5th Division position in stages, as he had done at Mons, the battalion commanders were able to respond to the gathering crisis by themselves reinforcing the line in turn, a military manoeuvre of the highest tactical skill and requiring the greatest courage. If von Kluck had been able to throw in a larger infantry force at one stroke, the British right would surely have been overwhelmed earlier. But Le Cateau, like Mons, was an encounter battle that did not give von Kluck the luxury of preparatory staff work for which the German Army was famed. If luck it was, the Germans had it early in the morning of the 26th when the mist enabled them to deploy their artillery in positions undetected by the British gunners. If luck it was, the British had it when the German infantry failed to press on down the vital highway of the Roman road at 2.00pm, when the 5th Division battalions had been fought to the limits of their endurance. If luck it was, Gen Snow had it on the left when the Germans failed to get round his flank. Smith-Dorrien had the luck, if it can be called that, to have had an artillery on the top of its form so that when the Germans did occupy the (abandoned) forward British positions the rear batteries, deployed in echelon, were able to register on the old line. This especially applied to 61 Howitzer Battery and 108 Heavy Battery in the 5th Division.

German infantry found on the 26th that to gain the enemy's front-line trenches was often an easier task – hard and costly as it was – than pushing towards the next, further objective; their natural instincts were to consolidate what they had rather than to court new danger in the cannon's mouth; even in these opening days of the war, this inherent feature of trench warfare was becoming apparent. But in any case the German infantry was already, in Major Becke's words, 'beaten to a standstill'. And these were von Kluck's best troops; his reserves he used on the flanks. French's luck held after the 26th when von Kluck failed to follow up the BEF with any real vigour. Gen Snow certainly thought that his 4th Division remained extremely vulnerable in the days following the 26th, but he never wavered from his view that the battle 'was worth the candle', in Smith-Dorrien's rather unhappy phrase, even if he had had 'little choice' but to fight. If 3rd and 5th Divisions had continued their retirement in the hours of darkness of the 25–26th, the 4th Division would have been overwhelmed, in Snow's certain view. But the experience of the battle, fought without his divisional signals and ambulances, with his hastily improvised retreat routes, dented Snow's natural optimism: he wrote later that 'it was the last time during the campaign that I took things easily and that ever after I always prepared for the worst'. He felt he had not been well served by GHQ. He may have felt that he received less than his due in despatches from GHQ.

And so the Retreat went on, now with von Kluck no longer snapping at the heels of the exhausted troops; in Wellington's words, he had been 'humbugged': outmanoeuvred as well as outfought. His cavalry in particular were much more wary when approaching British positions. But 'shattered' Second Corps were not, as French had convinced himself they were in his self-serving belief. Some infantry may have 'dribbled away', in Gen Fergusson's words, from the right flank towards the middle of the day (which was instrumental in his retreat suggestion), there were certainly wounded coming back to Reumont, helped by their mates; and there was certainly a near-mutiny at St Quentin, but in the simile that occurred to Smith-Dorrien at the time the troops going down the St Quentin road resembled a good-natured crowd leaving a race meeting rather than a rabble intent on escape. Sir John had employed the same simile himself a day later; it was a not uncommon one at the time. In the words of the *Official History*:

> The men looked upon themselves as victors, some indeed doubted whether they had been in a serious action, yet they had inflicted upon the enemy casualties which are believed to have been out of all proportion to their own, and they had completely foiled the plan of the German commander.

Maj Becke described the Roman road to St Quentin towards the end of the day as a,

> *Via Dolorosa* [with] a rudderless horde of men, guns, wagons, limbers without guns, carts, riderless horses. As units came into this stream they were engulfed in it, formations being broken up and cohesion lost. With nightfall it became harder to move and numerous long checks took place. Rain began to fall. The misery of hunger, thirst and extreme fatigue could hardly be borne. Yet these men were soldiers still. Wounded and exhausted men were assisted along by their comrades, others were carried on wagons, guns, limbers, and carts. All kept their rifles and ammunition: for none had abandoned themselves to despair. In fact it was not a rout or panic, merely extreme confusion. No one who took part in it could ever forget that Wednesday night. [The men were] sustained only by the knowledge that it was their duty to keep moving until they could be organized once more into their old historic units.

Capt Jack and Capt Dunn, both reliable witnesses, saw no panic on the Roman road. Both officers were good examples of the old military truism that leaderless and demoralized troops will respond well to a capable officer who seems to know what he's doing. Lt Roupell wrote of this time:

> I remember staggering along the road beside a gun limber, stumbling with fatigue, and at last being pulled up on to the seat of the limber by the gunner, where I fell asleep in his arms! He must have held me or otherwise I should never have remained perched on the small seat of the gun limber. It was dark when I was pulled on to the limber and the rest and sleep did me a power of good.

Dr Dolbey of the KOSB marched with the men:

> In a dream we marched, unconscious of the towns we passed, the villages we slept in; fatigued almost beyond endurance; dropping to sleep at the five-minute halt that was the reward for each mile covered. All companies, dozing as they marched, fell forward drunkenly on each other at the halts; sleeping men lay, as they had halted, in the roads and were kicked uncomplainingly into wakefulness again ... once more forward with feet that hurt like a hundred knives.

Lt Johnston, mainly one suspects from the selfless ethos of his officer class, marched with his men, although wounded ('unfits were sent back in the lorries'). He had, however, been reunited with his horse:

> I have never in all my life been so tired, it was my third night running without sleep, my leg was very painful, we had been retiring and marching enormous distances for the last five days, it was so dark that one kept tripping over stones, the men were simply drunk with fatigue and lack of sleep and reeled from one side of the road to the other. I first of all walked in order to try and keep awake, then owing to feeling so tired I tried riding a bit, but this rather hurt my wounded leg and also I kept on falling asleep in the saddle, and all the time I had a most awful thirst; altogether it was the worst night I ever spent. However at last we reached Ham in the early hours of the morning [28 August].

These descriptions could be recognized by those on the retreat to Corunna in 1808, Dunkirk in 1940 or back through Burma to India in 1942, although at the time the comparison that sprang to mind was Napoleon's retreat from Moscow. Second Corps troops could not know, of course, that later in their war the Germans would pass this way again, going west as they routed the British 5th Army around St Quentin on 21 March 1918 and pushed them back almost to Amiens in July. There would be very few of the 1914 men who would experience two retreats (which is why Frank Richards' and George Roupell's memoirs are so valuable). And of course the British were to come back here in October 1918 in the final victorious campaign, after crossing the Hindenburg Line.

When the troops later came across boxes of provisions – bully beef in 7lb tins, biscuits and the like – that had so thoughtfully been dumped beside the roads by Gen Robertson's quartermasters they often found that the Germans were hardly allowing them enough time to stop and open them. Gen Robertson's quartermasters also rather unhelpfully left great sides of beef by the road that the retreating soldiery were hardly in a position to serve up and to which the Germans were only too pleased to help themselves; from this they got the impression that the BEF was in a more desperate plight than it actually was. In the hasty retreat troops had attempted to make bonfires of piles of unwanted supplies and on one occasion German troops following on had found tins of bully nicely cooked for them; once again, troops in headlong flight do not take time to destroy supplies. In fact the only instance of panic that Smith-Dorrien came across in his car journey down to Noyon on that dismal night was among a rear-echelon ammunition column. The captain in charge had convinced himself that the ubiquitous Uhlans were upon him and jettisoned his load; it was his bad luck to have had the corps commander right behind him.

The official historian, Brig Sir James Edmonds, was at Le Cateau as a staff officer with the 4th Division at Haucourt, which gives his account some of its graphic quality and adds to its credibility.* Forever after the men of 4th Division considered that the stand saved them from encirclement and capture; Smith-Dorrien was guest of honour at their annual dinner for many years.

Losses

The total official losses were given at the time and accepted by the *Official History*, after the return of stragglers, as 7,812 men and officers (of whom 2,600 were captured) and thirty-eight guns. The problem comes in estimating the numbers of dead, missing and wounded out of the net total of 5,212 casualties (after subtracting the prisoners). The more seriously wounded were left behind in the best available care; this is the price of abandoning the battlefield. They should anyway be counted among the 2,600 prisoners. Walking wounded and those wounded that could be got away came back and should be counted among the 5,212 dead and wounded. In a retreat such as this with medical services overstretched or non-existent, a high ratio of dead to wounded would be expected, which is normally reckoned at one third to one quarter of the total. This would indicate between 1,750 and 1,300 killed. In fact the figure for those who died on the 26th and 27th (according to the Commonwealth War Graves Commission) is 1,200. This would mean that 4,012 got away wounded, in the care of the RAMC. The casualty figures therefore are:

Taken prisoner	2,600
Killed	1,200
Wounded	4,012
TOTAL	7,812

Nigel Cave (*see* Bibliography), with acknowledgement to Jack Horsfall, has calculated total Second Corps casualties as no more than 5,000, half of which were prisoners, giving a casualty figure of no more than 10 per cent of the troops actually engaged. His view is that the official figures for casualties were swollen by the failure to allow for stragglers returning over time to their units. Actual fatalities he reckons ('reasonably accurately') as no more than 500, or at the most 600 allowing for those who died of wounds at a later date. Jack Sheldon calculates, without giving sources, German casualties (killed and wounded) as under 2,000. This author prefers to accept the official figures for British casualties, and those of the Commonwealth War Graves Commission,

*Edmonds, never robust, according to Snow, had a physical collapse on the 28th.

145

with the figure of 1,200 British killed as the lowest estimate, taking as it does no account of those who died later than the 27th of wounds received on the 26th. German casualties of 2,000 seem to be an unrealistically low estimate; it is highly unlikely that German casualties at Le Cateau were only a fraction of those at Mons (admittedly unknown), especially since Second Corps artillery was not extensively engaged at Mons.

This lower than expected number of British deaths (1,200) at the battle greatly strengthens Smith-Dorrien's case; curiously, at no time during the battle of the memoirs did he make reference to them, always accepting the figure of 7,812 casualties. He had no staff to help him compile statistics and the records were not easily accessible.

The best estimate for German casualties was made in the 1933 War Department *Battle-field Tour Guide*, a guide written primarily for staff officers; this gave a figure of 8,970 killed and wounded. This must remain the official figure, based as they must be on the official German figures.* Other estimates have appeared at various times giving figures three times as high. The 'true' figure may well have been higher than the official British estimate, if only because the Germans were known not to include the lightly wounded in their counting. Cave and Sheldon's figure of German casualties (2,000) is given without explanatory or supporting evidence. There were no Germans taken away as prisoners, although no doubt the intelligence officers of corps and divisions would have liked to interrogate an officer or two. A few wounded Germans fell into 10th Brigade hands briefly; they were treated and left behind. Sheldon's figure of 2,000 German casualties is believable if we accept that a great many of those lightly wounded by British shrapnel are not counted; but the German system of counting applies equally to both Sheldon's figures and the War Department figures. However it is examined, there is a figure of 7,000 'missing' casualties that Sheldon does not explain: the difference of nearly 7,000 between his figure of 2,000 and the official War Department figure based on German casualty returns. If these casualties were not incurred on the 26th, when were they incurred?

Whichever figures for those killed at Le Cateau are nearest the truth, the fact remains that a British gunner or an infantryman stood a much better chance of surviving the day – even if he was in the 15th Brigade area – than his forebear in an infantry square on 18 June 1815. These better odds of survival were in spite of the nearly one hundred years of human scientific endeavour devoted to producing ever more efficient methods of killing troops on a battlefield.

Sheldon has, however, examined in detail casualty returns from the 66th Regiment (13th Brigade, 7th Division, IV Corps), the regiment that bore the

---

*German casualty figures were given for periods of ten days.

brunt of the attack in the late morning on the British right flank, and where casualties would be expected to be among the highest of all the attacking forces. He found casualties of eighty dead and 420 wounded, a rate of about 25 per cent: serious, but perhaps not as heavy as the British reports would have us believe, which had said, in biblical style, 'every gathering was laid low'. Opposing them were the firing lines of at most three British battalions (KOSB, KOYLI and the Suffolks) which could be brought to bear on them, say 300 rifles at the very most; there were the machine guns, none of which were in the firing line facing north. There were the 60-pounders and howitzers, one of the latter by late morning out of ammunition. And there were the shrapnel-firing 18-pounders, or those still firing. All the evidence, both British and German, indicates that shrapnel balls did not have the kinetic energy beyond 50yd to do much more than lodge themselves in clothing. The German first-hand accounts, collected by Jack Sheldon, make little mention of machine-gun fire. It is this shrapnel evidence, supported by the eyewitness accounts of Lt Roupell, Count Gleichen and others that gives credence to Sheldon's low figure of 2,000 German casualties for the battle as a whole. If battles can be reduced to arithmetic, then the sums, the accumulation of 5th Division fire, were not in the British favour. The truth was that the German soldiers did not simply walk into a storm of fire – with their *Pickelhauben* tilted against the shrapnel, their bugles blowing, their colours unfurled and their officers waving their swords – and carry on walking until they met a British bullet or shell. They did do all these things; but they also went to ground, they waited for British fire to abate and they returned fire. In short, they did all the things that they had learnt on manoeuvres and were learning to do against BEF infantry. The instinct for survival is a spur to quick learning.

It seems likely then that when the *Official History* recorded the German attacking lines going down under British fire and being instantly replaced by fresh troops fed in by their commanders, what was actually being witnessed was the attacking troops going to ground, disappearing from view and then re-emerging to carry on the fight, perhaps in a different part of the field. In short, the 66th Regiment was using fieldcraft, which is exactly what they would be expected to do and what the eyewitness accounts collected by Sheldon indicate that they did do. All of which suggest that Sheldon's figure of 2,000 German casualties is not so exaggerated, even if it still leaves an unaccountable shortfall.

We must remember that, as with so many battles in the war, for the majority of the men in the battalions on 26 August the battlefield would have appeared empty of enemy; the experience of the Suffolks, the Gordons and the Rifle Brigade was exceptional. The battle may have echoes of nineteenth-century ones, with major-generals on horseback up with the front line, but it was largely an artillery duel as far as most of the men were concerned. And mercifully only a relative handful of companies stood their ground to the bitter end. Most of the men of 3rd Division never saw an enemy soldier. On the German side, waves of attacking troops being mowed down by British machine guns, the received image of the war, simply didn't happen on 26 August. On the 3rd Division frontage advancing German infantry, well spaced out, 'used the available cover with considerable skill', in Major Becke's words, using the leafy shade of woods to camouflage their concentration. And British shrapnel was no more effective than German at detonation distances greater than 50yd. Gen Snow was unfortunately exaggerating when he wrote of seeing German infantry being cut down in their thousands by his 4th Div artillery. What he saw (from a considerable distance, it must be presumed) was not German infantry being killed in large numbers, but taking evasive action, throwing themselves on the ground, some of whom certainly having been wounded by the air-bursts of shrapnel but only a small number actually having been killed. On this occasion, the attack on Ligny, the Germans did not press their pursuit but went back rather than suffer needless casualties. Their tactics in August 1914 were nowhere near as sophisticated as their infiltration techniques of March 1918 – they could not be expected to be so – but what the BEF was witnessing at Le Cateau was these later tactics in embryo. We can be reasonably certain that had the Germans been mounting an attack like Le Cateau in 1918, they would have poured through gaps in the British line – for example between 7th Brigade at Caudry and 11th Brigade at Fontaine – and left those brigades to the attention of follow-on troops. In 1914 by contrast, their troops expended all their energy on fighting 11th Brigade and fought themselves to a standstill. But in both August 1914 and March 1918 the early morning mist favoured the attackers.

BEF brigade commanders like Hunter-Weston witnessed German attack tactics using all arms, and achieving success at acceptable cost against a determined enemy: a military lesson that could not have been lost on him when he became a division commander. It was a lesson that he unfortunately took too much to heart; he was always over-fond of the frontal daylight assault, and he very soon gave up leading from the front.

The Royal Artillery lost twenty-four officers and 201 other ranks as casualties, a higher proportion of officers than the infantry, as well as 274 horses. Only three RFA officers were at Torgau POW camp (including a doctor); this indicates that the gunners were able to get their wounded away in their transport, which of course infantry battalions do not have with them in their fighting positions. The gunners were anyway normally back from the lines and not in direct contact with the enemy; XV and XXVIII Brigades were exceptions. 5th Division was the hardest hit in the RA: they lost fifty ammunition wagons and fifteen limbers, and XXVIII Brigade came away with only two out of its eighteen field guns; twenty-seven guns, out of the thirty-six that were lost to enemy action, were abandoned on this flank. One of their RGA Heavy 60-pounders was lost when it overturned in a ditch trying to get away and had to be abandoned.

One 5th Division gunner, who lies buried near the place where he was killed on the 26th, Gunner Stanley Spillan of 124 Battery, was only sixteen years old. Bugler P.G. Martin, of 52 Battery XV RA Brigade, who held his captain's horse during the battle and saw him killed, was only fifteen years and eight months old.; he lived to old age. Out of eighteen officers in XV Brigade, only four remained unwounded and the command devolved on Capt Higgon of 80 Battery. And yet 122 Battery went into action again at 6.00pm with its two rescued guns against German infantry seen coming down the valley road. Lt Hodgson of 122 Battery wrote of how forlorn it felt to retreat with only two guns and then attempt a rearguard action. These equipment losses could not be replaced before the battle of The Marne.

The lack of ambulances in 4th Division was keenly felt; their casualty rate was swollen, of course, by losses in the Kings Own, which was avoidable. About 6–700 seriously wounded were got away in 4th Division using country carts, in addition to the walking wounded. The line of 4th Division survivors, retreating with their wounded in farm carts pulled by men and horses along the dirt country roads, presented a distinctly pre-industrial scene, reminiscent of Goya's Peninsular War sketches. As ever in the British Army, bandsmen acted as stretcher-bearers in battle. Capt Jack came across abandoned Argyll and Sutherland drums beside the Roman road on his way back to Le Cateau in the afternoon and thought at the time that he must make sure they were loaded back onto the limbers; he was a methodical man. The drums were unlikely to make it to Compiègne.

The 2nd Lancashire Fusiliers are a good example of the difficulties faced by adjutants when compiling their casualty reports. Their regimental history records 'an uncertain number of NCOs and men' killed, three officers and eighty-six other ranks wounded, and six officers and 402 other ranks missing; three officers and 143 other ranks subsequently rejoined. Even the methodical Col Bond of the KOYLI does not give a precise figure for those killed on the day in his battalion. Parents and relatives of those 'missing' had to wait an agonising length of time before learning their fate. The KOSB *History* attempts no casualty figures for Le Cateau at all.

These figures are very small when compared to the battles of Ypres that were to come in the autumn, by the end of which the casualty figures were equal to four-fifths of the original BEF. First Ypres was a protracted defensive battle where the British would not give ground, and where much desperate glory was won in counter-attacks. It was effectively a stalemate, but the town of Ypres remained in British hands. By the time it ground to a halt the total Allied casualties for the first months of the war were nearly a million men; German casualties were marginally less.

The casualty rate of approximately 25 per cent of the infantry engaged at Le Cateau for 5th and 4th Divisions, if we accept Major Becke's figures, is testament to the severity of the fighting. But these are figures expressed as percentages of those infantry actually engaged, the infantry battalions. 4th Division was at full strength, more or less, while 5th Division was more than 2,000 below strength in infantry due to losses at Mons: their losses of 3,150 and 2,350, respectively, hence work out at similar percentage losses of the whole divisions. 3rd Division losses of 1,796 in total and 1,450 (figures vary) in infantry represent 10 per cent of their nominal strength and 15 per cent of their actual fighting strength. Thus this one division – the division least seriously attacked – suffered the same casualties as the whole of Second Corps at Mons. The loss of the Gordons represents a large part of the total casualties in the Division.* The killed and wounded were accounted for largely by German shelling, but deaths in the 3rd Division could not have been more than 250 or so, and probably a good deal less, while those taken prisoner would have been nearer 1,000.

Walter Bloem, a captain in the 12th Prussian Grenadiers, was part of the mopping-up troops on the 27th. His grenadiers and some mounted hussars carrying lances were searching the cornstooks for British stragglers, the hussars spearing the stooks and making a great hue and cry. Perhaps because he was known as an English-speaker a couple of hussars came up to Bloem: 'Sir, we have taken prisoner a wounded English colonel.' The colonel was dressed in:

> ... a short khaki jacket, a dark blue schoolboy's cap with two long black silk bands hanging from it at the back, a short blue and black square-checked pleated skirt, between which and his stockings, which only reached to below the knees from a pair of brown shoes, was an expanse of muscular, hairy, naked leg.

Bloem recognized him as a highland Scot. He was defiant and uncowed. The colonel, 'an elderly gentleman', had a bullet wound in his shoulder and a bad graze on his knee; he was put in a horse-drawn cart and taken to a nearby farmhouse, but not before becoming the subject of much ribald laughter from the Germans, who assumed that someone had stolen his trousers. Bloem had to explain: 'He's a Scot; you'll see plenty of them in time. His checked ballet skirt, his stockings, and his naked legs are all part of the regulation uniform of Scottish regiments.' He could have been none other than one of the two Gordon Highlander colonels taken prisoner early in the morning of the 27th, according to the official records; probably Col Gordon. He was later

---

*Confusingly Brig-Gen the Hon F. Gordon [DSO], also of the Gordon Highlanders, took over command of 19th Brigade on 5 September.

exchanged for a German aristocrat. Lt Col Neish also ended up in the Torgau camp with Col Gordon, where the two colonels presumably avoided each other, as explained below. Neish was also repatriated via Switzerland, as was Col Stephenson of the KOSB. Most of the rest of the officers in Torgau were interned in Holland at the end of the war; by that time the Germans were happy to get them off their hands.

Before this eventful day the two Gordon Highlander colonels had been on the best of terms. But recriminations between the two resulted in a libel action and a court of inquiry, convened after the war when all surviving prisoners had returned. Gordon swore that Neish had been asleep in his trench, that he acted like 'a wayward child', that he didn't allow for the slower wounded on the breakout, and that it was he who had ordered the men to lay down their arms, which could be a court-martial offence. In the end the court decided that 'the column was captured owing to the chances of war'. The libel action resulted in a win for (Bt) Col Gordon of £500 against John Leng & Co., who had published an article stating that it was Gordon who had ordered the men to lay down their arms. Neish had been a shareholder in John Leng.

On another part of the field on the morning of the 27th – a sunken road just south of the Cambrai road near Audencourt, west of Beaumont – lay the wounded, paralysed and dejected Lt M.V. Hay, also of the 1st Gordons. We left him after the action of the night before wrapped in a greatcoat in the open, his two loyal men having been ordered back after making him as comfortable as possible and Private Sinclair the last to leave him. When light came, a straggler from the Royal Irish Rifles stumbled across him, but could do nothing more than move him a short way into better shelter. Some French peasants came along but passed by on the other side. Then German soldiers arrived:

> For some inexplicable reason I tried to get away. By seizing a tuft of grass in the left hand I could move along a few inches at a time. After advancing in this manner about a foot along the edge of the road, I collapsed from exhaustion, and drew the greatcoat over my head. I do not know how long I had been thus covered up when I heard a shout and, peeping through one of the holes in the coat, saw a German soldier standing on the top of the bank. He was gesticulating and pointing to his revolver, trying to find out if I was armed! But he soon saw that I was past any further fighting.
>
> He offered me a drink from his water bottle and pointed to the Red Cross on his arm. I can never hope to convey to anyone what a relief it was to me to see the cross, even on the arm of an enemy. The man asked me if I could walk, tried to lift me up, and when he saw I was paralyzed said he would go for a stretcher. 'You will go away and leave me here', I said. 'I am of the Red Cross', he replied, 'you are therefore my *Kamerad* and I will come back and I will never leave you.'

There then followed a curious incident that would be comic but for the fact that Hay was near death. While he was lying in the lane waiting for the German Red Cross orderly to come back with help, a party of well-meaning Frenchmen turned up with a stretcher. They put him on it. The Red Cross man came back, with a stretcher and an officer and two men. The French and the Germans then had an argument as to who should have custody of the paralysed Hay. The Germans clearly had found him first, but he was on a French stretcher. It was resolved by the officer asking Hay to choose. Hay answered, with a smile, '*J'y suis, j'y reste*'. The Red Cross orderly took him by the hand and said '*Adieu, Kamarad*'. The officer said 'We shall be in Paris in three days' and then gave him a piece of chocolate. He never said 'For you the war is over', or made any reference to Hay's kilted battledress. German military 'justice' could be arbitrary; while Hay was allowed to be taken away by the French, at Haucourt a priest was shot for harbouring British soldiers.

And so it was that Hay went off with the French, made a good recovery (after receiving the last rites), and ended up in Germany and eventual freedom in 1918.

By 27 August, after only four days fighting, Second Corps had suffered casualties of more than 20 per cent of its total strength (including 4th Division), a figure that is comparable to similar French formations in the battles of the frontiers. Stragglers took up to a week to be sorted out and sent back to their units. During the first five days of the Retreat between 2,500 and 3,000 men suffering from bad feet and exhaustion were sent to the base at Le Mans for treatment and recuperation; these men were of course also classified as casualties. First Corps had still not been seriously engaged as a corps (its total casualties were 1,636 by the morning of the 28th), although on the Aisne in September its losses began to take on the attrition rate that was to become such a distressing and recurring feature of the trench warfare to come; Haig's trial by fire had by then arrived.

Back at home at this time (28 August) morale was given a much-needed boost with victory at sea; three German cruisers were sunk and three others damaged in the Heligoland Bight. There were no British ship losses. A brigade of Marines had been landed at Ostend on the 27th in an attempt to shore up the Belgians and harry the Germans; it achieved neither. But the absence of any journalists with the troops at the front meant that the public could have no knowledge of the stark reality of modern warfare. For this reason the 'Amiens Dispatch' published in *The Times* on 30 August, which drew a very gloomy portrait of the infantry on the Retreat, came as a profound shock to the British public. Its author, Arthur Moore, was captured by a German cavalry patrol on 2 September, but released within a few days. It is unlikely that his release was a calculated propaganda move to spread despondency on the home front, given the normally inept handling by the Germans of any matter with a public relations aspect. The execution in October 1915 of Edith Cavell, the British nurse found guilty of helping escapees get to neutral Holland, was a case in point: her death inflamed opinion against Germany on both sides of the Atlantic. Arthur Moore went on to fight in Gallipoli.

Artillery and Machine Guns

Serious military lessons were being learned. Gen Wilson of the staff thought that Le Cateau proved the superiority of British gunnery and shooting, particularly by the cavalry arm. This may well have been so and certainly German cavalry treated British columns with greater respect after the 26th; Major Becke characterized the pressure on Second Corps after the 26th as a 'respectful pursuit by mounted troops only'.

We do know that the British heavier field gun shell was the envy of the German staff by the end of the year. The German 77mm shell was in fact a hybrid, or 'universal', shell with a mixture of HE and shrapnel. In any event the Germans later dropped it in favour of a solely HE shell that burst on impact, while the British persisted with the air-burst shrapnel shell. The British had no exact equivalent to the larger 5.9in German howitzer which, with the smaller field howitzer, may well have been responsible for the majority of deaths in the whole corps. It was certainly the most feared of the German weapons, according to all the eyewitness reports, although Lt Johnson, with typical understatement, was calling it 'our old friend the 5.9' by the time of the battle of the Marne. Its effectiveness was probably enhanced by the hard August earth of the fields south of the Cambrai road.

The losses of guns at Le Cateau – thirty-eight – were not easily replaced in the short term. Astonishingly, factories in Britain between August and the end of November produced just fifteen field guns and thirty-one field howitzers, although production picked up in December. Production of the heavy 60lb guns and the heavy howitzers, the equivalent to the German 5.9inch, was zero. The 13-pounder RHA gun, designed for support of fast-moving cavalry, was phased out, although it was used in the initial bombardment at Neuve Chapelle in March 1915. It is still used on ceremonial occasions today.

Gen Snow wrote that German gunners were extremely well served by their forward observers and by aeroplanes acting as spotters, something that the BEF had not even attempted. The fact that German gunners had been able to bring down fire onto the right flank of the 5th Division so early in the morning is a tribute to their fire direction and target acquisition; the RFA Brigades had at this stage merely offered themselves as gratuitous targets. It is surprising that the British experience in South Africa, when gunners had learned to shoot over hills with the aid of observers, had not been transformed into standard operating procedure in August 1914, but it is difficult to visualize how this could have been put into practice in the circumstances of 25–26 August.

Major Becke considered that Le Cateau proved the value of the RA training manuals but that the immediate lesson from the battle was the folly in having so many of XV RFA's guns so far forward. If they had been placed three-quarters of a mile further back, where in fact there existed an ideal valley, all the guns would have been saved and there would have been no loss of effectiveness; in fact they would have been able to fire into the Selle valley, which in the event was denied them. But the gunners were able to exploit the proximity of the infantry in one crucial respect: manhandling the guns. With the enemy closing in from the east, the gunners of 80 Battery got help from the Manchesters in turning the guns round to face the new threat and engage them at point-blank range. The infantry were undoubtedly encouraged by the willingness of the gunners to share the front line with them. For the gunners the experience of being under small arms fire was a novel, distinctly unpleasant and thankfully rare occurrence.

In fact it was not until April 1915 that the BEF equipped the 18-pounder gun with HE shells for use against trench fortifications. Until that time only the howitzers were so equipped. In the highly unnatural conditions of a demonstration laid on for the top brass Haig pronounced himself greatly impressed by the 'tremendous power' of the HE which proved itself 'most useful' against parapets. Unfortunately the reality of Western Front warfare and the shortage of munitions meant that even with this new fire-power it had become no easier to break through the enemy's front than hitherto.

In December 1914 Smith-Dorrien made a plea for the manufacture of a trench mortar to the Master-General of the Ordnance (von Donop). Haig's First Corps engineering workshops had led the way in producing a primitive trench mortar that could throw a 2lb bomb a distance of 300yd. A few were sent to Second Corps in December to try out, but there were pitifully few of them. Mortars had existed for at least fifty years and the Germans were by December using the *Minenwerfer* against the BEF with 'horrible effectiveness'. Later, infantry in the trenches had to resort to their own home-made mortar devices, which often proved fatal to those firing them.* In due course the Stokes Mortar became an invaluable part of the British armoury. The forward howitzers of 37 Battery, which could at a pinch have provided the role of mortars on the right, were out of ammunition by 1.30pm. This crucial and modern gun in the British armoury was to be beset by production delays and

*Rory Macleod witnessed just such an accident in the Neuve Chapelle sector in March 1915.

the BEF was to suffer grievously as a result. But a howitzer cannot play the role of a mortar – which is why mortars had to be re-invented – although interestingly it was a howitzer which knocked out the field gun which the Germans brought up to Landrecies on the 25th, using direct fire. A howitzer firing a shell say 750yd would have to fire with the barrel set at an elevation of around 85 degrees, and hope that the shell would explode within a few yards of its more or less dug-in target; there were simply too many imponderables, with friendly troops so close, to make the cutting opposite the Suffolks a profitable target for short-range howitzers or for the reserve howitzers. It was not until the next war that infantry battalions acquired their own portable mortar sections. The machine guns which the Germans brought up to the cutting were not in any case in the line of sight of the howitzer battery (37), which had no OP; they were much more of a target for XXVIII Brigade and the KOYLI infantry. The effective shoot which the gunners of XL RFA Brigade achieved against the German troops in the Cambrai road cutting north of Audencourt – only 400yd from the Gordons – was against a much more profitable target: massed infantry. The gunners of XV Battery understandably sought targets among the attacking infantry rather than the semi-concealed and out-of-sight machine-gunners. But the action at the end of the day, when 61 Howitzer Battery from its position in the rear put down an effective barrage in front of the abandoned infantry trenches, shows that even in the confusion of a pell-mell retreat infantry/gunner co-operation and spotting were still working.

More seriously for the long term, there was an immediate recognition that more and bigger guns, siege guns in fact, were going to be needed. Field guns firing shrapnel were well suited against troops in the open on the South African *veldt* or the fields of northern Europe but not against protected troops or fortifications. As gunners were to learn, they did not destroy enemy wire defences. The trouble for the British was that what siege guns there were back in the UK were themselves of Boer War vintage. The 60lb gun was liberally supplied with ammunition, but after 500 rounds its barrel had to be replaced.

The field guns fired an average of slightly more than 100 rounds per gun in 5th Division; it would have been more in some batteries if majors had felt free to be profligate in its use and if resupply had been easier. 100 rounds was the allocation of each gun at the start of the battle; in other words, they used up their entire allocation, on average, and could have used more if it had been available. Many guns were replenished by rushing up the ammunition wagons from the rear. A lot more HE and shrapnel ammunition was going to be needed if this rate of expenditure was going to persist; the shell crisis of 1915 was already in the making. It would appear that the gunners on the 26th fired as many as 25,000 rounds and could have fired more. On 18 August the Government had placed an order for 162,000 shrapnel shells; on 30 August the order was doubled. The appetite of the guns for shells was almost unlimited.

The British persisted with shrapnel shells for longer than other belligerents, which may have been due partly to the innate conservatism of military professionals, always pronounced in the British Army.

Allocations of the Vickers machine gun were increased in November to four per battalion, although Vickers struggled to meet the order and the Territorials had to wait until well into 1915 to receive their guns, and even their Lee-Enfield rifles. The new drum-fed, lighter Lewis gun was not yet in production at the time of Le Cateau, although arrangements were in hand for BSA Ltd to manufacture it under license. The pre-war equivocation over the role of the machine gun meant that mass production was not possible for many months. Both these machine guns and the Lee-Enfield used the same .303 ammunition, which helped mass production when it came.

But it was not simply a question of the numbers of machine guns, vital though this was. The tactical deployment of the Vickers, and the Lewis when it arrived, had to be thought through; the BEF had to think of it as both an offensive and a defensive weapon. In 1914 there was no idea of overhead fire in attack or distribution in depth. There was also a certain prejudice against machine guns because they were thought liable to jam. On the one hand they were thought of as weapons of opportunity that could cover a retirement (and even sacrificing themselves was visualized); and at other times they were thought of as best sited out of action in reserve (the East Lancs guns for example) or at best on the flanks. Good battalion officers, however, such as Major Peebles or the estimable Major Doughty of the Suffolks personally supervised the placing of the battalion machine guns in the firing line, ensuring they had good fields of fire against troops attacking from the east. It is possible that these officers did not place the guns to cover a retirement, as was accepted practice, knowing in their hearts even soon after dawn that there would be no retirement. The Rifle Brigade machine guns came into their own in the dash back to Ligny, but did not form part of the line.

The first machine-gun school was established before the end of the year. Lewis guns when they arrived at the front were also issued to gun batteries as anti-aircraft guns, which could at least force enemy planes to keep their height and distance. But in August 1914 there was no practice in the BEF of concentrating or brigading machine guns, which the Germans achieved so effectively against both the Suffolks and the Lancashire Fusiliers. In fact, the allocation of machine guns in German divisions was no greater than in British ones; rather it was their bold tactical handling in attack that accounted for their effectiveness. Lt-colonels in British battalions often thought of the firing line purely in terms of rifled infantry, as they always had been, although the Gordons had their machine guns up in their extended line, on the flanks. It is safe to say that the British were slow in recognizing the tactical uses of the machine gun, although it is not true to say, as popular belief would have us believe, that there had been an absence of debate. But as Paddy Griffith, the historian of small-scale tactics, has pointed out, pre-war regulars paid very little attention to 'tactics' as a specialist subject in its own right.

By the autumn of 1914 the War Office realized that it was going to have to find and train officers for the army on a scale never before envisioned. In August 1914, the hasty training of young infantry officers hardly prepared them for what they were about to face. Robert Graves, the future poet, was commissioned into the Royal Welch Fusiliers as a Special Reserve second lieutenant, by virtue of his experience in the OTC at Charterhouse and the recommendation of the secretary of the local golf club. His instruction consisted of 'regimental history, drill, musketry, Boer War field-tactics, military law and organization, how to recognize bugle calls, how to work out a machine gun, and how to conduct ourselves on formal occasions.' Graves was in France in good time for the battle of Loos, which was Sir John French's undoing and very nearly did for Graves. He did not serve as a machine-gun officer. But he had joined the regular army, albeit as a Special Reserve infantry officer, unlike those commissioned later into the New Armies, who received only temporary commissions, and were hence 'temporary gentlemen'. Training for officers commissioned into the Royal Artillery via the Special Reserve was equally rudimentary, compared with the regulars, at least until 1915.

Another entry route into the regular army for those seeking commissions was via the Public Schools Battalion or the Artist Rifles; the War Office regarded both as a source of potential officers.* But in the short term, in September 1914, among the all-too-few officer replacements sent to the BEF the vast majority were inevitably raw second lieutenants like the young Graves, to the consternation of Sir John French. These young officers, undoubtedly keen, willing and able to recognize bugle calls, were hardly going to be expert in the siting of machine guns. If they survived their initiation into the trenches, they learned on the job, dependent on helpful fellow officers and NCOs.

We must be aware that once in action a Vickers was not a very movable weapon; the gun alone with its tripod needed two men to carry it. The Germans had carts for battlefield handling (a practice they later abandoned), while the British had no specific machine-gun carrier, although they were of course carried on limbered General Service transport while on the march. For this reason, if for no other, machine guns were not sited in the most forward positions; to do so, for example in the KOYLI position, would condemn the team to an ultimate choice between abandoning the guns or being killed or

---

*The military career of the author's grandfather neatly illustrates the War Office's desperate search for officers. He was commissioned into the Artist Rifles as a Territorial, joined the nucleus of a New Army battalion (9th Berkshires) in November 1914 and was sent to Gallipoli as a replacement company commander in the regular 2nd Hampshires (29th Division). He was badly wounded on 4 June, after four days at the front, and medically discharged.

seeking surrender; there would be very little chance of getting away with the guns once close-quarter battle was joined and the abandonment of a machine gun was considered a very serious loss.* The surrender of machine-gun teams was not readily accepted by either side, at least later in the war. There are no figures available for the number of machine guns lost at Le Cateau; a likely figure could be as many as a quarter of them. Certainly the machine guns of the Suffolks, the Manchesters, the Argylls, the KOYLI, the 2nd Royal Scots, the Lancashire Fusiliers, the Hampshires and the Gordons were lost. There seemed to have an attempt to camouflage one of the latter's guns by painting it in blotches of various colours. The development of an individual automatic assault weapon was not perfected until the next war, although prototypes were made toward the end of the 1917.

The RA was clearly going to have to improve its counter-battery work, an area obviously linked to its relative neglect of forward observation. In XV Brigade, observers were put forward but telephone contact was soon lost; flags were then used. They did all they could in the short time available; rifle-fire had broken out even as they were digging in. In any case, when the infantry appeared they had all the targets they could engage. Later in the war great improvements in this area were made by the expanding RFC, as well as technical developments such as taking bearings of muzzle flashes, and acoustic direction finding. All this depended on accurate maps, and here the experience of August 1914 led to great efforts by the Ordnance Survey. When the BEF retreated due south instead of towards the channel ports they went off their maps; this was in spite of the fact that each brigade in 1914 carried three quarters of a ton of maps; the BEF had not been expecting to fight south of St Quentin.

Another lesson that should have been taken to heart, which is an issue common to all armies, was the degree to which officers throughout the chain of command should be allowed or even encouraged to use initiative and discretion in interpreting orders. Clearly it takes time for an army to adjust to wartime conditions; but by any standards Lt-Col Neish of the Gordons was an officer who should not have risen above the rank of lieutenant. If Major Salmon of the Rifle Brigade or Capt Hyslop of the Argylls had been in Neish's boots, the Gordons would not have been left in the lurch. Gen Snow singled out Brig Haldane of 10th Brigade who, when ordered to get out of Haucourt by the sunken lane, later complained to Snow that the lane was being shelled and that it was an unwise exit route but nevertheless stuck to it. Snow surprisingly blamed himself for his too-rigid order; but Haldane was hardly using his discretion, although *Field Service Regulations* would have exonerated him from disobedience. Haldane, paradoxically, was considered among the brightest of his generation, having been chosen as an observer at the Russo–Japanese War

---

*The Infantry Training Manual, 1914, laconically states 'In defence machine guns ... may lose their mobility'.

of 1905. The German Army, by contrast, encouraged initiative right down to the levels of its sergeants, who performed to a large extent the role of sub-alterns in the British Army. It is possible that the high standard of working-class education in Germany did something to increase military effectiveness among the other ranks.

The War Department in 1933 insisted and repeated as a kind of mantra the old military doctrine that:

> The most important lesson of all [from the battle of Le Cateau] is that no mat-
> ter how unfavourable conditions may appear, nor how desperate the situation
> may seem, the enemy is probably in a worse plight and the combatant with the
> real will to win will always achieve victory.

This is of course an eternal military truth applicable both to the offence and to the defence, and it was undoubtedly true that on 26 August 1914 the moral (as it was termed in those days) of the BEF was high, as it was throughout the Retreat, inasmuch as the BEF never lost confidence in itself. Without this moral factor Smith-Dorrien would not have demanded of his troops the extra exertions of fighting and withdrawing; and without it the men would not have done what they did. To take just one example, the machine-gun officer of the KOYLI, Lt Unett, was on the morning of the battle attached to brigade but asked to fight with the battalion guns, a request which was of course granted. This sort of action is not done in an army of poor morale. He survived the battle. The only comment on morale which Major Becke permitted himself was that the 5.9 HE was very bad for the morale of troops in towns. But even with high morale soldiers cannot win battles unless they have effective weapons to fight with, and with the 18-pounder field gun, the 4½in howitzer, the .303 Lee-Enfield and the Vickers they had weapons that proved themselves in a major European battle for the first time. Morale and good weaponry of course go hand-in-hand; without some degree of confidence in their weapons, the morale of the men will suffer. It is nothing short of extraordinary that in the winter to come, when the gunners were limited to a few rounds per day and the men had to make their own bombs, the morale of the BEF remained as high as it did. The holders of the Mons Star may have achieved semi-mythical status akin to the Spitfire pilots of 1940, aided by the pens of Brig Edmonds and Major Becke, but the skill exhibited on this day in what Smith-Dorrien himself admitted was a most difficult situation shows how richly deserving are the men of 1914 of their campaign medal.

The lesson that French took from Le Cateau was that his Second Corps com-mander was not to be trusted, any more than his allies. His wish that the BEF should be allowed a period to refit after the great Retreat was entirely under-standable, given the conviction that French and his staff now held that Second Corps was a spent force. He could hardly order First Corps into battle and give

Second Corps a time to refit at the hour of his ally's greatest need; at any rate this option was never considered at the time. Kitchener and Joffre had to cajole and implore him to get back into the war, but it was not difficult in the end to appeal to the martial virtues of an old cavalryman who was a professed admirer of Napoleon as a commander. The business of an army is to fight, after all. But even as late as 4 September French, supported by Haig and Smith-Dorrien,* was still urging the need to rest his troops and let the French take up the attack.

There is no doubt that on 26 August the heroism of the Suffolks with Major Doughty, the KOYLI and Major Yate, the Gordons, the Iniskillings, the Manchesters, the Argylls with Major Maclean and Capt Hyslop, the Rifle Brigade and Major Salmon, Lt Macleod and countless gunners, as well as others too numerous to mention, enabled so many to get away unmolested. The lesson here is that heroism is an eternal military virtue: one determined outpost can hold up a whole enemy division. Capt Bradbury, commanding L Battery at Nery on 1 September, scattered a whole cavalry division (4th) which played no further part in operations for a whole week. The 2nd Royal Munsters (First Division) under Major Charrier, together with two guns of 115th Battery RFA, held off for nearly twelve hours nine battalions and four artillery batteries at Etreux on the day after Le Cateau; the Munsters no longer formed part of the First Corps order of battle, but the Retreat went on. At the end the surviving 250 Munsters had formed themselves into a square in an orchard before being overwhelmed. But the feeling remains that had 5th Division attempted to retire an hour earlier, say at 12.30pm, then it might just have been possible for those Suffolks and KOYLI still unwounded to have got away, without sacrificing the rest of 5th Division.

Major Yate, Major Doughty and Capt Reynolds are acknowledged as the bravest of the brave for all time; others have no name that has been recorded. An unnamed motorcyclist in 5th Division RA was sent back to the ammunition park to collect some badly needed fuzes for the field guns. He did the round trip of 10 miles (16km) and the guns were able to carry on firing. All wars have their unsung heroes. Lastly, the lesson that the front-line troops had surely taken from their first experience of prolonged enemy shelling was that to survive they must dig.

In the words of Smith-Dorrien:

> In fact, had not the Suffolks and other intrepid troops refused to budge, there would have been nothing to prevent the enemy sweeping on to the scattered units of the division before they had had time to get on the road allotted for their retirement. Had this happened, the safety of the whole force fighting at Le Cateau would have been jeopardised ... the whole nation should be grateful to them.

*According to French but not Smith-Dorrien.

One reason that history has been kind to Sir Horace is that Sir John French effectively shot himself in the foot with the publication of his memoir *1914* (London 1919). This is not strictly speaking a work of historical reference at all; it is more of a polemic against Sir Horace and an attempt to build up Haig against Smith-Dorrien. In much the same way a generation later, Field Marshal Montgomery's inability to give credit where it was due undermined his reputation for all time. If Sir John had written in his memoir that Second Corps' battle on the 26th was fought against his better judgement and in the teeth of his military instincts, but that his worse fears were not realized, a great deal of unnecessary argument would have been avoided. It would have been a not unrealistic assessment. Field Marshal (as he became) Wilson's reputation similarly never recovered from the revelations in the biography by Gen Callwell.

Sir Horace's more dignified period of silence and his conduct as pall-bearer at Sir John's funeral in 1925 were effective in swinging the weight of opinion his way. In defence of French, his biographer has had to fall back on Churchillian quotes such as his 'sacred fire of leadership', whatever that means, although he did find evidence that the sickness rate in Second Corps was slightly higher in subsequent months. Other commentators can be found who have taken up the French cause: Col Repington of *The Times* wrote at about the time of Le Cateau that in his long talks with him, 'I was impressed with his complete grasp of the whole military situation, and by his intimate knowledge of all the details of his troops and their services.' Repington also had recourse to the 'fire of leadership' argument. French's own staff loyally supported him in his self-serving belief that the morale of Second Corps was never the same again after 26 August. Major Tom Bridges of the 4th Dragoon Guards shared this view, but he had of course been instrumental in heading off a near-mutiny of exhausted Le Cateau survivors with his tin drum in St Quentin late on the 26th, and so formed a jaundiced view of Second Corps infantry. He was also under the impression that Second Corps losses were 14,000 in 3rd and 5th Divisions alone (French's dishonest figures, taken from the losses from 23–27 August) which, if true, would have been truly staggering.

Understandably but perhaps unfairly French's supporters don't give him enough credit for the retreat decision on the night of the 23rd, the decision he got right (if a little late) and stuck to through thick and thin (and hung on to a little too long). This decision was taken in spite of optimistically low estimates of German strength by Wilson, who was still advocating an attacking posture as late as the evening of the 23rd, even putting forward the view that French attacks in the Ardennes and Alsace would somehow help the BEF position around Mons, a view that Haig marked with one of his asterisks in his diary. The preservation of the BEF, which was Britain's only field army at the time, as a fighting force was the focus of Sir John's priorities, as it quite properly should have been. It is after all true that under French's command the BEF got back from Mons to Compiègne with only 15,000 casualties. 'Such a casualty list can in the circumstances be considered as astonishingly light', says the *Official History*, a casualty list that fell out of all proportion on one wing of the BEF. It is true that in spite of this unequal burden on one half of the BEF, it had managed that most difficult of manoeuvres, a retreat without losing its cohesion and without losing its fighting ability. But without doubt the condition and position in which the BEF found itself on the night of the 25–26th was the most precarious of the whole Retreat, and its escape albeit with a casualty list of 7,812 officers and men on the 26th owes nothing to French himself. By contrast, the much derided Lanrezac, who also got the bulk of his 5th Army back to the Marne, played an active role in the tactical handling of his army on the 29th. If the Marne was a miracle, then the Retreat was a deliverance and the Ypres Salient became the altar of their sacrifice.

A week after the Retreat Gen Wilson said, with his unerring ability to get things wrong, that he expected the BEF to be across the German border in four weeks. And at Noyon on the 27th he had been heard muttering 'We shall never get to the sea.' As Gen Charteris, Haig's intelligence chief, candidly commented in 1915, 'His imagination seemed to take complete charge of his judgement.'* But to be fair, imagination in a soldier, leavened with a dash of common sense, could be argued to be a positive virtue.

Nigel Hamilton is no apologist for Smith-Dorrien, but no friend to French either; he is scornful of the leadership generally. He considers that the decision to offer battle on the 26th was fundamentally flawed, with the troops tired and 'dispirited' (sic). With 4th Division lacking so much of their support, there was more to be lost than gained by a stand; only luck saved Second Corps from disaster, inasmuch as von Kluck did not realize how close he was to a complete victory. Lt-Col Maxwell-Hyslop made more or less the same points in an article in the *Journal of the Royal United Services Institute* in 1921; too much was asked of the troops and the potential gain was not worth the cost. Spears curiously had a soft spot for French. But French has never had his Terraine.

When the marching orders did finally come for Sir Horace on 6 May 1915 during the crisis of Second Ypres (''Orace, you're for 'ome', in the words of Field Marshal Robertson, who had risen from the ranks, or alternatively 'Orace, you'll 'ave to 'op it') it was appropriate that it was ostensibly about his advocacy of a fall-back position, something he had put forward on his third day in France; but of course by that time it didn't matter how well-argued was Smith-Dorrien's paper in support of the proposed line and against the counter-attacks urged by Joffre and Foch: he was due for his comeuppance, from

---

*Although later in the war, Charteris' reports to Haig suggesting that the German armies were close to imminent collapse also verged on the fanciful.

French's viewpoint. His fall-back line was viewed as defeatist even though its logic in the face of the German gas attacks was impeccable; he was treated as Lanrezac had been treated by Joffre in September 1914. It was the army's loss if only because Smith-Dorrien's military instincts were extremely sound and allied to a decisive and adaptable mind, if a prickly one. Technically, Smith-Dorrien offered his resignation; in what was a move of military two-step he was replaced by Gen Plumer as commander of Second Army (which Second Corps had now become), the officer whom French had wanted in the first place, and who promptly accepted the logic of the fall-back line. French immediately accepted the new line, which he had previously called a 'retreat', showing once again that the source of the request was more important for him than the nature of the request itself. By this time Haig was already plotting the removal of French and his replacement by himself, and now there was no-one between him and the commander-in-chief. Haig was always more skilled in military politics than Smith-Dorrien, although the latter was no slouch in lobbying influential opinion in the war of the memoirs.

In many respects it would be tempting to see Smith-Dorrien as a British Pétain, at least in the latter's 1916–17 manifestation: essentially a general more suited to defence and concerned above all for the men, with his military doctrine rooted in his own down-to-earth common sense. Smith-Dorrien was fortunate that his reputation is untarnished by association with the bloodletting of 1916 and 1917; he was safely in Gibralter thanks to Sir John French, his posting to East Africa having been cancelled because of illness. And of course he never became the political general that Wilson was briefly before being murdered in 1922 and that Pétain so regrettably became.

An incident occurred on 28 August that shows a Pétainist touch. An order had gone out from GHQ to 4th Division, and copied to the other divisions, and had been endorsed by Second Corps staff, to the effect that spare personal kit (and ammunition!) should be jettisoned from the wagons and men and officers carried instead. The order (from Wilson to Snow) was intended to hurry the retreat along ('load up your lame ducks') but it smacked to officers of a panic measure that was quite unnecessary; it is not the sort of order that should be issued in an orderly retreat. This order was seen by Col Huguet, who relayed it to Joffre with his comments as follows:

> For the moment the British Army is beaten and is incapable of any serious effort ... the 3rd and 5th Divisions are nothing more than disorganized bands, incapable of offering the smallest resistance. Conditions are such that for the moment the British Army no longer exists.

Smith-Dorrien knew his men better than GHQ; nothing is more illustrative of the gulf between GHQ and the men on the march than this telegram. In fact, on the 28th Second Corps had no contact with the enemy at all and First

Corps only fleetingly. Even allowing for the fact that Huguet did not have a robust and sunny disposition in the first place, GHQ's mood had communicated itself to him, to the extent that when Joffre issued his orders for Lanrezac to counter-attack on the 29th he had told him to 'take no account of what the British are doing on your left'; in other words, you cannot rely on the British to help you in a tight spot. Such was the legacy of French's pessimism. But Huguet paradoxically was that rare Frenchman, one having an admiration for all things British.

Smith-Dorrien countermanded the jettison order, which he only learned about by chance, much to the fury of the C-in-C. When it reached Haig's HQ it was torn up by order of Brig Gough. In any case most troops sorted themselves out in their own fashion; the *Official History* states that on the 28th in the 5th Division 'as many men as possible were carried on vehicles of one kind or another.' It was the same with personal kit; when ordered to abandon all luxury items so as to lighten themselves for marching, one officer of the Rifle Brigade was not pleased to see his mother's tartan travel rug being worn later as a kilt by a highlander. One senior NCO in the Rifle Brigade (CSM F. McGahey) refused to be parted from his spare kit throughout the retreat; he survived the war and subsequently got married in it (presumably for sentimental reasons). Lt Roupell wrote of men taking the place of officers' valises on the limbers even before Le Cateau was reached.

One of the first things that Smith-Dorrien did when he reached St Quentin on the afternoon of the 26th was to organize the trains to carry out the wounded. In the confusion it clearly needed the firm hand of the senior officer to cut through the administrative deadlock. He had been expecting to see the C-in-C at St Quentin; he told Capt Dunn of the Welch Fusiliers that he had 'an appointment' with him. French would have to wait. There were trains to be got off to the south and wagons with rations to go up the Roman road to the troops; the latter left with an armed escort. Dunn left with a convoy of wagons for Noyon, with firm instructions to stop for nothing. Smith-Dorrien went back to St Quentin after the meeting with French at Noyon to carry on knocking heads together: very much a touch of Pétain in the night. It was his fourth night without sleep. The railway transport officers were going to have to look a bit sharp. Some of the Argylls managed to get on a train for Noyon.*

Of course, a feud between two red-faced generals with bristling moustaches (moustaches were compulsory for officers until 1915) is rather amusing, but by itself no more than a footnote in history. On the other hand, the fact that the Lords Lucan and Cardigan could hardly speak to each other does more than spice up the whole Balaklava debacle: it made its own contribution to

---

*According to Lt Ian Stewart's family history this train was 'commandeered' by the Argylls, who promptly fell asleep as soon as it left the station. When they woke up they had passed the British troops at Noyon and were almost in Paris.

the wrong guns being chosen by the Light Brigade as the target. One could speculate and imagine that one small part of Smith-Dorrien's decision in the early hours of 26 August was to cock a snook at his superior, whose military judgement he held in contempt in any case. But Smith-Dorrien was hardly likely to admit to this. His memoir and his diary (which he wrote at the behest of the King) are models of correctness.

When Smith-Dorrien, alone but for his driver, did finally track down French at 1.30am on the 27th at Noyon, after many hours motoring about (he got lost in Noyon) in the car lent him by Lord Derby, there was not likely to be a dispassionate setting-out of the facts as far as they were known. Horace had the nerve to turn up alive and well and full of optimism(!) with news that appeared to undermine the C-in-C's *amour propre*. Went the day well? Second Corps was retreating in reasonable order; the bulk of the Corps was away towards St Quentin, with only 5th Division seriously threatened in the battle. French already was aware of all this and didn't relish being told it by someone who seemed rather pleased with himself. Sir John was in danger of being made to look foolish. No one consciously wants to have his worst fears realized, but all day GHQ had been anticipating disaster. At 1.30am Sir John had to readjust his thinking, but one thing he was not going to do was to congratulate his *bête noir* on a miraculous deliverance and a great feat of arms. In time he would get his own back on this man who had undermined his authority. In two days' time French would be engaged in a row – with Haig – about liaison with Lanrezac, which was also about upholding his fragile authority, and from which French would make a tactical retreat in the face of an angry retort from Haig.

Now it was Sir Horace's upbeat, optimistic cheerfulness that seems to have grated most on the disgruntled French; Sir Horace made a point of this in his memoir. Curiously, or maybe not, none of the senior staff officers present at Noyon have published anything about this meeting. But one can imagine the veins standing out at the temples as the two commanders jabbed their fingers at the maps. French was probably still smarting from the humiliation he had suffered earlier in the day when his staff had had to admit to Joffre that they had not translated the latest *Instruction Generale* concerning the formation of 6th Army. All we know for certain is that Smith-Dorrien left GHQ at 3.00am to return to St Quentin. If French had a guilty conscience, as John Terraine has surmised, he had a lot to feel guilty about. It is possible also that in some atavistic corner of Sir John's brain – he had been schooled in the Victorian navy – there lurked the belief that Smith-Dorrien should have gone down with his ship.

Feuds, jealousies, the desire to get credit in the eyes of the public; all these are the stuff of life in high command. In the next war Gen Montgomery's prima donna, almost child-like behaviour and Gen Mark Clark's obsessive courting of newspaper fame were to cause frictions on a greater scale than those seen in 1914–18. Montgomery's staff officers, in particular De

Guingand, had to smooth things over with the Americans on more than one occasion. Both French at Le Cateau and Montgomery, particularly at the Battle of the Bulge, suffered from the same inability to recognize and give credit where it was due. It is a pity that Gen Murray couldn't do for French what De Guingand did for Montgomery, or what Alanbrooke did for Churchill.

The Retreat Continues

The greatest achievement that Smith-Dorrien can point to is that by dawn on the 28th practically the whole of Second Corps had been brought south of the Somme, 35 miles (56km) from the battlefield of the 26th, with only one serious attempt by the Germans to attack the columns. On the 27th a German field artillery battery had somehow got up to within 1,000yd of the 4th Division but had been driven off by a charge of the Hampshires, their colonel being wounded and captured in the action.* Bridges were blown by the sappers as the army retreated, which is of course normal military procedure in a planned retirement. There is no mention anywhere in the histories of any British attempts at booby-trapping, which is an accepted act of war in a retreat.

But the darkest hour is just before dawn. Capt Jack of the Scottish Rifles states bleakly in his diary that after leaving the Argylls at Honnechy, where as we have seen he was in the rearguard, he was too exhausted to remember details until the 28th, when he reached Pontoise. This was clearly the nadir of the retreat. His diary records these events:

> Rain was now falling. I soon joined groups of various regiments and some horse transport stumbling along, the men half-dazed from fatigue, being only kept together, and moving, by the exertions of their few remaining officers ...
>
> Some time in the night a motor lorry gave me a short lift before stopping to park with others. During this brief pause a little food purchased and devoured at an *estaminet* made me very sick; I lay down under a lorry to rest until it was ready to proceed with its neighbours. Soon somebody pulled me out saying they were going on; so I rose, numbed by the cold and rain, scarcely caring what happened ...
>
> About dawn I met, and reported for duty to, Lt-Col C.J. Hickie (HQ Second Corps). He was accompanied by one or two mounted orderlies and had also lost his headquarters. Both of us were now off our maps. We had I believe strayed west of St Quentin. Scarcely any troops were to be seen, but I managed to borrow a spare horse from a single battery and went with the colonel on a small tour to try and discover our whereabouts. Of soldiery we saw none, but heard heavy gunfire to the north-west (British and French rear-guards).
>
> Then we stopped in a village, loosened girths, watered and fed the horses, and bought for ourselves as well as the orderlies beer, raw eggs, rolls and butter.

*Lt-Col S.C. Jackson, who was to recover from his wound and join the Torgau prisoners.

This delicious breakfast was cut short by the approach of mounted from the north; so thinking they might be Prussians and that we might have wandered behind our rear-guard we girthed up and trotted away. The rain had now ceased, giving way to warm, bright weather.

Directing our way south by the sun we came across the main St Quentin–Ham road, straight, white, tree-lined, and running through open cultivated country. On it an endless irregular procession of infantry, batteries, transport and refugees tramped slowly towards Ham ...

A large number of valises and entrenching tools were absent, having been lost in action or thrown away by order or otherwise; all troops however had their arms, beside the residue of their ammunition. The officers were afoot, many of them carrying one or two of their men's rifles. The chargers bore equipment or exhausted soldiers, and towed a man hanging on to the stirrups on either flank. Transport vehicles gave similar assistance.

Frequently someone would fall or sit down for a rest, the first to be picked up by comrades and put on a wagon, and the second urged to his feet again. Here and there in this ghastly queue marched a fairly solid company, platoon or section.

Abandoned equipment littered the roadside; at intervals wagons had to be left for lack of teams.

During the morning things began to improve. Staff officers at road junctions distinguished the medley: 3rd Division on the right of the road, 5th Division on the left, 4th beyond the 3rd. There the different regiments were sorted out and formed into companies. Ammunition and rations, previously dumped by the transport, were issued.

I heard of one young staff officer being amused – until quelled – at the difference between this retreat and the Real Professional Retreat performed at Aldershot in perfect order.

In the twinkling of an eye organization and food produced a happier air; so when the improvized companies had devoured a meal from the cookers collected at these rendezvous, followed by an hour's sleep or a smoke and chat, they set out again like new men, soldierly and singing although dead-beat ...

As to the French peasantry: deeply concerned as they were about their own security, and bitterly disappointed at being left to the enemy's hands, their kindness by deed as well as word all the way from Mons can never be exceeded. At no time did I see on their faces, or hear in their remarks, anything but pity for our men. They stood at their doors with pails of water, sometimes wine, long rolls of bread and butter, fruit, just what they had. We must never forget them.

Late in the afternoon I crossed the Somme at Ham on foot, having relinquished my mount earlier – I could not ride with that wearied throng walking – and was directed to Ollezy, 4 miles eastwards, where nearly all the brigade was already assembled in bivouacs and barns.

The distance marched from Le Cateau was about 44 miles, the weather hot, and the men had had practically no proper meal or rest for thirty-six hours or more. Col Robertson estimated that the Cameronians covered 57 miles in that time. In the evening, when visiting the bivouac of my battalion I fainted – twice, I was told.

The condition of the troops on the 27th and 28th is in marked contrast to that only a few days later when a French civilian described a passing column as:

> ... phlegmatic and stolid ... their calm is in striking contrast to the confusion of the refugees ... As sportsmen who have just returned from a successful raid, our brave English eat with a good appetite, drink solidly, and pay royally those who present their bills ... and depart at daybreak, silently as ghosts, on the whistle of the officer in charge.

By contrast, on the same day Capt Spears witnessed a column of Lanrezac's Fifth Army troops 'shuffling' southwards:

> Dead and dying horses that had dropped in their tracks from fatigue lay in great numbers by the side of the roads. Worse still, horses dying but not yet dead, sometimes struggling a little, a strange appeal in their eyes, looked at the passing columns whose dust covered them, caking their thirsty lips and nostrils ... [men] utterly worn out, overcome by fatigue or sunstroke, dropped or lay where they had fallen, yet the spark of duty, the spirit of self-sacrifice, survived and bore the army on.

This was the army, let it be remembered, that French was unwilling to help.

All this time of course the cavalry had been active. Major Tom Bridges of the 4th Dragoon Guards had had a particularly busy time ever since the 24th. Many of the infantry had reason to be grateful for the often unseen exploits of the cavalry on the Retreat. On the 24th he had been swept up in the general action around Elouges. He had had a horse shot from under him outside Andregnies, was stunned and concussed, was taken into a friendly farmhouse, laid low while Uhlan patrols searched nearby, made good his escape next morning on a borrowed horse, and then had to shoot it when it went lame. He then found his friend Francis Grenfell of the 9th Lancers who sheltered him, got a ride with a signals officer in a motor car and rejoined his Dragoon Guards (2nd Cavalry Brigade). He took part in several brisk rearguard actions on the 26th on the right flank and then witnessed a bizarre sight. A car looking uncannily like a German staff car was spotted on a hill loaded with ladies having a good look round with binoculars. The 'ladies' were obviously

German staff officers who moved off sharply when Bridges sent a patrol galloping in their direction. Bridges made no further comment on the episode. But spy fever was endemic and even Bridges was not immune.

He then, late on the 26th, rallied the dejected infantry in the square of St Quentin by playing 'The British Grenadiers' and 'Tipperary' on a borrowed tin whistle and toy drum. The town mayor was desperate to save his town from bombardment and certain atrocities from the German soldiery; he had induced Montgomery's CO, Lt-Col Elkington, and another colonel to sign a surrender document. For a moment until Bridges' inspired intervention it looked as if British infantry and their commanding officer were going to surrender abjectly on the say-so of a defeatist French civilian, although at this point there were no German troops to surrender to. In mitigation it must be said that Sordet's troops were coming into the town swearing they were the only survivors of their regiment, the British were annihilated and the *Boche* were close behind them. A French cavalry officer accosted Capt Dunn outside the *Mairie* and told him to get out to Noyon 'or I would see some of the most atrocious things ever seen on this earth'. This was at about 4.00pm. GHQ had already left en masse. Smith-Dorrien passed through between 4.00pm and 5.00pm. Bridges had not yet arrived. 'Everything was chaos', in Dunn's words, and there was a leadership vacuum. But Bridges' resourcefulness saved the day. Although only a major, the troops responded to his mixture of threats, blandishments and the now famous tin whistle and were soon begging their saviour to stay with them. Col Elkington went off, joined the French Foreign Legion and redeemed himself.

One Somme crossing point used by Second Corps on the 28th – Voyennes – is that which Henry V had used on his way back to the channel from Burgundy in 1415. Field Marshal French should now have been sleeping more soundly; he had a major obstacle behind him, which had been his desire since Mons. Since 23 August the corps had fought two general actions, besides several minor affairs, and had marched just over 100 miles (160km). The worst trials of Gen Smith-Dorrien's force were now over. We will let Sir John French have the last word:

> I cannot close the brief account of this glorious stand of the British troops without putting on record my deep appreciation of the valuable services rendered by General Sir Horace Smith-Dorrien. I say without hesitation that the saving of the left wing of the Army under my command on the morning of August 26 could never have been accomplished unless a commander of rare and unusual calmness, intrepidity and determination had been present to conduct the operation personally.
>
> (Official Dispatch to Kitchener, 7 September)

Unfortunately this was not French's last word. In his memoir, *1914*, he wrote:

> In my despatch of September 1914, I refer eulogistically to the battle of Le Cateau ... [this despatch] was completed, of necessity, very hurriedly, and before there had been time to study the reports immediately preceding and covering the period of that battle, by which alone the full details could be disclosed ... I accepted without question the estimate made by the commander of Second Corps as to the nature of the threat against him ...

In sum, no tacit agreement was given to Dorrien-Smith to fight the battle which resulted in the Corps being 'shattered'. Even after the battle had started, 'staff officers were sent to Gen Smith-Dorrien carrying peremptory orders to break off the action and continue the retreat forthwith'. And as far as having given consent to the battle, 'there is not a semblance of truth in this'.

This was a continuation of his war by other means. It was French's tactical error to fight this last battle with his old enemy on matters of fact where he could be contradicted. French also rather missed the point. The losses at Ypres in the autumn were nearly eight times those at Le Cateau, and yet this disaster does not seem to have exercised his rage and spleen to anything like the same extent, even though it was the battle in which the old BEF effectively died. And of course Second Corps was not in the same condition it had been on the 22nd; how could it be after two major battles and two weeks of fighting retreat? One historian (Robin Neillands) has written that this row between French and Smith-Dorrien 'rocked' the British Army. Well, yes, but not to the extent that the Dreyfus affair had rocked the French Army a generation before. This also rather misses the point. The debate about the First World War, which grew in intensity as another war loomed, was not about whether or not the Battle of Le Cateau should have been fought or whether Sir Horace had saved the BEF; it was about how to fight the next war without incurring the same level of casualties as the last.

An interesting cast of players was drawn into the controversy. As well as the generals involved (although Hamilton was dead and Haig wisely kept his head down) such diverse characters as Sir John Fortescue (Smith-Dorrien's old school friend), Conan Doyle, Henry Newbolt, Wigram, the King's secretary, Lord Ernest Hamilton, Sir Frederick Kenyon and the editors of *The Times* and *The Daily Telegraph* all got involved at one time or another. Sir Horace undoubtedly came out the winner in the war of the memoirs, his role as the man who saved the BEF by his courageous decision in the early hours of 26 August receiving official recognition by Major Becke in 1919 and by Brig Edmonds in 1923. Sir Horace was also absolved from undue pessimism in September 1914 and April 1915.

In all the countless words written about the opening moves of the war perhaps the most bizarre comment of all was Lord Hamilton's in *The First Seven Divisions* (1916) in which he wrote: '... perhaps the main factor in deciding that Briton and German should cross swords at Le Cateau was the primitive impulse – always strong in the Anglo-Saxon breed – to face an ugly crisis and die fighting'. He must have thought that the French were lacking in primitive instincts or were better at keeping them under control.

Much ink was spilt over the role of Gen Sordet's cavalry in the war of the memoirs; French said he saved the left wing (because he loved cavalry and wanted to down-play Second Corps' achievement), Smith-Dorrien gave him official credit on the 29th and subsequently, and Gen Snow, who was in the position to know best, wrote that Sordet was never sorely tested and never exerted himself beyond showing a token presence, and that anyway d'Amade's gunners in Cambrai were more useful. Elements of Sordet's cavalry certainly behaved badly in St Quentin on the 26th, as witnessed by the always reliable Capt Dunn. (D'Amade retreated about the same time as 4th Division, about 3.00pm, by happy coincidence.) The truth was that von Kluck thought he was up against the whole BEF, he was in a hurry to defeat it in battle before it disappeared over the hill like it had before, and he didn't have the time or the intention to send his cavalry reserve formations several miles to the west in an attempt to fix his enemy to the ground: they had already done that for him themselves.

This was not a battle of large-scale manoeuvres. Von Kluck had military logic on his side, with his immediate attack on two flanks, given his three-to-one numerical superiority; and so, to be fair, did Sir John French with his insistence on the priority for retreat. Sir John's character flaws could be forgiven had he been a great general, as for example were Gen Patton's in the next war; but Sir John's mercurial temper was so bound up with his generalship that activity at GHQ became at once febrile and despondent. In much the same way, Smith-Dorrien's decision to fight, and Haig's decision to march on south, are both bound up in their respective personalities. We could hazard a hypothetical scenario and suggest that if Haig had been commanding Second Corps his prudence would not have allowed him to issue the 'stand and fight' order, but that if he had French's response both at the time and later would have been entirely different.

In any case French's actual contribution to the tactical handling of divisions, brigades and battalions in battle was zero. And for all of Col Macdonogh's vaunted expertise at GHQ's Intelligence Branch, he lacked the intimate knowledge that Gen Grierson had had of the German tactical deployment of troops, so that GHQ was operating without a compass. French's impounding of 4th Division's support train was extremely regrettable. Few of the major functions that GHQ was tasked to perform – intelligence, co-ordination of operations – were adequately fulfilled. Only its quartermaster role was well executed.

Actually, the French–Smith-Dorrien row does have its more revealing moments and was the subject of a book published in 1993, incorporating Sir Horace's statement of 1921 setting out his riposte to French's *1914*, previously only circulated privately. Its title, *The Judgement of History*, may be a touch overblown but useful facts emerged, for even in 1925 there still were gaps in the recorded chronology. With his usual disregard for facts, French claimed in 1919 that he was the first to perceive the need for the retreat and issued the orders accordingly at 8.17pm on the 23rd. He was not allowed to get away with that; an order was verified that went out to corps and cavalry at 8.40pm to 'stand this attack on the ground now occupied by the troops', referring to the expected German attack the next morning. The kindest thing to say would be that confusion of this sort is endemic to war, whereas generals in their memoirs like to appear as if they were in control of events.

The problem for both Smith-Dorrien and French over the vital timing of the retreat order was the role of (acting) Capt Edward Spears. French didn't want to acknowledge that it was the evidence of such a junior officer that was so revealing, and Smith-Dorrien didn't seem to know about Spears' presence at GHQ at all. So French had to present the 'facts' as showing that his perception of the new reality somehow predated Spears' visit. And Smith-Dorrien couldn't understand why he wasn't informed of the general retreat order earlier and was reluctant to cast blame on his chief of staff, Forestier-Walker. At the same time there was GHQ's reluctance to use the wire/phone when matters of great import were being transmitted. An excessive concern for secrecy is often the enemy of good decision-making; but at least the decision was made.

But while Smith-Dorrien got some fitful sleep, on the night of the 23rd–24th, before Forestier-Walker's return from GHQ, the seeds of his future defiance of French were being sown. If he had to get away it must be done soon. If he had to fight he would fight; but he was not sanguine about the outcome. He was 'chafing'; it was his 'tipping point', in language not current in 1914. The odds were better on the 26th with a shorter line to defend and another division under his command; and in any case the general who waits for every last gun and man to be in place will never fight. On the 26th Sir Horace was matched to his hour.

After all, the Retreat did not have a fixed objective, like the three retreats mentioned earlier: Corunna, Dunkirk and Burma. On the 26th the BEF didn't know whether it was aiming for Peronne as an objective, or Paris, or Amiens or Le Havre. On the 29th Haig was under the impression that the BEF was changing its base to Nantes. Perhaps Smith-Dorrien on the 26th could hear Wellington's cry from 1815: 'Now's your time! Up Guards and at them.'

The second convincing set of facts to emerge from the re-examination in 1993 was the reasons for the critical gap that existed at dawn on the 26th between the two corps. It amounted to several hours' march, unlike at Mons where the two corps were mutually supporting, but it was still possible even at this late hour for cavalry at least to have come to the aid of Second Corps. There is no denying the contrast between First Corps and their German opponents during the retreat to Landrecies/Le Cateau. The Germans, simply by sleeping on the roadsides rather than going in to billets, seemed to push on with more determination than First Corps, something that was acknowledged by the Torgau prisoners. The Guards were going into billets at Landrecies as early as 5.00pm on the 25th: they got to their billets before the German vanguard who were after the same accommodation. The Germans had moved through the Forest of Mormal whereas First Corps had not. First Corps casualties of nearly 1,200 on the 26th were due mainly to men falling out from exhaustion and crippled feet rather than to enemy action, although the corps was able to push on quicker without the weaker brethren, or 'wasters' as Lt Johnson rather cruelly called them. All this is true and merely illustrates the point that Haig's battalions, apart from the 2nd Connaught Rangers, were not seriously engaged on the 25th (and the 26th) and did not push on towards Le Cateau, which GHQ expected them to do: this is why Murray was baffled as to their whereabouts, in spite of Johnny Gough being in Le Cateau at the time.

To let First Corps march blithely on due south for the whole of the 26th when it would have been perfectly possible to get new orders to Haig by no later than 7.00am (by volunteer driver, for example) is 'eccentric', to say the least. The War Office in 1933 wrote that the 'altered' direction of Haig's Corps was 'acquiesced' in by GHQ. Altered from what? The truth was that Haig didn't exactly alter his route of march, he merely chose the middle route of the three on offer. The insistence on the Busigny direction was now watered down. We must assume that the staff officer who arrived on horseback at Haig's HQ at 6.00am on the 26th, did not come with the certain knowledge of Smith-Dorrien's stand decision. But given that, it remains the case that the only inference that we can draw is that French (or GHQ in general) was intent on saving at least part of the BEF from destruction, destruction that was being brought down on Second Corps by the foolishness of its own commander. Haig's choice of the middle route chimed well with his own acknowledged prudence and career calculations.*

If Haig was trying to conform to his interpretation of his orders he was not listening to his military instincts which must surely have led him closer to 'the main body'. Like Admiral Evan-Thomas at Jutland, he did not turn towards the enemy when the guns started firing in earnest. And like Evan-Thomas he was in receipt of orders that did not make clear the overall plan, because there was no overall plan, at least on the 26th.

It was perfectly possible to get an order to Haig in the early part of the morning of the 26th with a message saying in effect 'Second Corps are fighting for their lives on your right; can you send help [cavalry] to the south of Le Cateau town?' The Duke of Westminster, dispatched with his Rolls-Royce, could have saved the right flank of Second Corps. As it was, the two corps were even further apart on the day after Le Cateau than before, and were not to resume contact until 1 September.

Smith-Dorrien was entitled to feel mucked about; he was to receive support from neither his fellow corps commander nor his commander-in-chief on the day when it was most needed. Just one brigade of First Corps hard up on Le Cateau and blocking the exits from the town would have been very welcome to Brig Rolt of 14th Brigade, although they would have had to have got there by 10.00am. Smith-Dorrien could rightly claim, which he did, that on the 24th he had forcefully pleaded with Murray that orders to both corps be issued that would keep them in step. It was at this meeting that he had been told by French that he could 'do as he liked'. (Haig had been told he could 'do as I judged best'.) This remark to Smith-Dorrien was intended to refer to the details of the routes taken by different brigades, but could have at a pinch been used in justification for the stand on the 26th. But to be fair to French, micro-management of corps movement orders was not his way of doing things, a way that did however place a burden on the small corps staff.

First Corps' retreat can be summarized thus:

24 August (early morning): Haig makes his own arrangements for retreat to Bavai, under the general retreat order, received at 2.00am.

24 August: Haig retreats down two main roads, east of the Forest of Mormal, according to orders, at an average speed of 2mph (3km/h). Reaches Bavai.

25 August: The attack at Landrecies. Haig receives orders to retreat towards St Quentin (south-west) but goes due south in great haste next morning after the night action at Landrecies, under orders from French.

*Nikolas Gardner, in his study of BEF command in 1914, tends toward the 'conspiracy theorists' in his discussion of the post-Landrecies move, or rather the interplay of the rivalries between the main players, but also points out the role of poor communications. Dennis Winter (*see* Bibliography) also supports the conspiracy theorists. I make no apology for repeating these serious assertions.

26 August: Haig continues due south for Etreux, on a good, straight road, having rejected the proffered option (6.30am) of going south-west and not receiving, or not acknowledging, the order (1.00pm) to go toward Busigny/St Quentin. He has no difficulty rejecting the south-east option, an option that remains a mystery. He continues 'on the lines I already laid down'. His diary makes out therefore that the route taken was the only feasible route. It is a profoundly dishonest entry, and ends entry lamely with comment that 'I felt I could not do more than I had already done to comply with the spirit of [French's] orders.' His interpretation of the 'spirit' of his C-in-C's orders is entirely self-serving. He ends the night at a small inn run by an old man and his daughter, and enjoys 'an excellent dinner of fried eggs and stewed rabbit'. His insides had recovered; he was satisfied with the day's progress.

There was thus no 'alteration' to First Corps' route equivalent to von Kluck' eastern wheel of 2 September; he merely continued due south as if Second Corps was not there at all. It was purely good fortune that von Kluck did not do more to exploit the gap created by Haig's more or less wilful refusal to close up on his right. Haig had (rightly) judged that a stand at Bavai would be disastrous, and had not changed his mind at Landrecies/Le Cateau. He was therefore no different from Lanrezac, for whom this judgement had earned him the soubriquet of defeatism, and who had abandoned his ally at Mons in order to save his own army. The fact that Haig's abandonment of Second Corps was not unhelpful to his career could be called a conspiracy theory by those sympathetic to him. It is also a possibility that French's offering of the three choices of route to Haig was an attempt to prepare the ground for defence if the finger of blame should look for a culprit; if so, it was an abject piece of buck-passing. His 1.00pm order to Haig to turn south-west could easily have been mere window-dressing: knowing it could not affect the outcome of the battle, it nevertheless would look good in the court of history. All historians would agree that Haig for his part was skilled at institutional infighting and at covering his tracks.

On the 29th Lanrezac's 5th Army – consisting of three corps – for the first time struck with full force into von Bulow's 2nd Army, against which First Corps had already been fighting. Gen Franchet d'Esperey ('Desperate Frankie' to the British) personally leading a brigade (he was a corps commander at the time) on horseback, white-gloved, sword in hand, colours fluttering in the breeze and the music of the bands playing the 'Sambre et Oise' and the 'Marseillaise'. It was magnificent and it was war as it would never be seen again. It has been called the last Napoleonic battle of the French armies. First Corps stood by on the left flank, Haig receiving a reprimand from French for the sin of fraternizing with the despised Lanrezac. Franchet d'Esperey was to replace Lanrezac before the battle of the Marne; Joffre's sacking of Lanrezac, whose intellectual arrogance had endeared him to no one and whose defeatism made him an unlikely French general, was not unwelcome to Sir John.

The situation was the reverse of what had happened to the British at Mons, when Lanrezac had abandoned the BEF, as Spears wrote:

> .... nothing would persuade the British to co-operate. They were doing as they had been done by ... They had been misinformed on every single matter of importance from the numbers of the enemy to the result of the French operations. Where they had looked for support they had found only shadows; schemes, plans, operations, everything had melted away, leaving only one reality – the enemy who in overwhelming strength and with relentless purpose had driven home blow after blow ...

These, we must remind ourselves, are the words of an ardent Francophile; Sir John may be forgiven for feeling that the position of a junior partner in coalition warfare was not a happy one, as experienced between 23 August and 6 September 1914. Later, of course, after the 'Race to the Sea', when the trench lines became established, the BEF, the Belgians and the French had their own frontages, the British in 1916 becoming responsible for the front as far south as the Somme. But it was not until 26 March 1918 that a truly unified command on the Western Front was created, when Marshal Foch, at the Doullens conference, was given overall command of the Allied forces at a time when the German breakthrough seemed all too reminiscent of August 1914.

Joffre – who had hovered by Lanrezac's side throughout the morning of the battle on the 29th in a way unthinkable to Smith-Dorrien – was well satisfied and went off for lunch in the nearest railway station buffet. The next day – as a direct consequence of the battle of Guise – von Kluck, in defiance of his Supreme Command, executed his 90 degree left turn, which 'ultimately brought about his downfall', in the words of John Terraine.

But the whole Le Cateau debate does have a point: the battle fought on 26 August 1914 does have relevance for the next war. If the BEF in 1940 under Lord Gort had been able to mount a successful stand – a stopping blow – in conjunction with the French against Guderian's Panzer army, the history of the Second World War might have taken a different course. The battle of France in May 1940 never had its Le Cateau, and that was its tragedy. The tragedy of the British defeat at Singapore in February 1942 could conceivably have been averted had Gen Percival marshalled his British, Indian and Australian troops into delivering a similar smashing blow to the Japanese invaders. The 2nd Battalion Argyll and Sutherland Highlanders, who had the misfortune to be in that ill-starred campaign, were commanded by Lt-Col Ian Stewart, the veteran of Le Cateau.

Postscript

The successful penetration by the German armies of so much of north-east France and Belgium in August 1914, von Kluck's eastern wheel and the check they received on the Marne, and their subsequent pegging-out of territory right up to Nieuport, made inevitable the stalemate of the next four years; 1914 bears almost no resemblance to 1870 (and very little to 1940, except that the British started off both wars with a retreat). It does however have close similarities with the German offensive of March–April 1918, which threatened Paris again but which was finally blunted and thrown back by co-ordinated allied action. In September 1914, as in August 1918, the pursued became the pursuers.

Without a doubt Smith-Dorrien's smashing blow slowed the German momentum on its western flank as did the blow given to the 2nd Army at Guise by Lanrezac's 5th Army three days later. The German armies of the right wing reeled under the double blows. The Schlieffen Plan may have been over-optimistic for armies that relied on shoe-leather and legs for movement, but the German armies still had to be stopped somehow. Their retreat to the Aisne after the battle of the Marne may have been conducted in a less orderly manner than the British retreat from Mons, but it was not a rout.

As it was the Germans were able to establish positions largely on ground of their choosing from north of Ypres in Belgium in a great arc down to the Swiss border. The allies had the Herculean task of throwing them back over their border, an ultimately successful effort that cost the armies of the British Empire nearly nine hundred thousand lives on the Western Front, the lives of its best young men. There was no compromise possible and no way round. And at the very end of the bloodletting the British Army were back where they had started, in Le Cateau and Mons. Gen von der Marwitz, who rather ineffectively commanded the right cavalry wing on 26 August 1914 against Gen Sordet's cavalry division, was back in Le Cateau in October 1918 as commander of II Army, a record of service to rival that of Haig's. The British battalions that were back at Le Cateau in October 1918 were almost all New Army battalions, rather than the old regulars.

During the intervening years, of course, Le Cateau was under German occupation; it was liberated on 17 October 1918 by the 66th Division. It was not spared the devastation that all towns in the zone of war in northern France suffered to some extent. On the night of 26 August 1914 it entered on the dark night of its exploitation and martyrdom at the hands of the Germans, who administered the town and surrounding country without pity for the next fifty-five months.

Curiously, on the night of 26 August the population did not flood out en masse along the roads south; there was no panic. The traders and café owners that had served the British presumably carried on serving soldiers in field grey the next day. Capt Dunn noticed on that rainy night:

> ... a number of women ... [who] did not seem in the least alarmed, rather they were amused, probably – poor creatures – looking on the affair as affecting only the Germans and the English, and no concern of theirs, little thinking that they were about to entertain the Germans for the next four years.

They did not exactly 'entertain' the Germans for the next four years. That same night drunken German soldiery rampaged through the town, looting the shops and creating 'a nightmare I shall remember all my life', in the words of M. Guillot, later of the Musée Matisse. The Germans treated occupied France as a source of food, labour and materials, to be exploited to the maximum benefit of the German war effort. Rations were steadily reduced to near-starvation levels and men were deported to work on military tasks for twelve hours per day. American aid, like Red Cross parcels in POW camps, was a lifeline, but in many respects conditions were worse than in 1940–44, though it was in the war yet to come that the Germans added refinements such as deportation based on racial qualifications.

Auguste Matisse, Henri's brother, who with his family and mother spent the occupation in Bohain, near St Quentin where the young Henri went to school, developed tuberculosis as a result of his privations. Anna Matisse, Henri's 74-year-old mother, refused to disinter her valuables for fear of the rapacious Hun, who became more and more thorough in his looting. She was jailed for four days in the spring of 1918 for refusing to leave her home when the entire population was ordered out into the fields. She refused in the spring of 1918 to join the pathetic throng of refugees who trekked along the roads north when the Germans allowed the infirm and elderly to leave. Henri was one of the first civilians to return to Bohain when it was liberated by the British on 8 October 1918. His mother went down to the cellar and recovered her silver. She had been living there for months on turnips and dried beans while the battle swayed back and forth above her; she was unbiddable and unbowed. She had sold her piano to buy food and the sheet music had become wrapping paper. Above her was 'a landscape of the last judgement'.

The Germans garrisoned at Le Cateau for the duration – 350 men and officers for fifty-five months – naturally fed and financed themselves at the expense of the French. There was no attempt at winning over even some potential sympathizers. Eighteen hostages were taken as early as September and held as security by the German commandant. The threat to their lives was

German appeal for raw materials; the blockade was having its effect. (Peronne Museum)

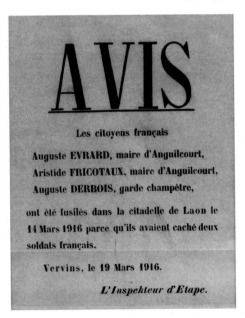

German proclamation. (Peronne Museum)

179

very real; on 2 September 1914 at Senlis, only 27 miles (43km) from Paris, the mayor and six other citizens were taken as hostages and shot in a field outside the town on the same day. In November 1914 three citizens of Cambrai and Catillon were shot for the crime of keeping pigeons. The last words of one of the condemned – M. L'Homme – were 'France shall avenge us!' A monument was erected to their memory and homage is still paid to them every year. All citizens were compelled to salute German officers. Jail sentences were imposed on boys who aimed their slingshots at electric cables.

The Germans attempted to control the black market by decree and threats. The town council was the mouth-piece of the commandant and as in the next war tried to extract what concessions it could in exchange for co-operation. It was decreed, for example, that bread should be made of not more than 30 per cent wheat flour; only one bakery in the town was allowed. Later in the war as the blockade of Germany became more effective the German authorities became desperate for new sources of material and offered a small price for washed nettles and fruit stones. The Germans were capricious in imposing levies on the conquered towns and cities: the burghers of Ghent, for example, were ordered at Christmas 1914 to provide one million cigars, ninety thousand pounds of tobacco, and the contents of every commercial wine-cellar.

In the final ten days of the fighting Le Cateau suffered a final orgy of looting by the departing Germans, followed by shelling which destroyed the majority of the town; the town hall and the church were spared only because the German sappers did not blow the charges they had laid. Even after the 66th Division (Third Army) had taken the town on 21 October the shelling continued for another ten days until the line was pushed back. All this was on top of the gratuitous shelling the town received on the 26 August 1914, well after the British had left the town. The fighting in October 1918 was very different from that in 1914. Cpl Cliff Lane of the 1st Battalion the Hertfordshire Regiment (37th Division) remembered:

> We made this attack just in front of Le Cateau. It was a night attack, and preparations were made to avoid chaos as far as possible. We all wore a silvery bit of metal on our backs so that anybody coming from behind would know who we were. We also carried red sort of candle things that would light to indicate our positions.
>
> We went over the top and we met no resistance. They came out with their hands up. One came running out of the trench waving a white shirt, he nearly knocked me over – he was screaming his head off – it was pathetic. You would never have seen that in the old days.

Today there is a drinking trough filled with flowers inscribed to the 66th Division just off the main square in Le Cateau. There is no memorial to the troops of the 19th Brigade and others who rested their blistered feet there so briefly in the early hours of the 26th. In the CWGC cemetery to the south of the town – Highland Cemetery, named partly for its height and no doubt partly for the thirty-two graves of the 13th (Scottish Horse) Battalion, Black Watch found in this plot – the visitor can look west towards Reumont over a battlefield almost untouched since 1914. There are no British soldiers who died at Le Cateau in 1914 buried here and very few at the International Cemetery to the north-west of the town. There are British soldiers, both known but mostly unknown, who lie buried at communal cemeteries at Honnechy, Caudry and Fontaine and other villages. These known graves, such as that of Major Rickman of the Rifle Brigade, buried at Fontaine, are mostly of men who received an honoured burial from French civilians in 1914; but most of those who fell on the battlefield on 26 August were buried without ceremony by the Germans, using impressed Frenchmen. Every year, on the first Sunday after All Saints' Day, a ceremony of remembrance is held, organized by the *Comite d'Entente* of Le Cateau, at the Highland Cemetery, the International Cemetery and the Communal Cemetery.

Nothing more graphically illustrates the tidal waves that engulfed the whole continent of Europe in the years 1914–18 than the forty-two Russian graves in the International Cemetery. The Russians had been conscripted into the German Army and were killed here by a foe with whom they had no quarrel. From this cemetery on the west of the town can be seen the embankment on the Cambrai road where the Germans brought up nine machine guns to the bottom of Suffolk Hill, aided by the concealed exits from the town, and part of Suffolk Hill.

An RA officer (Lt E.L. Armitage) who was wounded and captured at Ligny was taken through the battlefield five days after the battle. Wrecked guns, limbers, dead horses were everywhere to be seen around the village of Audencourt, where the Gordons had hung on until after midnight; this was 6 Battery, which had received the direct hit when limbering up. It looked as if the RFA Brigade had kept their transport up with the batteries, such were the number of wrecked limbers and dead horses. The hedgerows of the road were pitted with hastily scraped hollows containing the bodies of dead 3rd Division men and to the north of the village were four machine guns, their detachments and three British officers lying dead beside them. German gunners also lay buried where they had been killed, their helmets placed on the freshly dug earth on top of their bodies.

There were four more years of war when communications with the German POW camp authorities were possible only through neutral countries and the International Red Cross. In August 1914 the War Office had no department dealing with POWs. The relatives of those recorded missing had agonizing months of not knowing what had happened to their sons, fathers and uncles. Of the more than 100 Le Cateau officers held captive in the Torgau (officer) prison camp, 70 per cent were suffering from wounds of one sort or another. The largest unwounded group of officers were regimental medical officers who had elected to stay behind with their wounded, or who had been captured along with the front-line troops while tending the wounded in advanced aid posts. There was also a large contingent of RAMC officers (4th Field Ambulance) who had been taken on the 27th at Landrecies where they had stayed behind to tend the wounded guardsmen. The high survival rate of the Torgau prisoners must have been due to some extent to the large number of medical men in their midst. In their *Torgau History*, compiled by their joint accounts of the battle, there is no bitterness against the decisions which had led to their incarceration. Instead there is a less than grudging admiration for the ability of the German 1st Army to keep up its forward momentum and still be ready to offer battle at what seemed a moment's notice. The Torgau prisoners were interned in Holland towards the end of the war, much to their relief. Food was getting very scarce in Germany in 1918 and the blockade remained in force for several months after the Armistice. Perhaps surprisingly, for one officer the harshest deprivation of all during the four years of prison was not the poor food or the physical conditions but the absence of any horizon to look at – he said it affected his eyes.

Those with no known grave – the vast majority of those killed on August 26th – are commemorated at the CWG monument at La Ferte-sous-Jouarre, 66 miles (106km) to the east of Paris. This monument lies at the furthermost point of the Retreat and it is here that all those who died, without the known and honoured burial given to their comrades in death, between August, September and early October 1914 are listed by name, rank and regiment and date of death. There are nearly 3,500 of them. These soldiers' names are also inscribed on war memorials in villages, towns, cities, churches, schools and colleges throughout the British Isles.

There is a fine memorial (stele) to the men of the 2nd Battalion the Suffolk Regiment, the 2nd Battalion the Manchester Regiment, the 2nd Battalion the Argyll and Sutherland Highlanders and XV Brigade RFA. The vast majority of the men and officers listed here have no known grave. It stands today on the same ground on which they made their heroic stand on 26 August 1914. It stands, white and bright, in a small grass meadow and the monument is shaded by five pine trees and is fenced round. All those who died here on 26 August are listed by name and rank. The eighty Suffolk names are headed by their colonel, C.A.H. Brett DSO. The landscape is unchanged, the only difference on the knoll being that modern tractors and ploughs have evened out the hollows in the ground that were there in 1914, and a farm track that existed in 1914 running parallel to the Roman road has been ploughed over. The bank of the sunken lane obscures the Cambrai road to the north, as it did on 26 August 1914.

The clock-tower of the church in Le Cateau is still the main feature to the north-east. The sunken lane is how it was in 1914, with evidence that it is now used as a lovers' lane by the youths of the town. Trucks pass along the Roman roads with a perceptible noise but otherwise the rest is silence. The bells of the clock-tower were rededicated in 1934 but the XV RFA Brigade did not destroy it in 1914; the gunners and spotters in the tower in all likelihood scampered down the spiral stairs soon after the first shells whistled past, although there was one palpable hit. All the glass in the church has been replaced.

In the St Symphorien cemetery at Mons there are two graves side by side that have a singular distinction. One is that of Private J. Parr of the Middlesex Regiment, killed on 21 August 1914. The other is that of Private J.L. Price, a Canadian, killed on 11 November 1918, just before 11.00am while talking to a child holding a flower. They were the first and last soldiers of the armies of the British Empire to be killed in the war. They lie in mute testimony to all the lives cut so brutally short, a testament to a war that ended where it began, that was declared for Britain by Prime Minister Asquith against German militarism but that had to be fought again a generation later against the same foe. It is our sacred duty to ensure that their sacrifice is not forgotten and that we keep faith with those who died.

The Suffolk Memorial, on the knoll to the south-west of Le Cateau. The dead of the Suffolks, the Manchesters, the Argylls and XV RFA are inscribed here.

Appendix I
British Losses
23–7 August 1914

(Excluding missing who returned to their unit)

August	23rd	24th	25th	26th	27th
	(Mons)		(Le Cateau)		
Cavalry Division	6	252	123	15	14
I Corps					
1st Division	9	42	32	826	
2nd Division	35	59	230	344	48
II Corps					
3rd Division	1185	557	357	1796	50
5th Division	386	1656	62	2631	76
4th Division			65	3158	58
19th Infantry Brigade	17	40	36	477	108

Appendix II
The Order of Battle

The composition of the divisions at Le Cateau, 26 August 1914 and total casualties suffered by division.

3rd Division, Maj-Gen Hubert Hamilton

7th Infantry Brigade, Brig-Gen F.W.N. McCracken
3rd Worcestershire
1st Wiltshire
2nd South Lancashire
2nd Royal Irish Rifles

8th Infantry Brigade, Brig-Gen B.J.C. Doran
2nd Royal Scots
2nd Royal Irish
4th Middlesex
1st Gordon Highlanders

9th Infantry Brigade, Brig-Gen F.C. Shaw
1st Northumberland Fusiliers
4th Royal Fusiliers
1st Lincolnshire
1st Royal Scots Fusiliers

Divisional Troops
C Squadron 15th Hussars, 3rd Cyclist Company
Divisional Artillery, Brig-Gen F.D.V. Wing
XXIII Brigade RFA: 107, 108, and 109 Batteries and ammunition column
XL Brigade RFA: 6, 23, and 49 Batteries and ammunition column
XLII Brigade RFA: 29, 41, and 45 Batteries and ammunition column
XXX Howitzer Brigade RFA: 128, 129, and 130 Batteries and ammunition column
48 Heavy Battery RGA and ammunition column
3rd Divisional ammunition column

Royal Engineers, 56th and 57th Companies
3rd Signal Company, 3rd Divisional Train, and 7th, 8th, and 9th Field
Ambulances

Total at full strength = approx. 18,650 officers and men
Actual strength = approx. 16,650 officers and men
Total casualties = 1,796

5th Division, Maj-Gen Sir C. Fergusson Bt

13th Infantry Brigade, Brig-Gen G.J. Guthbert
2nd King's Own Scottish Borderers
1st Queen's Own Royal West Kent
2nd Duke of Wellington's West Riding
2nd King's Own Yorkshire Light Infantry

14th Infantry Brigade, Brig-Gen S.P. Rolt
2nd Suffolk
1st D.C. Light Infantry
1st East Surrey
2nd Manchester

15th Infantry Brigade, Brig-Gen Count Gleichen
1st Norfolk
1st Cheshire
1st Bedfordshire
1st Dorsetshire

Divisional Troops
A Squadron 19th Hussars, 5th Cyclist Company

Divisional Artillery, Brig-Gen J.E.W. Headlam DSO
XV Brigade RFA: 11, 52, and 80 Batteries and ammunition column
XXVII Brigade RFA: 119, 120, and 121 Batteries and ammunition column
XXVIII Brigade RFA: 122, 123, and 124 Batteries and ammunition column
VIII Howitzer Brigade RFA: 37, 61, and 65 Batteries and ammunition
    column
108 Heavy Battery RGA and ammunition column
Royal Engineers, 17th and 59th Field Companies
Total number of guns: 74

5th Signal Company
5th Divisional Train
13th, 14th, and 15th Field Ambulances

Total at full strength = approx. 18,650 officers and men
Total actual strength = approx. 16,350 officers and men
Total casualties = 2,366

4th Division, Maj-Gen T. D'O. Snow

10th Brigade, Brig-Gen J.A.L. Haldane
1st Warwicks
2nd Seaforths
1st Royal Irish Fusiliers
2nd Royal Dublin Fusiliers

11th Brigade, Brig-Gen A.G. Hunter-Weston
1st Somerset Light Infantry
1st East Lancs
1st Hampshire
1st Rifle Brigade

12th Brigade, Brig-Gen H.F.M. Wilson
1st King's Own Regiment
2nd Lancashire Fusiliers
2nd Inniskilling Fusiliers
2nd Essex Regiment

Divisional Artillery, Brig-Gen G.F. Milne DSO
XIV Brigade RFA: 39, 68 and 88 Batteries and ammunition column
XXIX Brigade RFA: 125, 126 and 127 Batteries and ammunition column
XXXII Brigade RFA: 27, 134 and 135 Batteries and ammunition column
XXXVII Howitzer Brigade RFA: 31, 35 and 55 Batteries and ammunition column
Total number of guns: 72

Total at full strength = approx. 18,650 officers and men
Total actual strength = approx. 18,000 officers and men
Total casualties = 3,158

19th Brigade (Independent Brigade), Maj-Gen J.G. Drummond

2nd Royal Welch Fusiliers
1st Middlesex
2nd Argyll and Sutherland Highlanders
1st Cameronians (Scottish Rifles)

Total at full strength = approx. 4,000 officers and men
Total casualties = 477

Cavalry Division, Maj-Gen E.H.H. Allenby

1st Brigade, Brig-Gen C.J. Briggs
2nd Brigade, Brig-Gen H. de B. de Lisle
3rd Brigade, Brig-Gen H. de la P. Gough
4th Brigade, Brig-Gen Hon C.E. Bingham

Artillery, Brig-Gen B.F. Drake

III Brigade
VII Brigade

Royal Engineers

Army Service Corps

Total strength = approx. 10,000 officers and men
Total casualties = 15

Total number of prisoners taken (included in above casualty figs) = 2,600

Appendix III
Notes on Some of the Veterans of Le Cateau

ALLENBY, General Edmund

After commanding Third Army on the Western Front, he became the architect of victory in Palestine against the Turkish–German forces of the Ottoman Empire in territory more suitable for the deployment of cavalry force. His record as Third Army commander is not considered a success. His nickname was 'The Bull'. He was promoted to field marshal and became High Commissioner in Egypt 1919–25. He died in 1936, aged 75.

BRIDGES, Major Tom KCB CB CMG DSO FRGS LLD

Bridges had a distinguished career as soldier and diplomat. During the Great War he was mentioned in despatches seven times, wounded three times and promoted major-general (19th Division). He was Head of Military Mission with the Belgian Field Army and in 1918 Head of British War Mission in the USA. He was Governor of South Australia 1922–27. The incident at St Quentin has become part of the mytho logy of the Retreat. He was also an accomplished painter, having studied at the Slade in his youth. He died in 1939, aged 68.

DOUGHTY, Major E.C.

Ernest Christie Doughty of Theberton Hall near Saxmundham was commissioned into the Suffolk Regiment in 1891. After being captured, severely wounded, on 26 August 1914 at Le Cateau he was held for a time at a POW camp in Cologne, transferred to Switzerland in 1916 and repatriated in September 1917. Curiously, although the *Regimental History* credits him with the award of the DSO, it was never gazetted. He epitomizes all that was best about the 1914 officer class.

DUNN, Capt J.C. DSO MC* DCM

Dunn was the self-effacing and courageous medical officer of the 2nd Battalion The Royal Welch Fusiliers for three years. In that most literary battalion, both Siegfried Sassoon and Robert Graves were proud to have known him. His book *The War the Infantry Knew* (published anonymously in 1938) is a unique chronicle of an infantry battalion during the war, a battalion that was always used late in action and over the bodies of those already fallen. He died in 1955, aged eighty-four.

FORESTIER-WALKER, Maj-Gen Sir George

Born the son of a general in 1866, Sir George spent almost his entire military career on the staff, apart from a spell of active command with the (New Army) 48th Division in Italy in 1918. At the time of Le Cateau he was senior officer in a staff of eight in Second Corps. He died in 1939.

FRENCH, Sir John (later Viscount French of Ypres OM)

After being sacked as C-in-C BEF in December 1915 and replaced by Haig (over the failure of Loos), French returned to England not in disgrace but to write his memoir *1914* and to become C-in-C Home Forces and then Lord Lieutenant of Ireland (1918). He was granted £50,000. He failed to impress almost all of his contemporaries except Churchill. The best that can be said of him is that up to September 1914 he enjoyed remarkable luck, but that after that time he was increasingly out of his depth. He was much better company than the dour Haig. He could have been the model for C.S. Forrester's book *The General*: his looks represent in late middle-age the archetypal 'donkey'. He died in 1925.

HAIG, Douglas (later Earl Haig)

Became C-in-C British Armies in France and Belgium in December 1915, holding that post until 1919. He led the British armies to ultimate victory in the hundred-day campaign of 1918, an achievement that has always been overshadowed by the losses of the previous years. To his detractors he was dour, unfeeling and unimaginative. His supporters can point to his early appreciation of the potential of tanks as an example of his flexibility. After the war he was granted £100,000 by parliament, and devoted himself to British Legion affairs. He was not very helpful to Smith-Dorrien in the French dispute. He died in 1928 aged 67.

HAMILTON, Gen Hubert DSO

He survived for only another six weeks after Le Cateau, being killed by a stray shell in the Bethune sector in October 1914 as he conferred with his 3rd Division staff officers. He was buried later that night in a churchyard only one and a half miles from the front, the padre having to read the familiar verses over the sounds of a night attack. Smith-Dorrien, who attended, was much moved. He was 53 years old at his death.

HODGSON, Charles and HODGSON, Victor

Twin brothers, both of whom served as gunnery officers at Le Cateau. They survived and served in both world wars, Charles in the second war as a staff officer in the Indian Army. He emigrated to South Africa after the war.

HUNTER-WESTON, Maj-Gen Aylmer

He soon abandoned his front-line bravery with 11th Brigade, even going on a pheasant shoot in October 1914 while a battle involving his brigade was in progress. He went to the Dardennelles in 1915 and commanded 29th Division, becoming known as the 'Butcher of Helles'. Invalided home with nervous exhaustion and sunstroke, he became an MP in 1916. He commanded VIII Corps in the Somme battle of that year, his corps suffering the highest number of casualties for the fewest gains. For some unknown reason, he let off his two mines earlier than planned, thus losing any possibility of gaining time on the enemy. He conducted the Court Martial of Colonels Elkington and Mainwaring, who had disgraced themselves at St Quentin. He died aged 75 in 1940.

HYSLOP, Capt Henry DSO

Hyslop served for three years of the war with the Argylls as a fighting soldier, rising to the rank of brigadier-general in August 1917 (59th Brigade). He was four times mentioned in dispatches and was awarded the DSO 'for services in connection with operations in the field'.

JACK, Capt James DSO*

Jack ended the war as a brigadier-general (28th Brigade). As Sidney Rogerson wrote in John Terraine's edition of Jack's diary, Jack was 'the best type of old regular officer, a type whose weaknesses have been unfortunately all too often seized upon and laughed at, but whose merits are far too little appreciated by any but those who have served under him he was worth his weight in gold'. He died in 1962, aged 82.

JOFFRE, Marshal Joseph

Known as 'Papa' because of his luxuriant moustaches and rotund belly. His one great contribution to military history, his finest hour, was his realisation that Plan XVII was not going to halt the German advance on Paris from the north, and his creation of the 6th Army under Manoury. Thereafter he had no more idea of how to throw the Germans back over their border than anyone else: his replacement as C-in-C French Armies, Gen Nivelle, launched the disastrous Champagne offensive in the spring of 1917. Thereafter Joffre played no part in the Wwr on the Western Front. But during the critical period of August–September 1914 his demeanour was the opposite of French's: calm and unruffled. He was always in bed by 10.00pm. He was almost an albino. He died in 1931, aged 78.

JOHNSTON, Lt Alexander

Johston was educated at Winchester College and RMC Sandhurst, from where he was commissioned into the Worcester Regiment in 1904, after a spell working as a cowboy in Colorado. At the time of Le Cateau he was serving as a signals officer at 7 Brigade, 3rd Division, although during the action he describes he was acting as an infantry officer. He recovered from his wounds at Le Cateau and went on to serve in many of the major engagements of the war, until badly wounded on 16 September 1917 while commanding 126 Infantry Brigade; he had been visiting the front-line battalions at the Sans Souci outpost during 3rd Ypres. Before the war he had played cricket at county level (for Hampshire) as well as for the Gentlemen v Players. He died in 1952.

von KLUCK, Gen Alexander

A veteran of the Franco-Prussian war of 1870–71, he has been criticized, from the German point of view, for losing the war in the first month by his premature eastern move around the north of Paris. Even so he was within 14 miles (23km) of the city (the Government had fled) when he was forced to retreat at the battle of the Marne (6–9 September). He was wounded in 1915 and took no further part in the war. He was never brought before any international court for his part in Belgian atrocities. He died in 1934, aged 88.

LANREZAC, Gen Charles

His handling of the 5th Army at Guise on 30 August, and in particular Gen Louis Franchet d'Esperey's bold tactical command, brought about the ultimate German abandonment of the Schlieffen plan. It was a larger battle than Le Cateau and drove von Bulow's Second Army back 3 miles (5km). But his pessimism – or realism, to be more accurate – resulted in his removal by Joffre on 3 September, denying him a role in the victory of the Marne (6–9 September). Both he and his army were by early September exhausted, but he saved many soldiers' lives by his refusal to engage in costly and futile attacks. He died in 1925.

MONTGOMERY, Bernard Law
(later Viscount Montgomery of Alamein) KG GCB DSO PC

Became Britain's most successful and highest ranked general of the Second World War, commanding 8th Army in North Africa and Italy. He commanded all Allied ground forces during Operation *Overlord* until after the battle of Normandy. Known above all for his careful planning of operations, it was said that he did 'much with much, but not much with little'. Badly wounded at First Ypres, he served on the staff of Gen Plumer's Second Army. He died in 1976, aged 89.

MURRAY, Maj-Gen Sir Archibald 1860-1945

Murray's active service was with the Royal Inniskilling Fusiliers; it was in leading his battalion in action in northern Transvaal in early 1902 that he was dangerously wounded in the abdomen. Thereafter he served mostly on the staff, although he commanded the 2nd Division for six months, until the outbreak of war in 1914. His appointment as Chief of Staff at GHQ was at the express wish of Sir John French. His physical collapse at the end of 1914 (he was replaced by Robertson) was short-lived and he was appointed to a command in Egypt where he arrived in Jan 1916. His forces were checked in Gaza and he was replaced by Allenby in June 1917. Allenby got the credit for the successful Palestine campaign, but Murray's preparations for it were widely acknowledged. He was known variously as 'old Archie' and 'Sheep' Murray. He married twice, his first wife dying in 1910; both wives were colonel's daughters. His house in Surrey was called 'Makepeace'. He died in 1945.

RICHARDS, Frank DCM MM

Called back to the colours in 1914, Richards served as a private with the Royal Welch Fusiliers throughout the war, surviving all the major campaigns virtually without a scratch. His memoir, published in 1933, became an instant success; he had the uncredited help of Robert Graves, who insisted on Richards retaining his own voice and avoiding any literary pretension. He died in 1961, aged 78.

ROUPELL, Lt G.P.R. VC CB DL

Roupell was commissioned into the 1st East Surreys, the regiment of which his father had been lieutenant-colonel, as he was in 1918, and of which he became the last colonel before its disbandment in 1959. He served as a battalion officer throughout the war, including a spell on the staff, returning to England only on leave, when wounded at Hill 60 in April 1915 (where he won his VC) and on compassionate leave in October 1916, when he made an extraordinary escape from the merchant ship taking him across the channel, which was captured and sunk by the German Navy. In fact his life was a series of daring escapes. In 1919, while serving with the British Military Mission to the White Russians, he was captured by the Bosheviks and nearly shot. He spent a year in prison in Moscow, which broke his health; he survived mainly due to the Red Cross parcels that got through. In 1940, now a brigadier (36 Infantry Brigade), he was cut off near Doullens by the German blitzkrieg and on his advice the brigade split up into small groups to try and get back to British lines. Roupell and a staff officer (Maj Gilbert) found a farm that gave them shelter and work, and treated them as part of the family. They made their way home in 1942 via the underground network. His fighting days were now over. He died in 1984.

SMITH-DORRIEN, Sir Horace KCB GCB DSO

After returning to England in 1915, Sir Horace was given command of the East African campaign but severe illness intervened, and he became Governor of Gibralter until his retirement in 1923. He then lived with his family in France for several years, mainly for financial reasons. He was well served by his life-long friend J. Fortescue in the French/Kitchener/Smith-Dorrien controversy. He was killed in a car crash in Wiltshire in 1930, aged 72. He has been called a fairly typical general of his era (*Dictionary of National Biography*), which is a less than helpful description.

SPEARS, Edward CBE MC

A passionate Francophile, he acted in Anglo-French liaison in two world wars, escaping in 1940 with de Gaulle to raise the standard of *La France Libre*. He was close to Churchill throughout his life, but fell out with de Gaulle. He was wounded four times in the war and in 1915 taken by French troops for a German. In his memoir *Liaison* he professes admiration for Joffre, Sir John French, even Huguet who had 'the greatest admiration for all things English'. Lanrezac exasperated him. He became MP for Carlisle and a director of numerous companies. In 1953 he visited the French outpost at Dien Ben Phu. He died in 1974, aged 88.

STEWART, Lt Ian DSO MC*

He had the distinction of being among the first troops to land in France in 1914 (on 10 August), the first to be mentioned in despatches, the youngest platoon commander in 1914 (18 years old) and the only one (probably) in his battalion to have endured and survived two retreats: Mons and Singapore, where he escaped capture by having been called away to Field Marshal Wavell in India at the last moment – he was reunited with his wife Ursula in Ceylon. He ended his career as a brigadier and in retirement actively farmed his estate at Achnacone, of which he was the 13th Laird; he died in 1987.

WILSON, General Sir Henry Bt

The second son of seven children of a prosperous Protestant Irish family, he had two guiding passions: Irish Unionism and the belief that Britain should be at France's side in the coming war with Germany. At the outbreak of war he became sub-chief of staff to Sir Archibald Murray and effective chief when Murray became incapacitated. He remained in close communication with Foch, a relationship forged before the war. His star rose when Lloyd George became Prime Minister in 1916, and Wilson became CIGS. After the war he became increasingly gloomy about the prospects for the British Empire, but would contemplate no compromise with the IRA (although he deplored the excesses of the 'Black and Tans'). His star was on the wane when he was gunned down by the IRA outside his house in London in 1922, a death which inflated his reputation. His reputation was left in tatters by the 1927 biography. He was 58 years old at his death.

The following senior officers of the BEF were killed, wounded or invalided before the end of 1914:

Gen Hamilton, 3rd Division, killed October

Lt-Gen Murray, GHQ staff, invalided September

Maj-Gen J.G. Drummond, 19th Brigade, wounded 26 August

Maj-Gen Sir Charles Fergusson, 5th Division, invalided October

Maj-Gen S.H. Lomax, 1st Division, wounded October

Maj-Gen T.D.O. Snow, 4th Division, invalided September but went on to command 27th Division

Brig E.S. Bulfin, 2nd Infantry Brigade, wounded November

Brig G.J. Cuthbert, 13th Infantry Brigade, invalided September

Brig R.H. Davies, 6th Infantry Brigade, invalided September

Brig B.J.C. Doran, 8th Infantry Brigade, invalided October

Brig Sir James Edwards, 4th Division GSO2, invalided August

Brig Fitzclarence, 1st Infantry Brigade, killed November

Brig R.C. Haking, 5th Infantry Brigade, wounded September

Brig S.P. Rolt, 14th Infantry Brigade, invalided October

Brig R. Scott-Kerr, 4th Guards Brigade, wounded September

Bibliography

Primary Sources

Imperial War Museum Sound Archives:
  Lt R. Macleod, XV Brigade RFA
  Cpl F. Atkinson, KOYLI
  Bugler P.G. Martin XV Brigade RFA)

National Archives:
  FO/383/280
  CAB/45/129 (the Torgau History, Gen Snow's memoir, Maj Peebles's
memoir, Maj Doughty's memoir, Col Swayne's memoir)
  WO/256/1 (Haig's Diary)
  WO 95/588 (First Corps Dispatches)

Arthur, Max, *Forgotten Voices of the Great War*, London, 2002 (for Private
  Charles Ditcham, 2nd Argyll and Sutherland Highlanders)

Ashurst, George and Holmes, Richard (ed.), *My Bit – A Lancashire Fusilier at
  War 1914–1918*, Marlborough, 1988

Astill, E., (ed.), *The Great War Diaries of Brig-Gen Alexander Johnston 1914–
  1917*, Barnsley 2007

Beckett and Donovan, *The Judgement of History*, Chippenham, 1993

Becke, Maj A.F., *The Royal Regiment of Artillery at Le Cateau*, Woolwich,
  1919

Berkeley, *The History of the Rifle Brigade 1914–1918*, Vol I, Winchester,
  1921

Bloem, Walter, *The Advance From Mons 1914*, Solihull, 2004

Bond, Lt-Col, R.C., *The King's Own Yorkshire Light Infantry In The Great
  War*, London, 1929

Bridges, Sir Tom, *Alarms and Excursions*, London, 1938

Callwell, Maj-Gen Sir C.E., *Field Marshal Sir Henry Wilson*, London, 1927

Cavendish, Brig-Gen A.E.J., *The History of the 93rd Sutherland Highlanders
  1799–1927*, private publication, 1927

Downham, Peter (ed.), *Diary of an Old Contemptible*, Barnsley, 2004

Dunn, CaptainJ.C. and Simpson (ed.), *The War the Infantry Knew 1914-1919*, London, 1987

Edmonds, Brig-Gen J.E., *The Official History of The Great War, Military Operations France and Belgium 1914*, London, 1933

French, Sir John, *1914*, London, 1919

Giddings, Robert, *Echoes of War*, London 1992

Gillon, CaptainS., *The KOSB in the Great War*, London 1930

Gleichen, Brig-Gen Count *The Doings of the 15th Infantry Brigade, August 1914 to March 1915*, 1917

Graves, Robert, *Goodbye To All That*, London, 1930

Hamilton, Nigel, *Monty, The Making of a General*, London, 1981

Hastings, P., 'The Diary of Major P. Hastings', *The Queen's Own Gazette*, No. 474 Vol. XXXIV, pp.3273–75

Hay, M.V., *Wounded and a Prisoner of War*, Edinburgh 1930.

Hodgson, C.F., *From Hell to the Himalayas*, Westville, South Africa, 1983

Murphy, Lt-Col C.C.R., *The History of the Suffolk Regiment 1914–1927*, London, 1928

Repington, Colonel, *The First World War*, London, 1920

Richards, Frank, *Old Soldiers Never Die*, London, 1933

Rimbaud, Isabelle, *In The Whirlpool of War*, London, 1918

Robertson, Sir William, *From Private to Field Marshal*, London, 1921

Roupell, G.R.P., *The Diary and Recollections of Brig G.R.P. Roupell*, VC CB DL, unpublished MS

Sheffield, and Bourne (eds), *Douglas Haig: War Diaries and Letters 1914–1918*, London, 2005

Smith-Dorrien, Gen Sir Horace, *Memories of Forty Years Service*, London, 1925

Spears, Edward, *Liaison 1914*, London, 1930

Terraine, John (ed.), *Gen Jack's Diary*, London, 1964

Vansittart, Peter, *Voices from the Great War*, London, 1981

War Office, *Battle of Le Cateau, 26 August 1914. Tour of the Battlefield*, 1933

Wyrall, E., *The History of The Duke of Cornwall's Light Infantry 1914–1918*, London, 1932

Wyrall, E., *The Somerset Light Infantry 1914–1919*, London, 1927

Secondary Sources

Ascoli, David, *The Mons Star*, London 1981

Babington, Anthony, *For The Sake of Example*, London, 1984

Barnett, Corelli, *The Sword Bearers*, London 1963

Blythe, Ronald, *Akenfield*, London 1969

Cave, N. and Sheldon, J., *Le Cateau*, Barnsley, 2008

Conan Doyle, Arthur, *The British Campaign in France and Flanders*, London 1916

Dictionary of National Biography

Egremont, Max, *Under Two Flags, The Life of Major-Gen Spears*, London 2002

Gardner, Nikolas, *Trail by Fire, Command and the BEF in 1914*, Westport, USA, 2003

Gentile, Major Louis, *Le Cateau 1914–1918*, unpublished

Gilbert, Martin, *First World War*, London, 1992

Griffth, Paddy, *Battle Tactics of the Western Front*, New Haven and London, 1994

Griffith, Paddy, *Forward Into Battle,* Chichester, 1982

Gudmundsson, *The BEF 1914–15*, Oxford, 2005

Hamilton, E.W., *The First Seven Divisions*, New York, 1916

Holmes, Richard, *Fatal Avenue*, London, 1992

Holmes, Richard, 'The Last Hurrah; Cavalry on the Western Front, Aug–Sept 1914', in *Facing Armageddon*, London 1996

Holmes, Richard, *The Little Field Marshal*, London 1981

Holmes, Richard, *Tommy*, London, 2004

Jackson, Bill and Bramall, Dwin, *The Chiefs*, London, 1992

Keegan, John, *The Mask of Command*, London, 1992

Lomas, *Mons 1914*, Oxford, 1997

Maxwell-Hyslop, Lt-Col, 'Le Cateau August 1914', in *RUSI Journal*, May 1921

Messenger, Charles, *Call to Arms, The British Army 1914–1918*, London, 2005

Bibliography

Neillands, Robin, *The Old Contemptibles*, London, 2004

Sheffield, Gary, 'Officer-Man Relations, Discipline and Morale in the British Army of the Great War', in *Facing Armageddon*, London, 1996

Smithers, A.J., *The Man Who Knew Too Much*, London, 1982

Spurling, Hilary, *Matisse, The Master*, London, 2005

Terraine, John, *Mons, The Retreat to Victory*, London, 1960.

Tuchman, Barbara, *August 1914*, London 1961

Winter, Denis, *Haig's Command: A Reassessment*, London, 1991

Acknowledgements

Without the all-round help, expertise, enthusiasm and research of my brother, Nick Bird, this book would not have been written, or at least not in the way it has. His knowledge of military history and publishing generally are the reasons he is such a useful and active member of the Royal United Services Institute and the Society for Army Historical Research, as well as a guide on conducted tours of the battlefields of Western Europe.

Dr Sanders Marble, of Springfield, Virginia, USA, one of whose specialities is gunnery in the Great War, has been more than helpful on all aspects relating to the artillery.

My special thanks are due to Mr Chris Roupell for lending me the invaluable diary of his great uncle, only short extracts of which have been published before.

Major Ken Grey of the Royal Green Jackets Museum, Winchester was most kind in making available the *War History* of the Rifle Brigade as well as excellent photographs. Mr R. Mackenzie of the Argyll and Sutherland Museum also kindly sent me the relevant parts of the 2nd Argyll's history, the battalion diary, CaptainHyslop's memoir, as well as memoirs by Lt-Col (as he became) I.M. Stewart MC* and Brig (as he became) H.J.D. Clark MC.

My brother-in-law, Col John Richardson RAMC, who is amongst many things a professor of military medicine, has been more than helpful and encouraging whenever I have had occasion to ask questions. His extensive library is a constant source of knowledge. His wife Susie is a self-taught computer expert with expertise far beyond those who charge for their services, and without it I would have been at a complete loss. My daughters Dr L.A. Bird and Dr E. Bird also gave me help on the computer. My father, T.A. Bird DSO MC* is knowledgeable on all matters relating to the Rifle Brigade and infantry tactics.

On our visit to the *Historial de la Grande Guerre* in Peronne, we (my brother and I) were most generously looked after by M. Dominic Frere. Nathalie Legrand of that excellent institution kindly provided us with the illustrations which so graphically amplify the text. We acknowledge the work of the photographer Yazid Medmoun in creating the photographic images.

I am grateful to Sally Nye for drawing the maps.

We declined the climb up the clock-tower of the church in Le Cateau, but discovered that it is perfectly possible to do so with a machine gun, if you are young and determined.

Antony Bird
Chichester, 2008

Index